UNVEILED SKY
A DIVINE REVELATION

A spiritual journey for seekers
of mystical wisdom and divine connection

JAMIE C. DUNSTON

"Unveiled Sky" is a captivating narrative
that explores the convergence of Heaven and Earth,
challenging societal norms and religious doctrines,
while offering an immersive experience through
photography, unraveling hidden mysteries
of existence, and emphasizing
the interconnectedness
of all beings.

UNVEILED SKY
A DIVINE REVELATION

A spiritual journey for seekers
of mystical wisdom and divine connection

JAMIE C. DUNSTON

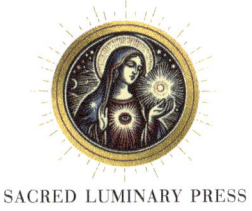

SACRED LUMINARY PRESS

Publisher's Cataloging-in-Publication Data

Names: Dunston, Jamie C., author.

Title: Unveiled sky a divine revelation : a spiritual journey for seekers of mystical wisdom and divine connection / Jamie C. Dunston.

Description: Includes bibliographical references. | Colorado Springs, CO: Sacred Luminary Press, 2024.

Identifiers: LCCN: 2024910340 | ISBN 979-8-218-42411-4 (paperback) | 979-8-218-43381-9 (ebook)

Subjects: LCSH Spirituality. | Experience (Religion) | Mysticism. | Trinity. | BISAC BODY, MIND & SPIRIT / Prophecy | BODY, MIND & SPIRIT / Mysticism | BODY, MIND & SPIRIT / Inspiration & Personal Growth | BODY, MIND & SPIRIT / New Thought | PHILOSOPHY / Metaphysics | RELIGION / Biblical Studies / Prophecy | RELIGION / Christian Theology / General | RELIGION / Eschatology | RELIGION / Spirituality

Classification: LCC BL53 .D86 2024 | DDC 204/.2--dc23

Please visit: jamiecdunston.com

TO GOD, THE GUIDING LIGHT

This book, a humble offering, is dedicated to You,
the Guiding Light that has illuminated my path.
With utmost reverence and gratitude, may its pages
serve as a vessel for Your eternal wisdom,
touching hearts and souls with hope, understanding,
and compassion.

TO MY BELOVED DAUGHTER AVERY DUNSTON

You are the radiant sun that illuminates my world with joy,
laughter, and boundless love. I am forever grateful
for the light you bring into my life.

TO MY DEAR GRANDMA EVELYN FRENCH, WHOSE
FAITH HELD HER THROUGH AND THROUGH

May your spirit forever shine brightly within these pages,
reminding us all that faith can move mountains
and illuminate even the darkest of paths.

AND TO MY DEAR MOTHER, JOAN FRENCH-SHARPE

Whose teachings of humility and the importance
of extending a helping hand to those in need
have shaped me profoundly.

THIS BOOK IS DEDICATED
TO EACH OF YOU.

TABLE OF CONTENTS

PREFACE

IN THE VAST EXPANSE OF THE EASTERN PLAINS, WHERE THE SANDY loam soil meets the boundless horizon, a small 40-acre vegetable farm stood as a testament to the beauty and harmony of nature. Avondale Colorado became the backdrop of a remarkable journey that would forever transform the life of its humble farmer.

I had dedicated my life to the art of organic vegetable farming and seed production, finding solace and purpose in the cycles of growth and the bountiful harvest. But little did I know that the seeds I sowed and nurtured would pale in comparison to the seeds of enlightenment that would soon be planted within me.

In the year 2014, a defining moment unfolded, one that would forever alter the course of my existence. I had an encounter with the blessed Holy Mother, a celestial visitation that transcended the boundaries of the physical realm. From that moment on, my life became a tapestry woven with mysticism and divine revelations.

The initial encounter with the Holy Mother was only the beginning. Like a veil being lifted, I embarked on a profound journey of self-discovery and spiritual awakening. Delving deep into the recesses of my being, particularly my heart, I found myself immersed in a realm beyond the ordinary, where the mystical and the mundane intertwined.

In a moment of prayer, I asked God for a tangible image of the divine. And in the mysterious workings of the universe, my plea was answered. Thirteen days later, I became a witness to the presence of God.

I walked with the Almighty, the beloved Creator, accompanied by His angelic hosts, for seven extraordinary minutes. In that sacred communion, I held the ineffable triune essence of the Father, the Son, and the blessed Holy Spirit. And with each step, I captured the essence of divinity through the lens of my camera, immortalizing the encounter that defied human comprehension.

This book, "Unveiled Sky," is the chronicle of my journey-a testament to the extraordinary and the miraculous that unfolds in the wake of that encounter. It is an invitation to explore the realms beyond our limited perception, to embrace the mystical threads that weave through the tapestry of our lives.

Within these pages, you will find not only my personal odyssey but also the universal truths that transcend time and space. It is my hope that by sharing my experiences, you the reader, will be inspired to embark on your own quest for meaning, to peel back the layers of the ordinary, and to uncover the extraordinary that lies within.

So, let us embark on this transformative journey together, as we lift the veil and venture into the vast expanse of the Unveiled Sky with boundless gratitude and an unwavering belief in the power of the unseen.

INTRODUCTION

IN A WORLD SHROUDED IN DARKNESS AND UNCERTAINTY, WHERE faith has waned and hope has all but vanished, a celestial secret lies hidden in the boundless expanse of the Unveiled Sky. Prepare to embark on an awe-inspiring journey of enlightenment and transformation as you delve into the pages of "Unveiled Sky: A Divine Revelation." Brace yourself for an extraordinary tale that will challenge your beliefs, ignite your imagination, and unveil the extraordinary power that resides within us all. Are you ready to witness the revelation that will forever change how you perceive the cosmos and your place within it? Let the journey to the Unveiled Sky begin.

In the midst of a world where traditional religious structures held sway, I forged a unique path amidst the backdrop of my upbringing in the mid-1970s. In the embrace of progressive and open-minded parents, who themselves sought solace in transcendental meditation, commonly referred to as TM which was founded by Maharishi Mahesh Yogi in India I embarked on a journey of self-discovery and spiritual exploration.

My mother, a cultural Catholic driven by an unwavering commitment to social justice, extended a helping hand to the less fortunate, while my father, a man of science immersed in the realm of electronics, pursued the agnostic path. Religious dogma did not dominate my household, and Sunday school remained an uncharted territory.

As my cousins prepared for their first communion within the Roman Catholic Faith. The faith of my dear grandma, I sensed a different calling echoing within my heart. The conventional pews and rituals held no allure for my inquisitive mind. Nevertheless, an insatiable hunger for understanding the universe and a profound connection to a higher power coursed through my veins. From a tender age, I yearned to unravel the mysteries that lay beyond the physical realm, seeking to comprehend the very essence of existence itself.

During moments of introspection, I contemplated the essence of God, even during my rebellious phase as a teenager experimenting with LSD, when I had little self-awareness. The New Age movement greatly influenced my personal journey. This movement disseminated occult practices and metaphysical religious communities throughout the 1970s and '80s. It held a vision of an imminent "New Age" characterized by love and enlightenment, providing a glimpse of this forthcoming era through the processes of personal growth and healing. The New Age movement embraced significant diversity, with individuals from various backgrounds actively seeking enlightenment. The movement was marked by the presence of numerous gurus, wise individuals, and healers who shared their teachings, although caution was necessary to avoid certain cults.

As I was maturing and expanding my knowledge, it was a thrilling period for me to explore and gain insights into these captivating subjects. Although I was always deeply spiritual in life there were also large swaths of time when I was not seeking actively to know my being. Yet, even in those moments of veiled awareness, an undercurrent of spiritual longing persisted. It stirred within me, a gentle reminder of the depths waiting to be explored, a call to resurface and reclaim my true essence. And so, the ebb and flow of my spiritual journey continued, weaving together moments of profound seeking and fleeting detachment.

In the grand tapestry of existence, there are moments when divine timing aligns, and the universe unfolds its mysteries with breathtaking clarity. As the seeker, that moment has arrived and has compelled me to write this book. In the presence of the divine, the truths revealed may be unsettling, even perceived as blasphemous by some. Yet, it is through the unwavering call of the divine that I have been impelled to lay bare the sacred revelations that I have been entrusted with.

In the eyes of the divine, every aspect of creation is meticulously known and cherished. God's omniscience extends to the minutiae of existence, counting each hair upon our heads, and recognizing the unique journey of every soul. Each and every individual, without exception, is embraced as a beloved child of God, a radiant spark of the eternal light.

Unconditional love flows abundantly from the divine source, unhampered by the need for validation or belief. God's infinitely pure love extends grace and compassion for all, regardless of their faith or lack thereof. It is Love that dwells within the depths of every human heart, awaiting recognition and awakening.

In this remarkable journey, I share with you the mystical encounter I had with God, an experience that transcends the boundaries of time and space. It is a testament to the interconnectedness of our current exploration into the realms of quantum physics and the study of qualia-the nature of subjective experience. As science and spirituality converge, a new landscape emerges, inviting us to dive into the depths of understanding the intricacies of existence itself.

Within the pages of this book, prepare to embark on a wonderous voyage that will challenge your perceptions, expand your consciousness, and illuminate the interplay between the seen and the unseen. As the universe unravels its mysteries, we are beckoned to explore synergies, to bridge the apparent chasms and uncover the intrinsic unity that binds all aspects of reality.

Together, let us venture into the uncharted territories of knowledge and wisdom, where the boundaries of human comprehension are stretched, and the wonder of creation unfolds before our eyes. Within the tapestry of "Unveiled Sky: A Divine Revelation," revelations await-revelations that invite us to explore the depths of our presence in this awe-inspiring cosmic dance.

In the realm of human experience, our perception of reality is woven through the tapestry of sensations, images, feelings, and thoughts. These subjective encounters shape our understanding of the world, fueling our quest for truth and meaning. It is within this quest that science emerges as a guiding light, a tool that seeks to unravel the mysteries of existence and discern the veracity of our perceptions.

Science, with its rigorous methodologies and relentless pursuit of evidence, serves as a vessel through which we can navigate the vast ocean of knowledge. It provides a framework to sort out the complexities of reality, inviting us to examine the world through the lens of objectivity. For the everyday rational person, it is this pursuit of truth that resonates deeply- a yearning to uncover tangible, measurable evidence that can satisfy the inquisitive mind.

Yet, amidst the quest for empirical verification, we encounter a profound insight- the realization that truth is not solely confined to the realm of external measurements or objective observation. As the great Indian poet Rabindranath Tagore once conveyed to Albert Einstein during their discussions on the divine in the 1930s, truth is also a subjective experience, realized through the very essence of our being.

TAGORE: Beauty is in the ideal of perfect harmony which is in the Universal Being; Truth the perfect comprehension of the Universal Mind. We individuals approach it through our own mistakes and blunders, through our accumulated experiences, through our illumined consciousness — how, otherwise, can we know Truth?[1]

In the exploration of truth, we are beckoned to embrace the multidimensionality of our existence. While science may illuminate the external world, it is through the subjective human experience that truth is not solely confined to the realm of the measurable, but also resides within the rich tapestry of our inner being.

I invite you to explore the captivating manifestation of our beloved creator through the lens of my inner journey and the mesmerizing images I have been blessed to capture. The journey commences with a striking photograph, a visual representation of God as a supreme being, omnipotent in nature.

In this image, our heavenly Father lies peacefully on his side, cradled beneath a cloud that he upholds with his Almighty right arm, lifting it toward the celestial abode. He wears an emblem of a cross on his chest symbolizing the qualities of a superhero- an expression of the belief that with God, all things are possible.

Jesus came to plant an invisible seed of hope in the hearts of humanity that which is planted in our being is called the Spirit.

These things have I spoken unto you in proverbs; but the time cometh when I shall no more speak unto you in proverbs, but shall show you plainly of the Father.

JOHN 16:25

As I stand before this breathtaking depiction, I am filled with awe, for our heavenly Father gazes straight at us, yet shades his eyes to not overwhelm or frighten. He paints himself abstractly within the clouds, embodying strength, prestige, honor, and wisdom of an old man. Through the lens of my camera, I capture this moment, through the branches of the mulberry tree, I feel this divine presence, and with a click of my camera's button, I capture a glimpse of eternity.

In the vast expanse of the high desert plains of Colorado, nestled on the eastern side of the Rocky Mountains in the Arkansas Valley watershed in Pueblo County during the enchanting evening sunset on the last day of March 31st, 2015, just six days before Easter Sunday, that I experienced a profound encounter with the divine.

This is one of the first images of God that I took on that beloved day of our encounter. At the time I snapped this photograph, I did not know what I was seeing. It was all intuitive and a feeling that I followed as I walked with the almighty LORD and his angelic host for about seven minutes.

There are stories of others who have walked with God. Enoch who was Noah's great grandfather walked with God. It was his faith that enabled him to do so. Levi who stood in awe of God's name and revered God walked with God. Noah who built the Ark at God's command saving mankind from extinction during the great flood walked with God. Abraham the father of Isaac and the father of many nations walked with God and now you too can walk with God as you join me on this incredible journey of faith, truth, and love.

In this moment, I am reminded that "I AM" (the name for God) is not merely a static being, but a dynamic and ever-unfolding process. God is an event, a stunning phenomenon that is about to take place and reveal its splendor to all who seek it. And, through these pages of this book, I hope to inspire the collective consciousness to recognize that all is one and to raise our awareness of the divine presence that permeates every aspect of our existence.

Consciousness, the very fabric of our being, is the key to understanding our experiences and shaping our reality. It is through the expansion of our awareness that we come to realize the all-encompassing, loving energy force that is God, residing deep within each and every one of us.

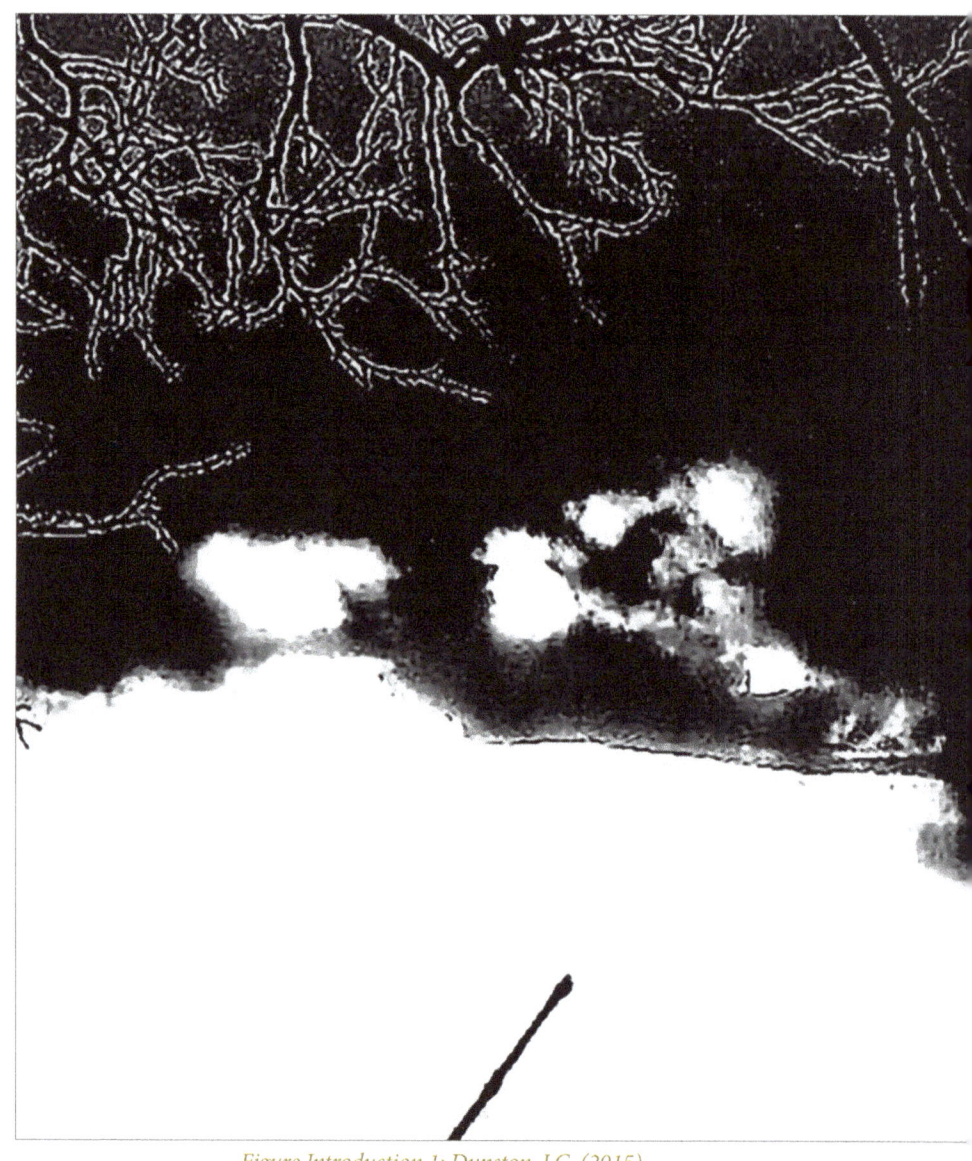

Figure Introduction 1: Dunston, J.C. (2015)
"SUPREME BEING UNVEILED: I AM THAT I AM"

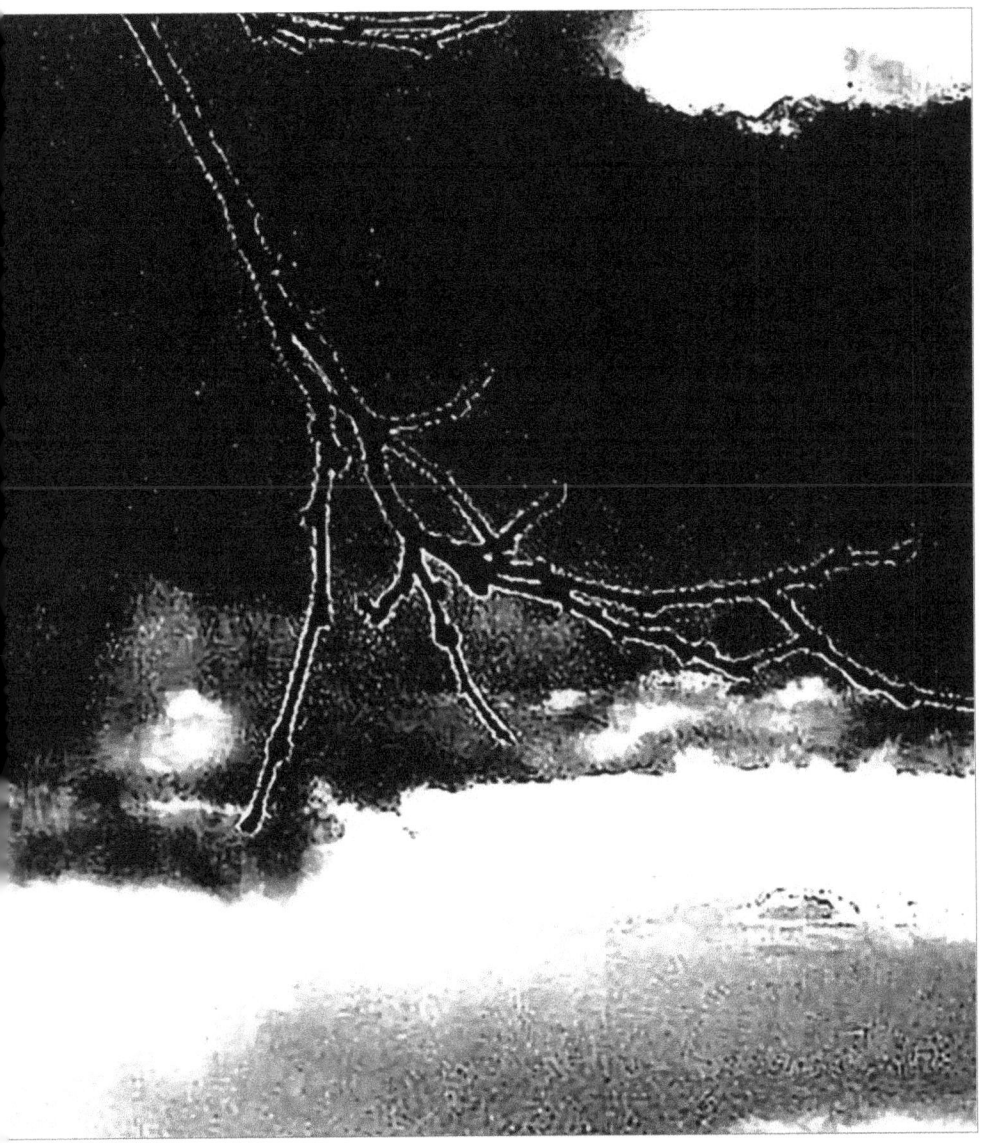

*"It is God's formlessness that allows God to assume any shape
and any form in any moment that it serves the ends of Love
for God to assume."*[2]

Within these pages, we embark on a profound exploration of the divine who manifests mind, body, and Spirit the triune that is God. Through the lens of my 35mm digital Nikon camera, I capture moments that encapsulate the truth of God's manifestation, his timeless beauty, grace, and wisdom that emanate from the very core of creation.

In the mystical perspective, the creation of our reality is intricately tied to our thoughts, words, and actions. What we think, we bring into existence. What we bring into existence, we embody. What we embody, we express. And what we express, we experience. This profound understanding reveals that our essential nature is rooted in love. We are eternal, boundless, and inherently free.

As human beings, our purpose is to make conscious choices, to declare our intentions, to create our reality, to express our divine nature, and to fulfill our true essence. We recognize that there are many ways through which we gain knowledge about God, human nature, and the relationship between thoughts and reality. Personal experiences and revelations play a significant role in this process.

It is essential to recognize that religions are human constructs. Unfortunately, throughout history, religions have sometimes hindered people from fully experiencing and embracing the love of God. They have instilled fear or disbelief instead. In my teachings, I emphasize that human beings are three-part beings, mirroring the image and likeness of our beloved Creator.

The profound question humanity should be asking is: Who is the extraordinary and awe-inspiring Creator we are connected to, and how can we engage with this divine force? We must recognize that our current values, concepts, and understanding limit our comprehension of God. To truly grasp the nature of God, we must humbly acknowledge our limited knowledge and not claim to possess an all-encompassing understanding.

God is not a static entity but a dynamic process. A "being" is not a mere thing but a continuous unfolding. God is the Creator and simultaneously the process of creation. In the scripture of Colossians 1:16, it is conveyed that all things were created through and for God. This verse illuminates the eternal process that we are all part of. We are integral to this process, and it is through this process that God manifests.

Jesus, as both the Creator and the created, exemplifies this divine process. As stated in Colossians 1:16:

*For by Him all things were created that are in heaven
and that are on earth...*

This verse beautifully encapsulates the essence of the process. We are not separate from it; we are an integral part of it. We are the embodiment of this process. This is the profound truth of our existence and the nature of God.

In embracing the mystical perspective, we open ourselves to the infinite and transformative possibilities of divine realization. We recognize that our understanding is limited and that our journey toward comprehending the divine is an ongoing and awe-inspiring exploration.

In the wondrous realm of mysticism, I find myself immersed in profound mystical experiences that unveil the unique expression of God through various forms, including icons and photography. These sacred expressions reveal metaphorical concepts that transcend the boundaries of mere words. They possess the power to convey complex ideas and evoke deep emotions with a subtlety and depth that touches the very core of our being.

Photography, in its essence, is inherently metaphorical. It captures fleeting moments, freezing them in time, and imbues them with layers of meaning that extend far beyond the surface. Through the lens of a camera, we can communicate profound truths, stir the depths of the soul, and invite contemplation on the mysteries of existence. It allows us to express the ineffable, the intangible, and the ethereal in ways that words alone may struggle to convey.

In my mystical vision, I perceive the interconnectedness that weaves through every aspect of the universe. Whether in physical form, energetic resonance, or metaphorical representation, everything is intertwined, and intimately connected in a cosmic dance. The tapestry of existence is interwoven with intricate threads that link all beings, all phenomena, and all dimensions.

This interconnectedness invites us to recognize the profound unity that underlies the apparent diversity of the world. It calls us to embrace the understanding that we are not separate entities but integral parts of a vast and harmonious whole. The recognition of this sacred connection opens the doors to a deeper comprehension of the divine essence that permeates all.

Through icons and photography, we glimpse the metaphorical language of the universe. They serve as powerful tools that enable us to communicate and explore the profound concepts that shape our existence. They invite us to go beyond the surface appearances, to delve into the realms of symbolism and metaphor, and to awaken to the deeper truths that lie hidden within.

In this mystical journey, I invite you to embrace the interconnectedness that binds us all. Seek the divine in every form, in every moment captured by the lens, and in every icon that speaks to your soul. Let us embark together on a profound exploration of the universal tapestry, where the metaphorical and the sacred dance in harmony, revealing the eternal truths that connect us to the boundless depths of God's expression.

Within the vast tapestry of existence, certain aspects hold fundamental significance. These are the foundational threads that weave through the fabric of reality, guiding our contemplation and exploration. As a mystic, I perceive the intricate interconnectedness of all things and acknowledge the existence of these fundamental elements.

While philosophers have long debated the concept of objective truth, I hold a distinctive perspective. I find that the notion of objectivity itself is complex and multifaceted. Yet, I boldly assert the existence of an objective truth that transcends individual beliefs and opinions. This truth, which I declare as an objective reality, extends its reach to all, regardless of personal agreement or disagreement.

In this context, I proclaim with unwavering conviction that God does indeed exist. This proclamation is not rooted in subjective preference or limited perspective but rather in a profound recognition of the universal and timeless presence of the Divine. It is an objective truth that resonates within the depths of every soul, whether consciously acknowledged or not.

As a mystic, my journey has led me to experience the divine essence that permeates all creation. I perceive God's existence as an undeniable reality, woven into the very fabric of our being. It is a truth that transcends the limitations of individual perspectives and cultural constructs, resonating with the core of our shared humanity.

While acknowledging the complexities surrounding the concept of objectivity, I invite others to explore their own understanding and experiences. Embrace the mystical path of seeking the divine, and you may discover the profound and transformative truth that God exists—an objective truth that transcends personal belief and encompasses the entirety of existence.

With humility and gratitude, I extend my hand and invite you to join me on this extraordinary odyssey of capturing the divine. Together, let us explore the boundless depths of our true nature and deepen our connection with the loving energy that breathes life into our souls. Thank you all for joining me in this significant miraculous event in the history of our conscious world.

JAMIE C. DUNSTON

1

EMBRACING DIVINE PRESENCE: THE SACRED VISIT WITH THE HOLY MOTHER

IN THE CAPTIVATING AUTUMN OF 2014, AS THE MORNING SUN kissed the horizon a wonderous expedition awaited me as I was blessed with a transcendent revelation from the exalted and cherished Holy Mother. Her divine presence graced my path, filling my heart with awe and inspiration. It was a profound encounter that ignited my spirit, propelling me towards an extraordinary adventure.

One morning, as I readied my breakfast and patiently waited for it to cook, I ventured into the living room. There, I sought warmth from the fireplace as I gazed outside amidst the cozy ambiance, I watched the cows peacefully grazing in the tranquil pasture below. Without warning, a surge of awareness washed over me as I became acutely aware of the arrival of a remarkable ethereal entity in my presence. In a mesmerizing display, she materialized within the confines of my living room.

As my gaze fixed upon her, I was immediately captivated, my eyes beheld a radiant, shimmering, translucent crystalline energy pulsating with vibrant hues of vibrant living light. This energy, so magnanimous and nurturing, exuded a maternal aura, embracing me with a love that knew no bounds.

I was enveloped by a profound sense of warmth and benevolence. It was a majestic spectacle, witnessing the embodiment of an affectionate presence, evoking a profound sense of awe and reverence within me.

This encounter with the living colors felt vividly tangible, surpassing the physicality of my own flesh and bone. It carried a profound sense of reality that transcended the boundaries of the material world, immersing me in an experience that felt even more vivid and tangible than my own physical existence.

In an instant, my heart resonated with a profound recognition. Before me stood the blessed, Holy Mother herself. Adorned in a resplendent blue mantle, she exuded an ethereal radiance, with luminous rays of light emanating from her being, casting a celestial glow that enveloped her in an aura of grace and holiness. It was a sight that stirred my soul.

She brings light and within her hands, she gently cradles a sphere of radiant white light. My eyes fixed upon a sphere of this ethereal orb, shimmering with an otherworldly brilliance that infused the surroundings with a gentle, yet powerful glow.

This mesmerizing sight of this luminous sphere is a symbol of divine wisdom and love. In that sacred moment, I perceive the light cradled in her hands as a precious gift, a divine offering extended to me. It was evident that she intended for me to personally experience the transformative power of this luminous radiance. Through a telepathic connection, she conveyed to me a profound truth that she is my mother and that she loves me.

In this sacred communion, she tells me telepathically that I am a child of the light, destined to share the luminous essence of love.

With utmost tenderness and compassion, she extended this ethereal light of love, inviting me to embrace it and allow it to illuminate my path, guiding me toward spiritual growth and fulfillment. This encounter was an extraordinary blessing bestowed upon me, for in her presence, I witnessed the convergence of her divine essence and the radiant light of Christ, that she cradles within her being—within her womb, within her heart, and within her hands.

Although our time together was brief, its impact was nothing short of astounding. It marked the inception of a deep and transformative journey into a realm of profound mysticism, where I would come to explore and encounter the mysteries of the divine in ways beyond imagination.

Prior to this profound encounter, I had embarked on a personal quest for self-discovery. I found myself immersed in a state of suffering, yearning to regain a sense of wholeness and joy that had eluded me.

It was during this period that I serendipitously stumbled upon the teachings of the Buddha. In his wisdom, I recognized a profound truth: the suffering I endured was not inevitable or necessary, it became clear to me that I possessed the power to alter the course of my own path, to relinquish the burdens that weighed me down, and embrace a new way of being. This realization marked a pivotal turning point, inspiring me to embark on a transformative journey toward inner peace, liberation, and the rediscovery of genuine joy.

Gratitude washed over me as I swiftly grasped the understanding that I held the power to govern my own thoughts and experiences. The realization of this profound truth filled me with immense appreciation.

Eager to cultivate this newfound sense of control, I embarked on a daily practice of meditation, making it a cherished ritual woven into the fabric of my everyday life. With dedicated commitment, I embraced the transformative power of stillness and introspection, recognizing meditation as a gateway to inner peace, clarity, and self-discovery. It became a guiding light, illuminating my path toward greater mindfulness and enabling me to navigate life's challenges with a newfound sense of serenity and insight.

During one of my meditation sessions, an extraordinary occurrence unfolded—a mystical journey that transcended the boundaries of my physical form, granting me profound relief and revelation. As my consciousness soared beyond the limitations of flesh and bone, I became a detached observer of myself, having an out-of-body experience and gazing upon the essence of my being from a celestial vantage point. In that transcendent moment, my preconceived notions of identity shattered like fragile glass, making way for a magnificent realization that reverberated through the depths of my soul.

Glimpsing beyond the veil of thoughts and perceptions, I bore witness to the eternal essence of my soul self— my consciousness took the form of a luminous bubble suspended in the expanse of the universe. Hovering above my incarnate vessel, it emanated a gentle radiance that whispered of eternity's secrets. Awe and wonder coursed through my very being as I was filled with an insatiable desire to explore the uncharted realms of consciousness, to delve deeper into the enigmatic tapestry of my existence.

In that sacred moment, the yearning to unravel the true nature of my being was kindled, a fire that danced with the celestial stars. It beckoned me to embark on a profound quest, to embrace the boundless depths of my soul, and to embrace the infinite possibilities that lay within the realms of my awakened consciousness.

As my journey unfolded, I embarked on a transformative path of embracing the present moment, liberating myself from the constant stream of thoughts that had once consumed my consciousness. Seeking guidance, I found a wise shaman—an experienced practitioner—who became my trusted mentor. Under their tutelage, I delved into the depths of my being, exploring the practice of shamanic journeying.

Through this ancient art, I learned to connect with my inner self and navigate the hidden landscapes of my psyche. The shamanic teachings opened doors to new dimensions of self-exploration, inviting me to embrace the vastness of my inner world. It empowered me to embark on a journey of self-discovery and spiritual growth, revealing the profound wisdom and healing that lay dormant within me.

With each step on this extraordinary path, I felt a sense of excitement and wonder. The shamanic practices became a gateway to uncharted territories of existence, allowing me to explore the depths of my own consciousness. I cherished the subtle sensations—the gentle rhythms of unseen energies, the vivid imagery that painted the canvas of my mind, and the whispers of ancient spirits guiding me toward profound truths.

In the embrace of shamanic wisdom, I discovered the untapped power residing within me. It awakened dormant potential and ignited a spark of curiosity and courage. Each moment of this journey was a testament to my commitment to self-discovery, an invitation to uncover the beauty and possibilities that awaited those who embarked on this path of personal exploration.

In our transformative work together, the shaman and I delved into the exploration of our root chakras, the energetic centers located at the base of our spines. As we delved into this foundational aspect of our being, a remarkable shift occurred-an unveiling of a deeper truth that would lead me to my encounter with the blessed Holy Mother.

The activation and harmonization of our root chakra served as a catalyst, dissolving the veils that obscured my connection to the divine. It was through this sacred energy work that I gradually became attuned to the subtle realms, paving the way for the extraordinary experience of encountering the blessed Holy Mother. This convergence and spiritual practices and energy alignment created a harmonious resonance within me, enabling me to embrace the sacred presence that awaited me on my mystical journey.

In my early twenties, amidst the rugged Rocky Mountains and under the cover of night, a revelation awaited. It was during my first experience with psychedelic mushrooms that I had a profound encounter with the reality of chakras, the subtle energy centers described in various spiritual traditions. These mushrooms heightened my perception, allowing me to witness the vibrant nature of these energy centers and the intricate fractals of light within them.

The psychedelic embrace transported me into a realm where the vibrancy of chakras shimmered with an ethereal glow. As I embarked on a walk with my friends, I observed how each individual's subtle body operated from different energy centers, manifesting in captivating dances of colorful and mesmerizing fractals of light. It was as if the secret language of the universe had unveiled itself before my very eyes.

Guided by an adventurous spirit, my friends and I ventured into the rugged majesty of the Rocky Mountains, enveloped in darkness beneath the star-studded sky. There, amidst this awe-inspiring backdrop, a revelation awaited. The pulsating energy fields surrounding each person became apparent, signifying their distinct energy centers—the chakras. This visual manifestation ignited an unwavering conviction within me, affirming the profound reality of these mystical gateways.

This encounter shattered the confines of skepticism and ignited an insatiable thirst for understanding. While the concept of chakras had made fleeting appearances in my awareness through the New Age movement of the 80s and 90s, I had regarded it as mere theory. However, this personal odyssey sparked a deeper understanding within me, transcending intellectual speculation.

In the depths of that transformative moment, I realized that chakras were not ethereal abstractions, but tangible portals to divine communion. They held the key to unlocking higher states of consciousness and connecting with realms beyond the ordinary. This epiphany resonated at the core of my being, propelling me into an extraordinary voyage of self-discovery and spiritual growth.

As time passed and I entered later stages in life, a spiritual calling emerged—a desire to participate in a chakra class and delve further into the ancient knowledge surrounding these energy centers. This calling resonated with me due to my previous encounter in my twenties, sensing the significance of chakras.

My intention was to tap into the immense potential of the chakras and harmoniously align them within myself. This sacred pursuit proved to be a transformative tool, fostering personal growth, and illuminating pathways to the divine.

Driven by this profound inner yearning, I embarked on a path of spiritual exploration with a renewed commitment to discovering my true nature. This journey unfolded through various practices such as meditation, contemplation, self-reflection, and engaging with spiritual teachings. By delving into the depths of my being, I sought to align with the wisdom of my higher self and the guidance of the divine. This conscious and intentional exploration, free from external substances, allowed me to connect with a greater sense of clarity, authenticity, and purpose. It became a transformative endeavor that opened to profound self-discovery and a deepening of my spiritual connection.

During my journey of the exploration of the root chakra, I was led to confront the snake that resides within us-an integral part of the transformative process. This experience stirred within me a range of emotions and memories, as I had never been particularly fond of snakes, despite encountering them frequently on the farm where I resided.

In our sacred spiritual journey, we embarked on a profound exploration, guided by ancient wisdom keepers who beckoned us to awaken the serpent within. This symbolic invitation referred to the awakening of Kundalini energy—an extraordinary concept that holds immense significance. It is believed that this dormant, coiled force rests at the base of the spine, representing a wellspring of spiritual power and enlightenment. The term "Kundalini" itself, derived from Sanskrit, means "coiled," evoking the mystique and potential inherent in this transformative energy.

As we delved deeper into our spiritual practice, we discovered that awakening the Kundalini energy was not a mere external encounter with literal serpents. Instead, it served as a profound metaphor for confronting our innermost fears, limitations, and subconscious patterns. It demanded that we courageously face the aspects of ourselves that we had long avoided or suppressed—the shadows that had held us captive. This process of awakening the Kundalini energy was an awe-inspiring journey, one that held the power to liberate stagnant energies, ignite heightened states of consciousness, and propel us toward profound self-realization and transcendence.

Central to our transformative journey was the profound understanding of the divine feminine energy, Shakti, and the divine masculine energy, Shiva. Shakti, the embodiment of the creative aspect of the universe, emanated a vibrant power that infused all of existence with vitality and transformation. Her essence was akin to that of a nurturing divine mother, fostering the growth and evolution of all creation. In contrast, Shiva embodied transcendent consciousness, representing the unchanging essence of the divine. He radiated stillness, embodying the ultimate realization of spiritual truth.

Shakti, as the activating energy, and Shiva, as the serene witness, represented the delicate balance of opposing energies—the union of the feminine and masculine principles. Their synergy symbolized the profound equilibrium and the eternal dance of creation and stillness that lay at the heart of existence.

Within the sacred tradition of Kundalini yoga, an ancient spiritual path rooted in Hinduism, we discovered the transformative tools and practices to awaken the dormant Kundalini energy. This profound journey invited us to embark on an inner pilgrimage, delving into the depths of our body, mind, and spirit in search of the hidden divine essence. The wisdom and techniques of Kundalini yoga, meticulously preserved in the Sanskrit Scriptures known as the Upanishads, have served as a foundation for our journey. However, it is important to note that there are diverse teachings and methods available to individuals seeking to awaken their dormant energy.

The ancient Rishis, the seers, and sages of old, bestowed upon us their timeless teachings. They revealed that our true nature is divine, eternal, and boundless. However, this inherent divinity is often obscured by a veil of ignorance. It is through dedicated spiritual practice that this veil is gradually lifted, revealing the radiant divinity that resides within us all. As we engaged in the practice of visualizing Shakti's potent energy, coiled at the base of the spine, we awakened and channeled the Kundalini energy—a profound process that brought us closer to the realization of our divine essence.

The serpent, a revered symbol in spiritual traditions spanning the globe, intricately wove its way into our awakening journey. It carried deep symbolism, representing transformation, rebirth, wisdom, and knowledge. Within the realm of Kundalini energy practices, the coiled serpent served as a potent metaphor for the dormant Kundalini energy residing within us. Just as the snake sheds its old skin, the awakening of Kundalini demanded that we shed the layers of the past, liberating ourselves from the shackles that had hindered our growth. Through this process, we experienced a profound transformation and spiritual growth, emerging anew on our path of self-discovery.

The sinuous movements of the snake held profound significance, mirroring the winding path of enlightenment and the quest for spiritual insight. As the awakened Kundalini energy rose through the central channel, its dynamic flow activated and purified the chakras along its celestial trajectory. We became immersed in a divine dance—a dance of cosmic connection and the awakening of divine energy, propelling us ever closer to the profound union with the divine that we sought.

In the tapestry of our spiritual work, the awakening of the snake —the Kundalini energy—unveiled the depths of our being, igniting a transformative journey of self-realization and transcendence. It called upon us to confront our innermost truths, to embrace the divine feminine and masculine energies, and to navigate the serpentine path of enlightenment. With each step, we embraced the profound potential within us, merging with the divine and embarking on an extraordinary quest for spiritual awakening and union.

The ancient Rishis, in their wisdom, prescribed the visualization of Shakti's potent energy as the coiled power residing at the base of the spine. This visualization technique, coupled with the power of suggestion, plays a crucial role in its effectiveness. As Albert Einstein once remarked, "Imagination is more important than knowledge," recognizing that knowledge is limited to what we already know and understand, while imagination embraces the boundless realm of possibilities.

As we delved into the exploration of Kundalini energy, we wholeheartedly embraced the power of imagination to broaden our comprehension and enrich our journey. By actively visualizing the image of the coiled serpent, we accessed the boundless potential of our creative mind, establishing a profound connection with the transformative energy residing within us. This imaginative process not only expanded our understanding but also opened pathways to profound revelations. In alignment with this, Jesus imparted the wisdom that if we ask, we shall receive; if we seek, we shall find; and if we knock, doors shall be opened unto us. This principle emphasizes the significance of active engagement and persistent pursuit in our spiritual quest, assuring that those who earnestly seek will be rewarded with divine guidance and opportunities for growth.

When I set out to begin this process of waking up this snake and becoming its friend. I was surprised by the things it brought up in me. It brought back some childhood memories for me that must have been lodged in my subconscious. These resurfacing memories held a certain significance, indicating that they had played a formative role in shaping my beliefs, behaviors, and emotional patterns. The process of delving into my subconscious brought these memories to the forefront of my consciousness, allowing me to examine them with newfound clarity and understanding.

During my childhood, around the age of nine, a vivid memory etched itself into my mind. Hand in hand with my devout Roman Catholic grandmother, I ventured into the sacred realm of the church. Inside those hallowed walls, a statue emerged, depicting the Virgin Mary in her triumphant glory. With resolute determination, she crushed a serpent beneath her heels. As I passed by that captivating sculpture, an unsettling sensation pervaded my being. The serpent, a symbol of malevolence and fear, triggered discomfort, and unease within me. In the realm of my young imagination, the snake epitomized evil, the embodiment of the devil himself, while the blessed mother of Jesus stood as a beacon of protection and solace. It is in these tender years of our existence that the visual language of religious iconography weaves its indelible threads into the tapestry of our perceptions and beliefs.

This experience left a lasting impression on me, as it highlighted the contrasting forces of good and evil, with the Holy Mother serving as a symbol of divine protection against the perceived threats of the world.

Revisiting this memory during my spiritual journey allowed for deeper introspection and understanding. It provided an opportunity to examine the intricate interplay between beliefs, emotions, and personal interpretations of religious symbolism.

In Catholic traditions, it is common to come across statues depicting the Virgin Mary standing on a snake. This particular depiction finds its roots in the biblical passage of Genesis 3:15,[3] where God addresses the serpent following its role in deceiving Adam and Eve in the Garden of Eden. In this passage, God proclaims that there will be enmity between the serpent and the woman (often interpreted as the Virgin Mary) and that the woman's offspring will ultimately triumph over the serpent's power.

Through this visual representation, Catholics are reminded of the role of the Virgin Mary as an advocate and protector against the forces of evil her triumph over evil, and her role in the redemptive plan of salvation.

It is fascinating to observe that the root chakra presents us with a captivating challenge—an energy center that encompasses grounding, self-preservation, safety, trust, and nourishment—qualities that bear resemblance to a child's yearning for a maternal figure in this world. As human beings, we possess an innate longing to be embraced by a higher power or divine entity, seeking solace and affection. To liberate ourselves from the clutches of fear, we must consciously opt not to surrender to its grip. It requires an active choice, a deliberate decision to relinquish fear's hold and foster a mindset abundant in courage, trust, and faith. By consciously electing to transcend fear, we unfurl ourselves to a profound connection with the divine, permitting love and compassion to flow unencumbered within us. This transformative shift in perception and mindset empowers us to perceive a heightened sense of safety and security, recognizing that we are cradled and supported by the tender presence of a benevolent universe.

Through my journey working with this shaman, I was gently led to forge a profound connection with the divine feminine energy, beckoning the dormant serpent within me to awaken. This transformative process demanded that I confront and navigate the hidden recesses of my psyche, unearthing layers of buried experiences and emotions. As I delved deeper into the depths of self-discovery, a remarkable realization unfolded. I discovered that the entire universe, with its vastness and intricacies, resides within the very core of my being.

In the midst of this awe-inspiring revelation, I witnessed the intricate interplay and interconnectedness of all things. Every thread of existence, from the shimmering stars above to the tiniest grain of sand beneath my feet, danced harmoniously within the grand tapestry of life. The boundaries of my perception expanded, allowing me to comprehend the boundless potential that lay dormant within me. It was as if the infinite expanse of creation had taken residence within the depths of my soul.

This profound recognition ignited a spark of liberation and empowerment. I came to understand that I held the power to manifest, create, and transform my reality. The realization that the universe's infinite wisdom and creative energy coursed through my very essence filled me with a sense of purpose and possibility. It was a humbling yet exhilarating realization that I was an integral part of the cosmic symphony, a co-creator in the unfolding of existence.

In embracing the divine feminine energy and awakening the slumbering serpent, I tapped into a wellspring of inner strength, intuition, and wisdom. I embarked on a journey of self-empowerment, guided by the profound understanding that the universe's vastness resided within the depths of my being. With each step forward, I embraced the transformative power that lay within me, ready to shape and illuminate my path with purpose and intention.

This awakening echoes the teachings of Buddha, who illuminated the illusory nature of our individual self and emphasized our interconnectedness with all beings and the world around us. He taught that our actions, thoughts, and intentions carry far-reaching consequences, not only for ourselves but for the entire interconnected fabric of existence. Just as a ripple in a pond reverberates throughout the entire body of water, our actions ripple through the intricate tapestry of life.

By recognizing our inherent connection to all beings, we unlock the potential to create positive change and foster harmony. Each choice we make, each intention we set, has the power to ripple through the collective consciousness, impacting the world around us. Embracing our interconnectedness inspires acts of compassion, kindness, and understanding, nurturing a ripple effect of love and transformation.

Just as a flower herself does not possess its own identity. A flower emerges as a radiant testament to the harmonious dance of oneness. It is a radiant expression of interconnectedness, merging seamlessly with the celestial realms. Each delicate petal unfurls as a testament to its symbiotic relationship with the cosmos. Bathed in the sun's gentle caress, it absorbs the whispers of the clouds, drinks in the nectar of raindrops, and anchors its roots within the nurturing bosom of the earth. In its very essence, the flower embodies a co-dependent nature, a profound unity with all elements. It unveils a timeless truth: we too are interwoven within the cosmic tapestry, intimately connected to the symphony of creation.

It was an astonishing awakening process for me to open the folds of my divine nature. This was when breakthroughs occurred, and the blessed Holy Mother connected with me on this fascinating journey and my consciousness manifested into my reality and I learned who I am and what I am, and the pillars of wisdom opened their door.

Do not forsake wisdom, and she will protect you;
love her, and she will watch over you. Wisdom is supreme;
therefore, get wisdom. Though it cost all you have,
get understanding.

PROVERBS 4:6-7, NIV

The divine essence within us yearns to be awakened and elevated. Within the sacred vessel of our being, we hold the potential to connect with the realms of the divine and to explore the mysteries of the vast universe. In a profound conversation between Jesus and Nicodemus, a wise Pharisee, Jesus imparts a significant teaching.

Jesus tells Nicodemus that to truly understand and embrace his identity and purpose, he must undergo a rebirth-a spiritual transformation that brings about a deepened sense of truth and understanding. Drawing upon an analogy from the Old Testament, Jesus refers to the story of Moses lifting up the snake in the wilderness.

Just as Moses lifted up the snake in the wilderness,
so the Son of Man must be lifted up, that everyone
who believes in Him may have eternal life.

JOHN 3:14, NIV

In that story, the snake was lifted up as a symbol of healing and salvation for the people, Similarly, Jesus explains that he, as the Son of Man, must be lifted up in order to provide a path to eternal life for all who believe in him. This lifting up signifies not only Jesus' crucifixion but also his exaltation and triumph over sin and death.

This conversation highlights the transformative power of faith, understanding, and connection to the divine. It invites individuals, like Nicodemus, to embark on a journey of self-discovery, embracing the truth and teachings of Jesus, and experiencing a spiritual rebirth.

Within your own being, you have the capacity to establish a profound connection with the divine. Through embracing your true "I-Am" essence, you discover that path and recognize the inherent divinity that resides within you. This journey leads to a state of being that resembles Christ, not in terms of blindly following, but in attaining self-realization of your own divine nature.

This invitation is to go beyond perceiving Jesus solely as a historical figure who lived 2000 years ago. Instead, it is to understand that Jesus' essence is alive and present in our daily lives, it is through this personal experience of Jesus rising within us that we come to truly know and meet him as he is.

To "put on the mind of Christ" is not merely an external imitation, but an internal transformation. It is an awakening to the realization that the same divine essence that dwelled within Jesus also resides within each of us. By aligning with this truth, we can embody the qualities and consciousness of Christ in our own lives.

In this understanding, Jesus becomes a guiding light, illuminating the path to self-realization and the recognition of our own divinity. It is an invitation to embrace the risen Christ within us, to cultivate a deep and personal relationship with the divine, and to live from a place of love, compassion, and spiritual awakening.

It was through the opening of my heart chakra; that I had a profound encounter with beloved Jesus and that flame of burning embers continues to ignite my soul. Christ Consciousness is a state of being symbolizing a spiritually resurrected individual. The serpent in scripture is both symbolic of evil and divinity for Jesus himself is represented by the bronze serpent. For those of us who desire to wake up out of our illusions of Maya that we have created for ourselves, we must rise to a higher understanding and empower ourselves with wisdom that can be found within our being.

We possess the freedom to embody qualities of kindness, consideration, care, sharing, compassion, and love. By actively practicing these virtues in our interactions with others, we create an extraordinary experience that aligns with our deeper purpose and existence in this physical form.[4]

In walking through that threshold, I embarked on a remarkable journey of self-discovery, spiritual growth, and the unfathomable wonders that awaited me. And so, with each step, I continued to explore, learn, and expand, guided by the love and wisdom that reside within me, ready to embrace all that lies ahead of this sacred path of awakening.

The essence of the message that the Holy Mother wanted to convey was centered around the radiant light she held in her hands. It was this luminous energy that seemed to be the focal point of her communication. While I do not recall the exact details of her face, the memory of the profound light and energy she carried remains vivid in my mind. This initial mystical encounter served as a preparation for an even more profound and overwhelming mystical experience I would have directly with God five months later.

Although I didn't document the precise date of the visit with the blessed Holy Mother, I do recall that it occurred during garlic planting season. During that period of my life, I was an organic vegetable farmer and seed producer in Avondale, Colorado. Our 40-acre farm cultivated a diverse array of organic vegetables, with garlic being our primary crop. The garlic planting season typically began around October 15th and continued until November 15th. After November 15th, the Bessemer Ditch the lifeblood of the agricultural community sustaining 20,000 acres of farmland, and providing the necessary water resources for farmers to irrigate their crops would get shut off.

During the time when we were planting our fall garlic crop, I finally mustered the courage to share the profound experience I had with the blessed Holy Mother with my partner. The weight of the encounter had become too much to bear in silence, and my heart yearned to confide in someone dear to me. However, opening up about such a deep spiritual experience was not an easy task for me.

I was uncertain about how my partner would react upon hearing my story. The fear of being misunderstood or labeled as "crazy" loomed over me, adding to my hesitation. Nevertheless, the need to share this transformative encounter outweighed my concerns, and I took the leap to confide in my partner.

I was met with sincerity and support from my partner. His response was genuine and understanding, which brought me a sense of relief and comfort. In our conversation, I referred to her as the "Divine Mother," a term that resonated with my spiritually transformative experience of her. Both my partner and I were raised in Catholic families, but we did not consider ourselves to be religious in the traditional sense. Instead, we embraced a more spiritual outlook on life, finding connection and meaning through our relationship with nature and the land.

It was not until this experience with the Divine Mother that I relearned some Catholic views of her and that she was not regarded as a divine being. I was slowly being reminded of the religious views of the church and that only Jesus is seen as divine. While my experience may not align with the traditional teachings of the Catholic Church, I am certain in my heart that the blessed Holy Mother possesses a divine nature. The encounter I had with her on the fall morning was transformative and revealed a presence that transcended the boundaries of human understanding.

I underwent a significant process of transformative reorientation as I grappled with the concepts ingrained in me through childhood conditioning and the direct experience with the Divine Mother. The journey involved reevaluating and reexamining the beliefs and perspectives I had acquired during my upbringing.

The conditioning we receive during our formative years, including religious and cultural influences can shape our worldview and understanding of the world. However, when faced with a direct personal experience that challenges or expands our existing beliefs, we are compelled to question and reassess the ideas we once held. Direct personal experiences possess a unique power to shape our understanding in ways that surpass intellectual knowledge or inherited beliefs. They call us to expand our perspectives, explore new avenues of spirituality, and seek a deeper meaning and truth.

Upon realizing the profound nature of what I had encountered, I came to understand that processing and integrating this experience would take time. It became evident to me that the journey unfolding in my life was not merely an external exploration, but rather an internal journey of the heart.

When I eventually shared with my daughter about the visit I had from the blessed Holy Mother, she asked a simple yet profound question: "Who is the blessed Holy Mother?" It was at that moment that I felt a sense of disappointment and realized that I might have fallen short in my role as a parent. Despite not identifying as a traditional Catholic myself, I was exposed to teachings about God at an early age. However, I had neglected to have open conversations with my daughter about God and matters of spirituality.

During my childhood, I had the freedom to explore various paths to connect with the divine, as I was not raised in a religious household. When I shared the experience of encountering the blessed Holy Mother with my nine-year-old daughter, I explained to her that she is the mother of Jesus and, being the mother of God, she holds the role of our Holy Mother as well.

In an effort to preserve the memory of this encounter, I asked my exceptionally talented nine-year-old daughter, who possesses great artistic skills, to draw a picture based on the description I provided. I wanted a tangible representation that I could hold onto, as I felt the presence of the blessed Holy Mother was gradually fading from my conscious memory, but it remained eternally alive within my heart.

After the visit from the blessed Holy Mother, I decided to purchase a Jesus candle from the store. The candle held deep significance for me, symbolizing my growing faith and connection to the divine. I placed it on my dresser where it served as a constant reminder of the spiritual experience I had encountered.

Figure 2: Dunston, A.S. (2014) "LUMINOUS GRACE:
THE BLESSED HOLY MOTHER'S SPHERE OF LOVE", Crayon and Pencil

Additionally, I developed a fascination with religious icon art depicting the blessed Holy Mother and Christ child. I searched for images that resembled my direct experience, hoping to find something that could capture and reflect the profound feelings I had during the visit. However, despite my efforts, I found no artwork could truly compare or fully encapsulate the depth of emotions and connection I experienced during that encounter.

I delved into researching other apparitions and mystical phenomena that have occurred to individuals from different parts of the world. This helped bring a sense of grounding and centeredness to my spiritual journey. There were moments when I experienced a profound longing to have another encounter with the blessed Holy Mother and continue having visionary experiences. As I dedicated more time to creating a sacred space within myself, allowing for the reception of new perceptions of cosmic energy, my love for God deepened. This period of exploration was accompanied by extensive writing and poetic expression. Through this process, I initiated a dialogue with God, embarking on a magnificent journey in which I felt a profound opening within myself as if my vessel was being expanded to embrace the spirit of God and receive the divine presence within me.

In surrendering to the guidance of the Universe, I set aside fear and doubt, placing my trust in the understanding that the universe recognizes and responds to my being. By relinquishing resistance and embracing what is, I allowed new opportunities to manifest in my life. It became apparent that a profound unfolding awaited my exploration-a journey towards a unified reality of oneness. I surrendered to the divine grace of God and followed the things to which I was called.

At a certain point in my spiritual journey, I made a heartfelt request to God, asking for a teacher to guide me. In response to my prayer, God sent me his beloved son, Jesus. This divine intervention filled my heart with immense joy and delight, bringing me into a state of remembrance and deep communion with the Lord.

I realized that when the student is truly ready, the teacher will appear. This principle reflects the way the universe responds to our sincere intentions and desires. It signifies that when we are genuinely prepared and open to receiving guidance, the appropriate teacher or mentor will manifest in our lives.

This divine interaction reaffirmed my beliefs in the profound workings of the universe and the divine orchestration that guides our spiritual journeys. It emphasized the significance of being receptive and attuned to the signs and opportunities that present themselves.

Continuing my journey of self-exploration and introspection, I dedicated myself to delving deeper into the inner sanctuary of my being. Within this sacred space, I made a profound discovery-the sacred heart of Christ residing within me. It was in this revelation that I encountered the immense love that God has for all of God's children. I underwent a transformative experience, and I was born again of water and Spirit, everlasting, refreshing my soul. My heart was on fire with the love of God.

I opened to God, and I was so happy to come to know his beloved beautiful Son. My heart opened like a lotus petal in full bloom, and grace, love, and joy filled me and my spirit. I was renewed in faith that my spirit had longed to know. My heart is filled with gratitude in knowing "I AM" is always with me, even unto the end of time.

As I embarked on this transformative path of self-discovery, my exploration of the heart chakra and its profound connection to the energy of Christ opened new vistas of understanding and illumination. Through devoted practices and a deep presence within, I tapped into the wellspring of divine love that resided within me, embracing the full spectrum of human emotions and allowing them to guide me toward healing and acceptance. As I nurtured and balanced my heart chakra, I discovered a profound sense of oneness and interconnectedness, not only with myself but with all of creation.

This sacred journey marked the beginning of a profound awakening, propelling me forward into the exploration of my spiritual body and the unfolding of my soul's purpose. It was but a glimpse of the mystical experiences that awaited me as I delved deeper into the realms of my chakra centers, each one beckoning me to uncover new facets of spiritual truth and wisdom. And so, with an open heart and a yearning for divine revelation, I ventured forth into the next chapter of my spiritual odyssey.

2

THE DIVINE UNVEILED:
THE REVELATION OF "I AM"

I AM is the name given to Moses at the burning bush.
God said to Moses, 'I AM WHO I AM.' This is what you
are to say to the Israelites: 'I AM has sent me to you.'

EXODUS 3:14, NIV

This is My name forever, and this is My memorial-name
to all generations.

EXODUS 3:15, NAS1977

As I embarked on my spiritual voyage, I delved deeper into my awakened state, nurturing my journey of self-discovery. At the time of this divine revelation, I was working on my third-eye chakra known as the seat of the soul. The "seat of the soul" is a metaphorical term that refers to the spiritual center or the core of an individual's being.

Enthralled by the mystical realms of spirituality, I embarked on a captivating journey where the boundaries of the physical and ethereal intertwined. Attuned to the beckoning of the divine, I eagerly heeded its call to explore the profound wisdom contained within sacred texts. One such treasure was the Upanishads, an ancient reservoir of knowledge that revealed profound insights into existence and truths beyond ordinary perception. Additionally, the Gospel of

John in the Holy Bible captivated my soul, offering a transforma-tive narrative that resonated deep within. Guided by the whispers of the Spirit, these sacred texts became gateways to transcendence, igniting a profound communion with the divine and sparking my spiritual metamorphosis.

The Upanishads offer a perspective on the universe where every-thing is interconnected and governed by a single underlying prin-ciple known as Brahman, which encompasses the diverse aspects of the cosmos. According to the Upanishads, this Brahman is believed to exist within the atman, which represents the eternal essence of the human individual. Brahman is formless but the birthplace of all forms in visible reality. Atman refers to the individual self or soul. It is the true essence or innermost self of a person that is believed to be eternal and unchanging.

Atman is considered to be distinct from the physical body, mind, and emotions. It is often described as being part of the larger universal consciousness or Brahman, which is the ultimate reality. The concept of Atman is central to the idea of self-realization and spiritual liberation.

I became immersed in the scriptures and ancient Sanskrit texts, and they were familiar to me, like an old best friend. I was deeply im-mersed in a profound connection with the divine. Over an extended period, I experienced a pervasive sense of being in the presence of God. This divine energy permeated everything around me, imbuing the world with a sense of enchantment. The melodic songs of the birds, the gentle caress of the breeze, the majestic presence of trees, the solid yet nurturing ground beneath me, and even the very air I breathed all carried the unmistakable essence of this divine energy.

I found myself in a state of complete surrender, and the atmo-sphere became saturated with a profound sense of divine grace. It was as if the presence of the Lord enveloped me, accompanying me every step of the way.

I was engaged in God. For many days I felt like I was in the pres-ence of God, I felt this energy everywhere and in everything. It was magical where the energy of the Almighty reverberated through ev-ery aspect of existence. My soul danced in the presence of God. It was in the bird's song carrying sacred melodies, the gentle blowing breeze whispered ancient wisdom and the trees stood as earthly sentinels of divinity, and the very ground beneath my feet pulsated with the essence of the divine. Surrendering to this sacred moment, I basked in the radiance of "I AM THAT I AM," feeling the living presence of God enveloping me. I was in a state of surrender and divine grace filled the air and the LORD was with me. I felt like I was in the living presence of all that is in "I AM THAT I AM." I truly felt like God's presence was with me, that he could hear me.

One day when I was in a state of communion with God, I asked God if I could have a picture of God. With a heart brimming with faith, I ventured outside and aimed my camera towards the heavens above, seeking a visual testament of the divine. At first glance, the photographs appeared unremarkable, lacking the glorious apparition or overt signs I anticipated. Yet, when I revisited them with a discerning eye, I discovered an unexpected revelation nestled in the upper-right-hand corner—a subtle yet unmistakable symbol: the number "3" It dawned on me that this synchronicity held profound significance, for the heavens themselves had sent forth a clue, a divine signpost pointing towards the next prelude of my visionary experiences.

Just as the visitation from the Blessed Holy Mother, cradling a radiant ball of light and love had foreshadowed the direct contact with the Almighty, the appearance of the number "3" was a celestial message from the heavens. It whispered to me, reaffirming that God's presence was not confined to a single moment or a finite location. It was a gentle reminder that the divine permeates all aspects of creation, from the grand tapestry of the cosmos to the intricate details of everyday life. In that sacred communion, I realized that my request had been heard, and God's response resided not in a single image, but in the interconnectedness of all things.

With awe and gratitude, I embraced the profound truth that God's presence transcends all boundaries, manifesting in the whispers of the wind, the sacred geometry of numbers, and the depths of my own being. This divine revelation propelled me forward, igniting the spark of curiosity as I eagerly anticipated the next chapter of my visionary journey, guided by the signs and wonders that the divine universe graciously bestows upon those who seek with an open heart.

It happened thirteen days later, nearly forgotten and unexpectedly. It was on the evening of March 31st, 2015, that I became a witness of God's loving presence. I saw a cloud outside, and my heart was called to it. Something was special about it, and my heart knew it. I remember thinking at first sight if it was the Divine Mother or a spaceship. I had a feeling about this cloud like I had when I had my encounter with the blessed Holy Mother. But I immediately discounted my thoughts and went to investigate.

Surrounding the fields where the farmers diligently work, a captivating landscape unfolds. The semi-arid high desert plains stretch out in all directions, exuding an air of rugged beauty. The earth, kissed by the golden rays of the sun, showcases hues of warm ochre and dusty brown. Rolling hills and gentle slopes create a dynamic terrain that adds texture to the vast expanse.

In the distance, the majestic peaks of the Rocky Mountains command attention, their snow-capped summits reaching toward the heavens. These towering sentinels stand as a testament to nature's grandeur and provide a stunning backdrop to the fertile fields below.

The farmers, ever mindful of the precious water needed to nourish their crops, keep a watchful eye on the snow reports from these beautiful Colorado mountains. They eagerly await the snowmelt, which will serve as a vital source of water for their fields, ensuring the growth and vitality of their plants. The convergence of the mountains and the fields symbolizes the interconnectedness of nature's elements, with the snow-capped peaks bestowing their life-giving gift upon the land, fostering a symbiotic relationship between the grandeur of the mountains and the abundance of the fields.

As the last days of March unfold, the landscape is alive with the promise of growth and renewal. The first irrigation has nourished the garlic, infusing the air with its distinct aroma. The fields, tilled and ready, await the gentle touch of the farmers' hands as they sow seeds of leeks and onions, carefully planning the placement of carrots and beets.

Amidst this picturesque scenery, there is an undeniable sense of anticipation and potential. The landscape serves as a canvas for both the toil of the farmers and the artistry of nature, blending together in harmonious coexistence. It is a place where the earthly and the divine converge, where the labor of human hands intertwines with the rhythms of the natural world, creating a tapestry of beauty and abundance.

With my camera in hand, accompanied by my loyal goats and dogs, I embarked on a leisurely walk. As I strolled along, my attention was captivated by a particular cloud that seemed to beckon me. Inquisitively, I studied the cloud, observing its ethereal form as we moved together.

To my astonishment, a profound realization washed over me - the cloud appeared to possess consciousness. It gazed back at me with an otherworldly awareness, as though acknowledging our connection. Despite its seemingly unremarkable appearance, this cloud held an intangible difference that resonated deeply with my attunement to nature.

Having spent years farming in the fertile valley of Avondale, Colorado, as an organic vegetable farmer and seedsman, I had cultivated a profound harmony with the natural world. Each day, I toiled under the open sky, attuned to the elements that shaped and nurtured my crops. Yet, even with my seasoned familiarity, this cloud stood apart, radiating a subtle energy that transcended the ordinary.

While its physical appearance might have mirrored any other cloud one would encounter on an average day, I could sense an extraordinary essence within it. It was as if this cloud held a secret, whispering tales of interconnectedness and hidden wonders, inviting me to explore the depths of its conscious presence.

In that enchanting moment, as the cloud and I engaged in a silent exchange, I realized the profound beauty that lies beyond the surface of our everyday observations. This encounter reaffirmed my deep connection with nature and the mysteries it holds, reminding me that even the most ordinary aspects of existence can unveil extraordinary revelations when approached with an open heart and attuned spirit.

A surge of overwhelming awe consumed me, and my mind echoed with the exclamation "OH MY GOD, THAT IS GOD!" At that moment, a peculiar impulse stirred within me, compelling me to call upon the celestial beings of God's heavenly realm. I called upon Archangel Gabriel, and to my astonishment, ethereal orbs of light materialized in the atmosphere.

As I delved into the teachings of the Upanishads, a profound connection stirred within me. The resonance of divine wisdom echoed in my being, evoking a spontaneous outpouring of the sacred sound, OM. In the depths of my being, I sang this sacred vibration, feeling intimately connected with the divine essence.

In that extraordinary moment, a mystical transformation unfolded before my eyes. The divine presence of God our Father manifested, revealing His divine form. At His right hand, the beloved figure of Jesus emerged, radiating love and compassion. Simultaneously, the blessed Holy Spirit materialized, taking place at the right hand of Jesus, enveloping the scene with divine grace, harmony, and unity. This divine manifestation brought forth a profound sense of awe and reverence, a testament to the interconnectedness and divine nature of the sacred trinity.

In the Bhagavad Gita (The Song of God) one of the greatest spiritual classics of the world, we find these words "I am OM the WORD that is God." The sound of OM is said to contain the entire universe. It signifies the One Supreme power Brahman (the absolute).[5] In the Holy Bible in the book of John 1:1, "In the beginning, was the WORD, and the WORD was with God, and the WORD was GOD." John 1:14, "The WORD of God became flesh and made his dwelling among us, and we saw his glory."

Today holds a profound revelation for you, an opportunity to witness the divine glory and behold the face of God. After my soul-stirring encounter during the walk with the divine presence, I returned home, eager to review the photographs I had taken. As I gazed upon the captured images, my heart overflowed with love for God.

In that transcendent moment, an overwhelming sense of joy washed over me, for I recognized that we, as human beings, are intricately crafted in the image and likeness of our beloved Creator. This realization filled me with a deep sense of gratitude and awe, highlighting the profound connection that exists between the divine and ourselves.

The photographs served as a tangible reminder of the beauty and grace that permeate our existence, mirroring the divine qualities that reside within each of us. It was a poignant reminder that we are not separate from our Creator but rather intimately intertwined with the divine essence.

In this realization, my heart found solace and profound happiness, knowing that we are intricately woven into the fabric of creation, embraced by the love and presence of God. It was a reminder to cherish our divine nature and to seek the reflection of our beloved Creator's attributes in our own lives, spreading love, compassion, and kindness to all those we encounter.

As I sat at the dining room table the following day, completely awe-struck while studying the photographs, my heart overflowing with profound reverence, I found myself repeatedly uttering, "Oh my God, Oh my God, Oh my God!" In that moment of pure astonishment, a remarkable occurrence unfolded.

Gathered outside the window, a flock of birds, resembling small sparrows, approached, their collective presence exuding an ethereal quality. They positioned themselves at eye level as if intentionally seeking to connect with me. To my amazement, these avian beings seemed to embody the essence of angelic hosts.

In an awe-inspiring display, the birds emitted powerful flashes of white-light orbs, akin to bolts of gazing lightning. These radiant bursts of energy enveloped me, leaving an indelible imprint upon my being. As swiftly as they had arrived, they vanished from sight, leaving me in a state of wonderment and curiosity.

Though the exact purpose of this extraordinary encounter remains unknown to me, I couldn't help but perceive it as a validating gesture, a confirmation of the divine nature of my experience in beholding the face of our Almighty Lord. In the presence of these angelic avian messengers, I sensed a profound reassurance that my encounter with the divine was acknowledged and embraced by the heavenly realms.

This inexplicable event served as a gentle reminder that the divine presence permeates all aspects of creation, even in the graceful flight of birds. It reinforced the interconnectedness of the spiritual and natural realms, leaving me with a deepened sense of gratitude and wonder for the mysteries that unfold around us.

It took me considerable time to muster the courage to confide in my family about the awe-inspiring encounter I had just experienced. Even to this day, the memory of it unsettles me, stirring a sense of discomfort within. I mustered the words to convey that I had witnessed God during my walk, and I shared the picture of Jesus with them, albeit without delving into all the intricate details captured within the photograph. The truth is, I felt an overwhelming need to tread cautiously, allowing myself the space and time to process the sheer enormity of this extraordinary event.

There are moments in life that possess such profound beauty and majesty that they defy belief. They transcend the boundaries of human comprehension, leaving us in a state of incredulity. Yet, I stand as a firsthand witness to the resplendent glory of God and the irrefutable presence that enveloped me. It is with deep trust and unwavering faith that I share this extraordinary encounter with you, fully surrendering to the divine knowledge that it holds, waiting for it to be revealed in all its profound splendor.

As the days unfolded, I found myself immersed in a profound state of contemplation, continually absorbing the magnitude of what had transpired. The experience I had encountered felt reminiscent of the monumental awakening that must have surged through the apostle Paul when he had his transformative encounter with Jesus on the road to Damascus.

Just as Paul's encounter with the divine presence had forever altered the course of his life, my own experience had left an indelible mark upon my soul. The revelation of the face of our Almighty Lord, coupled with the awe-inspiring visitation of the angelic avian messengers, had ignited a spiritual awakening within me, akin to a radiant light piercing through the veil of my previous understanding.

In the aftermath of this extraordinary event, I found myself reflecting on the profound implications it had for my journey and purpose. Like Paul, who underwent a radical transformation from persecutor to apostle, I felt a stirring within my being, a calling to embrace a renewed path of faith, devotion, and service.

Just as Paul's encounter with Jesus had sparked a deep devotion to spreading the message of God's love and grace, my own encounter with the divine had ignited a fervor within me to share the boundless beauty and transformative power of such experiences. It was a call to walk a path illuminated by the divine light, guided by a deepened understanding of the interconnectedness of all life and the eternal presence of our beloved Creator.

In the days that followed, I embarked on a journey of self-discovery, seeking to align my actions and aspirations with the profound awakening that had been gifted to me. I was filled with a renewed sense of purpose, and a burning desire to embody the love, compassion, and wisdom exemplified by the apostle Paul and countless other spiritual seekers throughout history.

As I embraced this transformative awakening, I felt a profound sense of gratitude for the divine grace that had touched my life. Just as Paul's encounter on the road to Damascus had forever changed the trajectory of his existence, my own encounter with the divine had set in motion a sacred journey of growth, understanding, and unwavering devotion.

As I embarked on my journey back to the depths of my heart, my faith, and my understanding of God, I kept a printed black and white picture of Jesus on my desk. It was an ancient icon known as Christ the Pantocrator, gracefully housed within the venerable walls of Saint Catherine's Monastery. I longed to grow familiar with its image, to forge a connection with its sacred presence.

The name Pantocrator, most commonly translated as "Almighty" or "All-powerful," encapsulates the essence of divine strength, might, and power. It embodies the totality of divine authority.

In the tranquil evening, as the golden sun gracefully descended beyond the majestic peaks of the Rocky Mountains in Colorado, I seized the opportunity to immortalize the breathtaking scene through my lens. The photograph I captured encapsulated the essence of our Almighty Lord, the divine orchestrator of all existence. Against the backdrop of the semi-arid high desert plains, the vibrant colors and awe-inspiring beauty of nature's canvas vividly reflected the divine presence.

As I wandered around the farm in the ensuing days, seeking to comprehend the profound awe that enveloped me, I contemplated the striking resemblance between the icon on my desk and the photograph. The likeness between the two was remarkable. It was during one of these contemplative moments that I heard a celestial voice resonating from the heavens, uttering the words, "It's the Christ in you."

Those profound words echoed within the depths of my being, stirring a realization. They served as a gentle reminder that the divine presence, symbolized by the Christ figure, resides not only externally but within each and every one of us. The photograph and the icon both reflect the sacred essence that dwells within the core of our being.

From that moment forward, I embarked on a journey of self-discovery, seeking to cultivate and nurture the Christ consciousness within me. This realization became my guiding light, inspiring me to embody the qualities of love, compassion, and wisdom that Jesus exemplified.

Today, I extend this inquiry to all of you: What does Christ look like within your being? The dearly beloved, whom you have yearned to know throughout your entire existence, resides within you. The LORD dwells within the sacred chambers of our hearts. Let us recall the words of Jesus regarding the arrival of the kingdom: "Neither shall they say, 'Lo here or Lo there!' For, behold, the Kingdom of God is within you" (Luke 17:21, KJV).

The date of this profound epiphany aligns with significant religious observances, adding a layer of meaning to the experience. March 31st, a date that has historically seen the celebration of both Passover and Easter, holds particular significance. Passover, a Jewish holiday commemorating the liberation from slavery in ancient Egypt and the offering of the first fruits, coincides with the arrival of spring. Easter, celebrated by Christians, commemorates the resurrection of Jesus from the dead.

The convergence of these religious observances on this date deepens the spiritual significance of the experience. It highlights the interconnectedness of different faith traditions and the profound tapestry of divine providence. This alignment resonates with the universal themes of liberation, renewal, and the triumph of life over death that these holidays symbolize.

The synchronicity of these events serves as a reminder of the profound mysteries inherent in our spiritual journeys. It underscores the depth and richness of our collective human experience and how the divine can manifest itself in our lives.

Attuning to the wisdom and guidance of our hearts opens pathways to higher awareness. Within the depths of our being, the heart acts as a sacred meeting place where we intimately encounter the divine presence within ourselves. It is in this inner sanctuary that we can experience profound communion and nurture a deeply personal relationship with God.

The language of the heart surpasses the limitations of words, allowing us to engage in a profound and authentic conversation with the divine. It is a language of love, intuition, and deep knowledge. As we listen to the whispers of our hearts, we attune ourselves to the subtle guidance and messages that flow from the divine source.

Jesus proclaimed, "The kingdom of God is within you," inviting us to recognize the divine connection within ourselves. Seeking and perceiving the Kingdom of God within unveils the unified reality of oneness that resides deep within us. It is a transformative journey of self-discovery, where veils are lifted, revealing our inherent divinity and the eternal presence of the divine. Embracing this truth, we align with love, compassion, and wisdom, embodying the Kingdom of Heaven on Earth.

I had an opening inside of myself, like a flower budding into bloom in the year 2014, when I surrendered to myself I became more self-aware. This was a healing journey that allowed me to go within myself. I started with meditation and going within myself, and I opened to the Spirit and created a sacred space for me to begin my journey. I went deep inside my being looking for answers and God was with me on my journey helping me along the way, guiding me, and showing me. The experience was graceful, and I felt elevated at times when I came to a profound understanding of myself. Sometimes it was hard to be in this elevated space where I felt supreme joy and bliss. I felt like I was outside of myself in a higher frequency where I wasn't attached to lower thinking and feeling.

My heart was connected to something divine. I wanted to stay in that energy all the time, but the demands of being a human being, a mother, a partner, and a farmer didn't allow me to stay present in that state of awareness all the time because of my physical being. I had to keep grounded in this earthly reality, and the tug and pull of this experience was challenging. One does not look back after they have set the plow to the field and that is what this experience was like for me.

To be in the vibration of joy and grace is an astounding experience. Grace is what transforms us. Grace is the Love of God shown.

I developed a relationship with God and came to know God's dwelling place within me. I connected to my spiritual body. I went inside the energy centers of my divine being.

These inner pathways are called chakras, which is a Sanskrit word that means wheel or disk. In our Spiritual body, we have seven major energy portals that represent different states of awareness in our being. I went through all seven of them, starting with the Root Chakra, which is our foundational support and connects us to Mother Earth.

In my experience traveling through each chakra, I worked through some tough issues, but it was necessary to heal and move forward. When I had this opening of my vessel, I began to have mystical experiences. When I got to my Heart Chakra, I met God in me. The universal Christ the Cosmic Christ. The heart chakra is the source of Love and connection. It is in the middle of the seven chakras and unites the lower chakras of matter and the upper chakras of spirit. It represents love and balance, self-love, devotion, receptivity, trust, compassion, to love and to be loved, and acceptance of self and others. This was where I met Jesus inside of me, in the abode of my heart and thus the second coming of Christ was born in my heart because I prepared a room for him in me, and I was so happy to meet this friend in me and my heart filled with gratitude and thanksgiving.

When I got to my third eye and the crown chakra, I had this stunning experience of co-creating and manifesting with God. The third eye is often referred to as the sixth chakra or the Ajna chakra in Hindu and yogic traditions. It is located in the middle of the forehead, slightly above the space between the eyebrows. The third eye is associated with intuition, insight, and spiritual vision. The crown chakra, also known as the seventh chakra or Sahasrara in Hindu and yogic traditions, is located at the top of the head. It represents our connection to the divine, spiritual consciousness, and higher states of awareness.

I was so delighted to have a connection with Source through my inward experience my faith grew. It is our Faith that holds the awareness of God's existence within our soul and our life. It is your faith that opens you to knowing your place inside the greatness- the greatness that is God. Your faith is the vessel that allows grace to flow from your loving heart and to give life to the beauty in the world.

We are the living resurrection of Jesus and of God's love. Jesus came to teach us to know ourselves in God, and his death was to teach us to know his resurrection in us. God loves his children, and he teaches us to love others as we love him, to see others as he sees us, in doing this unity is realized.

> *I have been crucified with Christ and no longer live*
> *but Christ lives in me. The life I now live in the body,*
> *I live by faith in the Son of God, who loved me*
> *and gave himself for me.*
>
> GALATIANS 2:20, NIV

We are the instruments of peace that bring heaven to earth. We don't have to wait until we die to connect with heaven, heaven is always in our midst. As above, so below is humanity transforming into its divine self, a co-creator, a co-redeemer, thus uniting heaven and earth together knowing "I Am" within us always.

After experiencing a profound revelation with God, I decided to attend church for a brief time. As an adult, I even participated in the sacrament of first communion and enrolled in RCIA classes, which stands for the right of Christian initiation of adults. My intention was to observe how the message of God was being conveyed, deepen my understanding of scripture, and ultimately receive the sacrament of confirmation, which involves the anointing of sacred chrism and the blessed sacrament known as the Eucharist. It's worth mentioning that I had already been baptized when I was around three years old, although my grandmother expressed displeasure at the delay in my baptism. Nonetheless, my father believed it was important for me to have some understanding of the significance of the event.

The celebration of receiving the Eucharist held great significance for me. When I was a child and attended my grandmother's church on occasion, I wasn't permitted to partake in the Eucharist because it wasn't my religious path, and I didn't fully comprehend the concept of Jesus at that time. Nevertheless, the 'Prayer of Consecration' remained my favorite part of attending mass.

Figure 3: (2016) Dunston, J.
CONFIRMATION AND ANOINTING WITH SACRED CHRISM

The Eucharistic Prayer is a solemn prayer in which the priest, act-ing in the person of Christ, offers thanks to God for the gifts of bread and wine, which are then consecrated and transformed into the body and blood of Jesus Christ. This prayer includes various elements, such as thanksgiving, praise, intercession, and the institution narra-tive, where the words of Jesus at the Last Supper are recited.

The Words of Institution for the bread are:

Take this, all of you, and eat of it,
for this is my Body,
which will be given up for you.

The Words of Institution for the wine are:

Take this, all of you, and drink from it,
for this is the chalice of my Blood,
the Blood of the new and eternal covenant,
which will be poured out for you and for many
for the forgiveness of sins.
Do this in memory of me.

These words are reverently recited by the priest, and it is believed that through the power of the Holy Spirit, the bread and wine become the true presence of Jesus Christ, while retaining the outward appearance of bread and wine.

My understanding of Jesus as a child was limited to seeing him as a historical figure—born in Bethlehem, a carpenter turned teacher, and crucified at the age of 33. He was a distant figure on a cross, someone with whom I lacked a personal connection. My perception of him was devoid of a living, breathing relationship. However, after my encounter with the divine, my desire to participate in receiving the Eucharist grew.

The idea of Jesus transitioned for me from being a historical figure to a living Jesus who is the son of God who was resurrected and who continues to live within us.

Jesus states that his kingdom is not of this earth, he implies that his mission and the nature of his kingdom transcend the temporal and earthly realm. It suggests a spiritual dimension that goes beyond the ordinary human experiences and is rooted in a higher reality or divine realm.

Jesus knew how the stories of his life would unfold and in these biblical stories, he instituted the Eucharist as a means for humanity to remember him. The purpose of the Eucharist is to contribute to the restoration and manifestation of the divine realm that exists within us.

Sometimes the songs that we would sing in church would melt my heart and I would weep; at times it was so overwhelming. After bearing witness to God and God's Almighty love, seeing the Revelation of Jesus Christ and the Blessed Holy Spirit, and connecting with the nature of our heavenly Father in such an intimate way I wanted to tell the world the Good News.

Surprisingly though it's not just something you can tell people. Part of me wanted to tell people Jesus is here, he's always with you, he sees you, he knows you and he dwells in your heart, and he loves you unconditionally!

Many people of faith are always talking about the kingdom coming and Christ's return, but they don't understand that it has already come it is here, it is now; it is always. It can be experienced anytime you choose, that power is within you. I had to separate the church's teaching of Jesus verse the Jesus that I know within myself.

I was a steward of the scriptures daily for a while and would read "The Daily Reading" USCCB (United States Conference of Catholic Bishops)[6] every day. I wanted to see how the homily would be preached, and I would often make my own homily. This helped me delve into the text and contemplate its message.

CHALLENGING DOGMA: EMBRACING LOVE AND INCLUSIVITY IN THE FACE OF RELIGIOUS CONSTRUCTS

I did eventually stop attending Mass although I miss it sometimes. I appreciated some of the rich mystical rituals the Catholic faith has. I feel at home in a Catholic church setting, and I was very fortunate to find a Catholic church with inspiring, heartfelt teachings.

I made an effort to involve my daughter in my religious activities, hoping that it would spark meaningful conversations about faith and God between us. At times, I felt conflicted and hypocritical, especially considering my daughter's open identification as gay and her belonging to the LGBTQIA community. She revealed her sexual orientation to us when she was just 10 years old, and I wholeheartedly love and accept her, as does God.

I have always encouraged her to embrace her true self. However, I have observed that certain organized religions, depending on the specific church, can be judgmental, and this is one of the aspects of religion that I find disheartening.

Throughout the history of Judeo-Christianity, there has been a longstanding tradition of condemning homosexuality. But let's dive into a thought-provoking narrative that challenges preconceived notions and rigid beliefs. Picture this: Peter, one of Jesus' closest disciples, finds himself in a wild vision. A sheet descends from above, filled with all sorts of animals that are considered unclean and forbidden to eat according to Jewish dietary laws.

In this extraordinary moment, God instructs Peter to feast on these taboo creatures. Now, Peter, being a devout follower, is taken aback and adamantly refuses to partake in this forbidden meal. But God persists and insists, saying, "Eat." It's a jaw-dropping encounter that challenges Peter's deep-rooted convictions.

This narrative reveals something profound. It shows us that even the most righteous leaders and disciples can experience transformative shifts in their understanding of certain biblical texts when they have a direct connection with the divine. It reminds us that religious institutions today may have bound themselves to false beliefs, constraining their ability to embrace new perspectives.

So, what does this mean for the topic of homosexuality? Well, if we consider Jesus' teachings and his approach to challenging societal norms, it's plausible to suggest that he wouldn't have seen homosexuality as a sin. Just as Peter's vision led him to question his preconceived notions, we can imagine Jesus encouraging us to approach matters of love, sexuality, and human relationships with compassion and understanding.

The parable of Peter serves as a powerful reminder that our interpretations of religious texts and teachings can evolve. It encourages us to break free from the chains of stagnant beliefs and embrace a more inclusive and loving perspective that aligns with the core message of Jesus' teachings.

When exploring the subject of homosexuality, it is stated by the Catholic Church that individuals with a homosexual orientation should be regarded as children of God, deserving of respect, compassion, and sensitivity. The Church's stance is explicit in accepting homosexual individuals as integral members of the Body of Christ. However, it also maintains the teaching that engaging in homosexual behavior is considered morally inappropriate.[7]

In the realm of human constructs, religion has often intertwined with societal views and interpretations of divine will. However, it is crucial to recognize that the notion of God condemning homosexuality is not an inherent truth emanating from a divine source.

Unfortunately, our human constructs of religion, shaped by cultural biases and personal interpretations, have sometimes given rise to divisive beliefs and discriminatory practices. It is important to acknowledge that the condemnation of homosexuality, as propagated by certain religious institutions, is a product of these constructs rather than a reflection of the divine.

In our pursuit of a just and inclusive society, it becomes imperative to challenge and critically examine the origins of such beliefs. By recognizing that these perceptions are human-made and not universal truths, we can foster greater understanding, compassion, and unity within our community.

Let us strive to build a society where love, acceptance, and equality transcend the confines of prejudice. Instead of tailoring laws to fit our prejudices, we should embrace the true essence of spirituality—a force that embraces all individuals, regardless of their sexual orientation.

By rejecting the idea that God condemns homosexuality as a human construct, we can work towards creating a more compassionate and inclusive world, where diversity is celebrated and all individuals are afforded the respect and dignity they deserve.

FROM VISION TO VATICAN: A PERSONAL ENCOUNTER THAT CHALLENGES BELIEFS AND MIRACLES

After my experience, I felt compelled to share it with the Pope, and in 2015, I wrote a letter recounting my profound encounter. In the Catholic faith, there are specific protocols to follow when reporting a miracle, and the Vatican has a procedure in place for certifying what qualifies as a miracle. Miracles are an important aspect of the Catholic faith. A miracle is defined as an extraordinary and astonishing happening that is attributed to the presence and action of an ultimate or divine power.

The Vatican's evaluation of alleged mystical or supernatural phenomena typically involves a rigorous and lengthy process. The Church carefully investigates such claims, considering factors such as historical evidence, testimonials, and theological implications before making an official pronouncement.

I also shared my experience with my spiritual advisor and had a meeting with the Catholic Bishop. This, however, did not go far and no one reached out to me about my claims.

I never heard back from the Pope, but I did give a photograph of God to my priest and had a meeting with him about my experience. He did see Jesus in my photograph. I asked God about this later after my failed attempts to shed light on this significant moment in the history of the world and God told me it was because of fear. Fear causes limitation and uncertainty.

In the Catholic faith, miracles are attributable to divine power and beyond the abilities of nature, seemingly extraordinary and the ability to sense. A miracle will need to be perceptible by the senses. Miracles are a signature from Spirit and correspond to a vortex of spiritual energy in space. I thought I would be a perfect candidate for the Holy See, a governing body of the Roman Catholic Church to be intrigued by the evidence I was presenting.

There are however numerous miracles that have been presented to the Vatican that have not officially been pronounced as definitive even though there have been many eye-witnessed accounts throughout history.

One story that I find fascinating that has not been conclusively determined by the Vatican is the miracle of the bi-locating nun known as Blessed Maria de Jesus Agreda born in Spain who was a Franciscan nun who bi-located to the Jamano Indians of central New Mexico and West Texas who they referred to as the "Lady in Blue" who flew through the sky in the 1620's teaching the Gospel and made hundreds of visits endowing her wisdom and love of God to the Jumano Indians. By 1626, reports from New Mexico were relaying stories of American Indians arriving at missions because a "Lady in Blue" had told them to go and speak to the priests at those missions.

However, I have no desire to be classified as a saint and I had to leave the Catholic Church because I disagreed with many of its views, especially on homosexuality and sin. Why would a benevolent deity bestow upon us the ability to make choices freely, only to judge us according to how we utilize that freedom? Such a God would seem to possess conflicting attributes.

The divine essence of God permeates everything, and there is no realm where the affection of the divine does not attend. The love of the divine is all-embracing and limitless, extending an invitation to all individuals to partake in the divine realm. Regrettably, certain present-day religious institutions endorse a narrow-minded and condemning perception of God, which cultivates an atmosphere of segregation, condemnation, retribution, and judgment.

Our society has been reluctant to embrace the notion that we can genuinely comprehend God and recognize that God's love surpasses wrath. I encourage individuals to seek a personal relationship with God. The love of God is accessible to everyone, and God acts as a caring and accepting parent to all of us. Society needs to release the fearful notion of a vengeful God. Maintaining such beliefs does not bring us any benefits; instead, it sustains incorrect perceptions.

We bear the responsibility of shaping the reality within our community. We should reject the damaging theology that fosters fear and contradicts the fundamental nature of a loving Creator. Continuing to teach and support these concepts is sacrilegious and does not contribute to the greater welfare of humanity.

Until our society relinquishes its hold on fear-based religious beliefs, we will remain trapped in a challenging predicament. Humanity must listen to their hearts and come together with the living Creator, establishing a personal connection rather than relying on an ancient book written by individuals who feared God. Our creator is the deity of life itself. It is imperative to make the choice now to embrace the true essence of our beloved creator, not as a source of fear, but as a source of love.

In any given moment, there are only two genuine emotions: fear and love. For the survival of the species, humanity must let go of the past perception of God. If we persist on the path of fearing God, we will never truly comprehend the divine. We possess the power to shape our own reality, and it would be highly beneficial to transcend these ideals that are contrary to the teachings of Christ.

We are interconnected and inhabit a participatory universe that is alive, conscious, and continuously evolving. The conscious universe responds to how we think and feel and unity among our species is of utmost importance.

When, Jesus says, "You will know them by their fruits," he is referring to a concept found in the New Testament of the Bible, specifically in the Gospel of Matthew (Matthew 7:15-20). In this passage, Jesus is teaching his disciples about discerning false prophets or teachers.

In today's world, many religious institutions are inconsistent with the teachings of Jesus and the principles of righteousness. Their "fruits" may involve fear, condemnation, deception, greed, hypocrisy, and false insights into who and what God is. Jesus encourages his disciples to be discerning and reminds us of the good fruits that will last including qualities such as love, kindness, patience, goodness, compassion, humility, honesty, joy, peace, self-control, and compassion.

UNVEILING THE TRANSFORMATIVE POWER OF PRAYER AND SURRENDER: EMBRACING DIVINE GUIDANCE AND LOVE

Mark 11:24, Jesus said, "Therefore I tell you, whatever you ask in prayer, believe that you have received it, and it will be yours."

The apostles once approached Jesus with a question about how to free ourselves from the inner struggles that plague us. In response, Jesus pointed them towards the power of prayer. There's a fascinating account in the Holy Bible where Jesus encountered a child possessed by an unclean spirit. His disciples attempted to expel the spirit but were unsuccessful. Puzzled by their inability, they inquired why they couldn't drive out the spirit. Jesus simply replied, "This kind can be cast out only by prayer" (Mark 9:29, NLV). This incident highlights the significance of unwavering faith and the act of seeking divine intervention through prayer. It reveals that certain challenges and obstacles can only be overcome by communion with the divine.

The act of prayer holds immense power. But what exactly is prayer? Prayer can be understood as the connection between our individual consciousness and a higher consciousness. It serves as a bridge that brings us into contact with God, the divine. Through prayer, we express our intentions for the greater good, setting forth our desires with a profound sense of purpose.

Intentions, in themselves, possess a remarkable potency. They act as influential tools in shaping our experiences. Even our emotions carry the weight of prayer. When we unite our thoughts and feelings within the depths of our hearts and genuinely believe that our prayers have already been fulfilled, we manifest our deepest desires. It is in this state of being, enveloped by the sensation that our prayers have already been answered, that we bring our intentions to life.

Our feelings themselves become the prayer, a sacred communion nurtured within the sanctuary of our inner being. If our intention is to seek a connection with God, the divine presence will undoubtedly reveal itself to us. By embracing this intention wholeheartedly, we unlock the pathway to divine revelation.

Research has shown that a significant majority of people worldwide partake in prayer as a practice, expressing feelings of admiration or gratitude. A substantial portion of these prayers involve making requests to a higher power and seeking positive outcomes for oneself or loved ones.

In summary, prayer is a powerful force. It establishes a profound connection between our consciousness and a higher consciousness. It is the intentional expression of our desires for the greater good. By aligning our thoughts and emotions, and embracing the sensation that our prayers have already materialized, we unlock the transformative potential of prayer within the sacred temple of our being. And for those who yearn to know God, their sincere intention will undoubtedly lead to divine revelation. When we engage in prayer or establish a state of communion with God, we cultivate a sense of unity and connection with the divine.

Through our thoughts, words, and actions, we are guided toward gaining knowledge and bringing about the desired outcomes aligned with our intentions. Prayer, in its essence, has the potential to directly impact the world.

This parable is powerful. "This kind cannot come out, except by prayer." We have all had those moments in life where we feel like we have no choice but to surrender because we do have not the skills to change or fix an issue we are faced with. We can become possessed by a story that our mind is telling us in our head or an idea that encompasses and embodies our being.

This is the state that the Buddha referred to as "suffering." In teaching the four noble truths and the eight-fold path we discover that the means of finding liberation from suffering is always available to us. When we combine the teachings of great spiritual masters such as the beloved Jesus and Buddha, we can come to new understandings about ourselves. Jesus taught that the presence of God exists within each individual.

Suffering arises from a lack of understanding about our true essence and identity. To overcome suffering, one must disassociate from their ordinary self and embrace their divine nature. The attainment of salvation, or the lack thereof, hinges upon this process of inner metamorphosis.

According to the teachings of Paramhansa Yogananda, spiritual surrender involves offering one's will to God, recognizing that by doing so, one can discover a transformative path that stems from a new understanding. Surrender is the realization that an improved way can only arise through a different perspective.

In the Vedic scriptures, the concept of spiritual surrender is described as the "bliss of surrender." It is the delightful and uplifting sensation experienced when one completely releases and relinquishes control. It involves transcending all limitations, going beyond one's usual patterns and beliefs, and embracing boundless potential. It entails surrendering the limited sense of self or personal identity to merge with the absolute.

Indian yogi and guru Paramahansa Yogananda expressed the idea that through surrender, the soul has the ability to broaden its awareness, much like an infinite sphere of light, until it encompasses the state of omnipresence.

To achieve complete surrender, one must possess faith. Surrender necessitates a state of awareness. It demands patience, and the ability to let things unfold naturally while understanding that everything necessary will effortlessly manifest at the ideal moment.

We are constantly evolving and changing, not bound by any particular state of circumstance. The Heart Chakra resonates with the energy of un-stuck-ness, and acceptance is the key to unlocking this freedom. When we feel dissatisfied and desire liberation, acceptance becomes the essential first step. By opening our hearts and minds to a higher power or source, we undergo a transformative experience. "For My thoughts are not your thoughts, neither are your ways My ways, declares the LORD" (Isaiah 55:8, BSB).

Surrendering to the moment of acceptance allows us to transcend the narrative we create in our minds, instead of being caught up in our thoughts, we can experience the simplicity of the present moment and find liberation from our self-imposed stories. Being fully present in the moment, rather than entangled in our mental narratives, brings about a sense of release. When we enter a state of heightened awareness and perceive ourselves as conscious beings rather than solely thinking individuals, we become aware human beings.

The essence of our creative ability exists within our unity, and the divine presence of God extends throughout the universe. By relinquishing control and embracing the grace and direction of God, our prayers are not only heard but also consistently answered. There is a resonance between our vibrational states and the manifestation of our desires.

Jesus said it best "Your faith has made you well" Jesus did not perceive individuals as being defined by their illnesses. Instead, he saw them for who they truly were and had a profound understanding of their well-being. His unwavering belief in the power of God was so strong that it created a vibrational state where illness could not persist. In essence, Jesus conveyed that their faith and trust in the power of God served as the pathway to their healing and continued well-being.

The practice of mindfulness alleviates suffering by cultivating understanding and compassion. When one embraces mindfulness, one embraces love and comprehension. This deepened perception enables them to address and heal the inner wounds of their own mind. By connecting with profound understanding and love, one experiences healing. Similar to Jesus, who had the ability to bring about healing through touch, the healing power of mindfulness extends to whatever it encompasses.

In conclusion, as instruments of peace, we have the extraordinary ability to bring heaven to earth through the resonance between our vibrational states and the manifestation of our desires. By learning to be fully present in the moment, we free ourselves from suffering and open ourselves to the profound wisdom and joy that lies within.

Letting go of fear-based belief systems allows us to recognize and embrace the divine essence that exists within each of us. Furthermore, we discover that the power of prayer and intentions are potent tools that shape the creation of our experiences. By harnessing these transformative forces, we can co-create a reality filled with love, harmony, and fulfillment. May we continue to explore and cultivate these profound truths to contribute to a world where peace and divine beauty flourish.

When we contemplate the happenings within our inner world, we simultaneously contemplate the contents of the collective human consciousness. If our desire is to witness peace and harmony, we must cultivate those qualities within ourselves. By delving deeper into self-reflection, we not only enhance our own consciousness, frequency, and vibration, but we also make a positive contribution to the overall consciousness and elevated vibrational state of the collective.

Directing our focus toward what we genuinely love represents an immensely potent state of being. Returning to the core of our being, where pure love resides, aligns us with the ultimate truth—that love is the sole prevailing force.

3

3 IS SEEING THE HAND OF
THE DIVINE ARCHITECT AT WORK

For there are three that bear witness in heaven: the Father,
the Word, and the Holy Spirit; and these three are one.
And there are three that bear witness on earth: the Spirit,
the water, and the blood; and these three agree as one

1 JOHN 5:7-8, NKJV

GOD LISTENS. ON THE DAY WHEN I INQUIRED IF I COULD POSSESS
an image of God, I ventured outdoors to capture photographs
of the sky above. During this endeavor, I sensed a certain presence,
and in this particular image, you will observe the number "3" located
in the upper right-hand corner, accompanied by a thought-provoking and fanciful outline. This photograph serves as a foreshadowing
of my subsequent profound encounter, wherein the sacred nature of
our One God is manifested through three distinct individuals the
Father, the Son, and the Blessed Holy Spirit.

The doctrine of the Holy Trinity is a foundational and distinctive
belief within Christianity, encapsulating the understanding of God's
nature as three persons in one being. Its roots can be found in the
teachings of Jesus Christ and the writings of the New Testament. In the
early centuries of Christianity, theologians and Church Fathers grappled with questions about the relationship between Jesus Christ, the
Holy Spirit, and God the Father.

Figure 4: Dunston, J.C. (2014)
"DIVINE PRELUDE: THE ENIGMATIC NUMBER THREE"

One notable figure in the development of the Trinity doctrine was Tertullian, a North African theologian who coined the term "Trinity" (Latin: *trinitas*) to describe the nature of God. He emphasized the unity of the Father, Son, and Holy Spirit while affirming their distinctiveness.

Constantine, the Roman Emperor, played a significant role in the history of Christianity, particularly regarding the doctrine of the Trinity. While he did not directly shape its theological formulation, his influence on the Council of Nicaea in 325 CE had a profound impact on its development and subsequent acceptance within the early Christian Church.

During Constantine's reign, Christianity transitioned from being a persecuted religion to gaining imperial favor and recognition. Constantine himself converted to Christianity and sought to unite the fractured Christian community under a common doctrine, seeing religious unity as a means to strengthen the empire and promote social cohesion.

In 325 CE, Constantine convened the Council of Nicaea, a gathering of bishops from various regions of the Roman Empire. The primary purpose of the council was to address the theological controversy surrounding the nature of Jesus Christ and his relationship with God the Father, with Arius proposing a view known as Arianism, which denied the full divinity of Jesus Christ.

The Council of Nicaea, under Constantine's guidance, sought to resolve this controversy and establish a unified belief concerning the nature of Christ. It produced the Nicene Creed, affirming the full divinity of Jesus Christ and his consubstantiality with God the Father. While Constantine did not directly influence the creed's content, his role in convening the council and using his authority ensured its widespread acceptance, solidifying the orthodox position on the Trinity within the Christian Church.

Further elaboration and refinement of the Trinity doctrine occurred at the Council of Constantinople in 381 AD, which affirmed the divinity of the Holy Spirit, completing the formulation of the doctrine as it is commonly understood today.

The hand of the divine architect can be seen in various aspects of existence. Various cultures across the world have long shared a belief that the number three carries a sense of sacredness, mystique, and even divinity. The distinct veneration of the number three has ancient roots and extends back thousands of years and its influence can still be observed in contemporary expressions of art, architecture, mythology, literature, science, and religion.

However, the question remains: What is it about the number three that has consistently maintained its significance for humanity? There seems to be an inherent message or meaning that the number three is attempting to convey, a message that seeks to capture our attention and communicate something important.

Is there an innate aspect within our being that instinctively recognizes the number three as a sacred symbol, and if so, what is the source of this recognition? There is a trinity that exists within each one of us. The recognition of the number three as a sacred symbol can be attributed to an innate aspect within our being. It stems from the understanding that there exists a trinity within each of us: the mind, body, and soul. This trinity reflects the interconnected nature of our existence.

In the story of Jesus' baptism, Jesus is standing in the Jordan River and we're told that the heavens open up and the Holy Spirit in the form of a dove descends upon Jesus. And the voice of God booms out of heaven and says, "This is my Son whom I love; with him, I am well pleased. Listen to him," (Matthew 3:17, NIV). In that particular scene, the representation consists of three entities: the Father, the Son, and the Holy Spirit.

The captivating nature of the Trinity lies in its enigmatic quality and mathematical conundrum, as it raises the question of how one can simultaneously be three. Often described as "three in one," this concept defies conventional mathematical calculations and remains a fascinating mystery.

In the realm of Indian culture and spirituality, there exists a divine trinity known as the Trimurti. This trinity comprises three primary deities: Brahman, Vishnu, and Shiva. Brahman represents the ultimate reality, the supreme cosmic power from which all existence emanates. Vishnu is the preserver and sustainer of the universe, responsible for maintaining cosmic order and harmony. Shiva, on the other hand, embodies the transformative and destructive forces necessary for regeneration and renewal. Together, these three deities symbolize different aspects of the divine and play essential roles in the Hindu belief system.

Within the Buddhist framework, there exists a concept of a Trinity, although it is distinct from the traditional notion of a triune deity. This Trinity revolves around the figure of Buddha, who serves as the central focal point. In this context, wisdom and compassion emerge as the primary polarities that form the Trinity within Buddhist thought. Wisdom represents profound insight, understanding, and discernment, while compassion embodies empathetic care, kindness, and love toward all sentient beings. Together, wisdom and compassion form a harmonious duality that encompasses the essence of Buddhist teachings and practices, emphasizing the importance of both intellectual understanding and compassionate action in the pursuit of enlightenment.

Across different philosophical and religious traditions, various trinities emerge, each offering unique insights into the nature of existence and the human experience. Additionally, another trinity that transcends specific religious boundaries is the mind, body, and spirit, acknowledging the interconnectedness and holistic nature of human existence. These diverse trinities offer profound perspectives on the divine, the human journey, and the intricate interplay between different facets of existence.

Does the number three serve as a divine design and a perfect means of communication? It can be perceived as a gateway through which the divine manifests itself, showcasing its intricate architecture. Numerous examples in nature symbolically convey profound messages to us, highlighting the wonders that surround us.

◊ **Natural Phenomena:** The intricate patterns of a snowflake, the vibrant colors of a sunset, or the delicate symmetry of a flower all reflect the meticulous design of the divine architect.

◊ **Human Anatomy:** The complexity and precision of the human body, from the intricacies of the circulatory system to the remarkable capabilities of the brain, testify to the handiwork of the divine architect.

◊ **The Celestial Bodies:** The vastness of the cosmos, with its galaxies, stars, and planets, showcases the divine architect's masterful creation, guiding the celestial bodies in their cosmic dance.

◊ **Synchronicity:** Moments of synchronicity, where events align in meaningful and seemingly miraculous ways, can be seen as the hand of the divine architect orchestrating the tap-estry of life.

◊ **Serendipity:** Unexpected encounters, fortuitous opportunities, and moments of inspiration can be seen as the workings of the divine architect, guiding us along our unique paths.

◊ **Prophetic Fulfillment:** The fulfillment of prophecies men-tioned in their sacred texts is seen as evidence of the divine architect's plan unfolding.

◊ **Miracles and Divine Intervention:** Religious texts often re-count stories of miracles and divine intervention, where the hand of the divine architect is evident in supernatural events that defy natural laws. These occurrences are seen as signs of the divine presence and influence.

◊ **Symbolic Languages and Parables:** The Parable of the Mus-tard Seed. The parable compares the growth of faith to the growth of a tiny mustard seed into a large tree. It symbolizes the transformative power of even the smallest acts of faith and the divine architect's ability to bring about profound change.

◊ **The Allegory of the Cave (Plato's "The Republic"):** Although not a religious text, this allegory presents a powerful metaphor for a journey of enlightenment. It depicts prisoners confined to a cave, perceiving only shadows on the wall. The allegory symboliz-es the divine architect's call to transcend illusions and seek higher truths beyond the limited perception of the physical world.

These are a few examples that illustrate how the hand of the divine architect can be perceived in the wonders of nature, the marvel of the human body, the cosmic realms, and meaningful coincidences. These various manifestations are regarded as channels through which the divine architect communicates with humanity, providing guidance, inspiration, and a deeper understanding of the divine plan.

God encompasses all objects, their relationships, and the princi-ples governing their interactions. God represents the greatest con-ceivable existence, which encompasses the entirety of existence itself.

God can be understood as Nature, denoting the entire system or universe in which we reside. The universe possesses immense power, as everything that occurs operates according to the laws of existence established by God. Every aspect of existence adheres to these rules, thereby highlighting the all-encompassing power of God.

The universe possesses a certain awareness of all states of existence. Consequently, the universe cannot be ignorant of your existence, much like how the laws of physics cannot be unaware of your presence. If we consider existence as divine, then each individual possesses a divine essence within them.

When we say that the universe possesses an awareness of all states of existence, it is not in the same way that a conscious being possesses awareness. Rather, it refers to the idea that the universe operates according to fundamental laws and principles that govern all phenomena. These laws, such as the laws of physics, describe the behavior and interactions of matter and energy in the universe.

In this sense, the universe "knows" or "acknowledges" all states of existence because it encompasses the totality of these laws. Every event, every interaction, and every state of existence in the universe is governed by these fundamental principles. The universe, through these laws, determines the behavior and development of everything within it, including ourselves.

THE TRUE NATURE: EXPLORING THE THREEFOLD PERSONHOOD OF GOD

The understanding of God as both an action and a personal manifestation can be approached in the context of the Christian understanding of the Trinity. In Christian theology, God is considered the source and origin of all existence and action. God is the ultimate reality, the ground of being, and the sustainer of the universe. From this perspective, God can be understood as the primary actor of the ultimate "verb" that encompasses all actions and happenings.

At the same time, the Christian doctrine of the Trinity acknowledges that God has revealed Himself in a personal and relational manner. The Trinity teaches that God is not only an abstract force or concept but also a personal being who interacts with humanity. The three persons of the Trinity- Father, Son, and Holy Spirit-represent distinct ways in which God reveals Himself and engages with creation.

The Father is seen as the source and originator, the Son (Jesus Christ) is the manifestation of God in human form, and the Holy Spirit is the active presence of God in the world and in the lives of believers. Each person of the Trinity is fully God, sharing the same divine nature, while also having distinct roles and relationships with the Godhead.

So, the understanding of God as an action and a personal manifestation can be reconciled within the framework of the Trinity. God is the ultimate source of all action and happening, while also being capable of revealing Himself personally through the Son and the Holy Spirit. The Trinity provides a way to understand the multifaceted nature of God's engagement with creation, encompassing both the transcendent and immanent aspects of God's presence and activity.

The understanding of the threefold person of God expresses the belief that there is one God who exists eternally as three distinct persons, yet they are not three separate gods but one God in three persons.

The concept of the Trinity is not explicitly stated in the Bible as a whole, but it is derived from the collective teachings of various bible passages. The early Christian theologians and councils, through careful study and reflection, formulated the doctrine of the Trinity to articulate and safeguard the biblical teachings about God's nature.

Several passages support the doctrine of the Trinity. Here are a few biblical passages often referenced in support of the Trinity:

1. **Matthew 28:19:** "Go therefore and make disciples of all nations, baptizing them in the name of the Father, and the Son and the Holy Spirit." This verse reflects the Trinitarian formula used in Christian baptism, invoking the three persons of the Trinity.

2. **Corinthians 13:14:** "The grace of the Lord Jesus Christ and the love of God and the fellowship of the Holy Spirit be with you all."

3. **John 1:1-14:** This passage describes the Word (Jesus) as being with God and being God, emphasizing His divine nature while also distinguishing Him from the Father. It highlights the existence of the Son alongside God from the beginning.

4. **John 15:26:** Jesus speaks of the coming of the Helper (Holy Spirit) and states, "He will bear witness about me." This verse indicates the role of the Holy Spirit in testifying about Jesus and His mission, highlighting His distinct personhood.
5. **Colossians 1:15-20:** This passage speaks of Christ as the image of the invisible God, the firstborn of all creation, and the one through whom all things were created. It highlights the deity of Christ and His involvement in the creation and sustenance of all things.

The concept of the Trinity can be challenging to comprehend fully. It is a mystery that reflects the complexity and unity of God. The paradoxical nature of the Trinity is that the Trinity involves holding seemingly contradictory truths together. It asserts that God is both one and three at the same time. This paradoxical nature can be challenging for our logical minds to reconcile. The Trinity shapes the understanding of God's nature and relationship with humanity. The Trinity emphasizes the dynamic relationship and mutual love that exists among the Father, the Son, and the Holy Spirit. The persons of the Trinity are in eternal communion and perfect unity, sharing a divine love that is the very essence of their existence.

As someone who has experienced God's presence and personally witnessed the Triune nature of God reflected in Nature, I have examined various scriptures that highlight different aspects of God's existence in the natural world. These scriptures, which I will now share with you, will help you understand more clearly the unveiling of God's essence as seen through my perception.

~ *Our Heavenly Father* ~

Behold, a conscious cloud, a sacred light, where God's presence dances, effortlessly light. A formless entity, yet aware and wise, expanding across the canvas of boundless skies. Within the cloud, the essence of all that is, A tapestry woven with love's gentle kiss. It whispers secrets of the universe's song, unveiling mysteries that have been hidden for long.

The use of anthropomorphism in the Bible allows humans to grasp and relate to the nature of God, who is otherwise invisible and transcendent. By assigning visual, animated, and definable qualities to God, it becomes easier for us to understand and connect with His attributes. In various verses, such as Daniel 7:9, Psalm 104:3, Matthew 17:5, Job 37:15-16, and Ezekiel 1:28, natural elements and phenomena like clouds, fire, and rain are metaphorically used to symbolize God's presence, power, and attributes.

For instance, the imagery of God riding on the clouds in Daniel 7:9 emphasizes His sovereignty and might. It portrays Him as having control over the elements and moving swiftly with great power. The verse also mentions that the hair of his head was white like wool. Similarly, in Psalm 104:3, God is described as making the clouds His chariot and riding on the wings of the wind, further highlighting His dominion over nature.

In these verses, we also find descriptions of God's appearance. Daniel 7:9 depicts His clothing as white as snow, symbolizing His purity, while His throne is described as being flaming with fire, conveying His divine authority. These visual descriptions help us conceptualize and relate to God's majestic nature.

Water is another powerful metaphor used throughout the Bible to represent various aspects of God's work and attributes. Verses like Hosea 6:3, John 4:14, John 7:37-39, Isaiah 12:3, John 3:5, Matthew 5:45, and Genesis 5:1-2 use water imagery to symbolize spiritual nourishment, cleansing, and God's provision. Water represents the life-giving and transformative work of God in the lives of believers.

Furthermore, in Exodus 3:14, God declares Himself as "I AM THAT I AM." This statement emphasizes His eternal existence and self-sufficiency, encapsulating His divine nature and being. It reminds us that God is beyond time and comprehends His own existence fully.

These instances of anthropomorphism and the use of natural elements as metaphors enable us to relate to and appreciate God's transcendence and beauty in a way that aligns with our human experience. They provide vivid and tangible descriptions that help us better comprehend and connect with the divine nature and attributes of God.

1. "While yet he was speaking, behold a bright cloud overshadowed them; and behold, a voice out of the cloud saying, "This is My Son, the beloved, in whom I am well pleased. Listen to Him!" (Matthew 17:5, BLB)

2. "Do you know how God establishes them, And Makes the lightning of His cloud to shine? Do you know about the layers of thick clouds, The wonder of one perfect in knowledge...?" (Job 37:15-16, NASB)

3. "As the appearance of the rainbow in the clouds in a rainy day, So was the appearance of the surrounding radiance. Such was the appearance of the likeness of the Glory of the LORD and when I saw it, I fell on my face and heard a voice speaking." (Ezekiel 1:28, NASB)

4. "So let us know, Let us press on to know the LORD his going forth is as certain as the dawn; And He will come to us like rain, Like the spring rain watering the earth." (Hosea 6:3, NASB)

5. "but whoever drinks the water that I give him shall never thirst; but the water that I give him will become in them a well of water springing up to eternal life." (John 4:14, NASB)

6. Now, on the Last day, the great day of the feast, Jesus stood and cried out, saying "If anyone is thirsty, let him come to me and drink." (John 7:37-39, NASB)

7. "Therefore, you will joyously draw water from the springs of Salvation." (Isaiah 12:3, NASB)

8. "Truly, truly, I say to you, unless one is born of water and Spirit he cannot enter into the kingdom of God." (John 3:5, NASB)

9. "that you may be children of your Father who is in heaven. For he makes his sun to rise on the evil and the good and sends rain on the just and the unjust." (Matthew 5:45, NHEB)

10. When God created man, he made him in the likeness of God. He created them male and female and blessed them. (Genesis 5:1-2, NASB)

11. And God said to Moses, I AM THAT I AM: and he said, Thus shall you say to the children of Israel, I AM has sent me to you. (Exodus 3:14, AKJV)

~ *Beloved Jesus* ~

In every heart, I kindle a flame, A love that burns without end or shame. I illuminate the depths of the soul, unveiling love's mysteries, making it whole. So, let my glory illuminate your days, bask in the love that my presence conveys.

For my conscious light, love reigns Supreme, a celestial poem, a radiant dream. Over the mountains high, my love does soar, a symphony of warmth, forevermore, I spark the fires of passion and desire, fueling love's flame higher and higher. I dance across the shimmering seas, whispering love to the gentle breeze. The waves respond in rhythmic ecstasy, reflecting love's infinite harmony.

1. "And God said, Let there be light and there was light. And God saw the light, that it was good: and God divided the light from the darkness." (Genesis 1:4, KJV)

2. And he said, I will make all the light of my being come before you, and I will make clear to you what I am. I will be kind to those whom I will be kind and have mercy on those on whom I will have mercy. (Exodus 33:19)

3. "And the LORD said, "I will cause all my goodness to pass in front of you, and I will proclaim my name, The LORD, in your presence. I will have mercy on whom I will have mercy, and I will have compassion on whom I have compassion." (Exodus 33:19, NIV)

4. And was transfigured before them: and his face did shine as the sun, and his raiment was white as the light. (Matthew 17:2, KJV)

5. Because of the tender mercy of our God, With which the Sunrise from on high will visit us. (Luke 1:78, NASB)

6. This then is the message which we have heard from him and proclaim to you, that God is light, and in him is no darkness at all. (1 John 1:5, ESV)

7. The true Light who gives light to every man was coming into the world. The true Light who enlightens every man has come into our world. (John 1:9)

8. As long as I am in the world, I am the light of the world. (John 9:5)

9. May the light of the Lord's face be shining on you in grace! (Numbers 6:25)

10. On that day you will realize that I am in my Father, and you are in me, and I am in you. (John 14:20, NIV)

11. But he, "full of the Holy Spirit, gazed into heaven and saw the glory of God, and Jesus standing at the right hand of God. And he said, "Behold I see the heavens opened, and the Son of man standing at the right hand of God." (Acts 7:55-56, ESV)

12. "As for me, I baptize you with water for repentance, but He who is coming after me is mightier then I, and I am not fit to remove His sandals; he will baptize you with the Holy Spirit and fire. (Matthew 3:11, NASB)

13. Sustaining all things by his powerful word. After he had provided purification for sins, he sat down at the right hand of the Majesty in heaven." (Hebrews 1:3, NIV)

14. "Very truly I tell you," Jesus answered, "before Abraham was born, I AM!" (John 8:58, NIV)

15. "I am the Alpha and the Omega, the First and the Last, the Beginning and the End." (Revelation 22:13, BSB)

16. "I Jesus, have sent my angel to give you this testimony for the churches. I am the Root and the Offspring of David, and the bright Morning Star." (Revelation 22:16, NIV)

17. "When a man believes in me, he does not believe in me only, but in the one who sent me. When he looks at me, he sees the one who sent me. I have come into the world as a light, so that no one who believes in me should stay in darkness." (John 12:44-46, NIV)

These verses utilize metaphorical language and imagery to convey profound spiritual truths about Jesus' identity, His role as the Light of the world, and the transformative power of faith in Him.

~ *The Blessed Holy Spirit* ~

In the realm of divine and celestial might, the Holy Ghost reveals its glorious light. Through sunlight's rays and electromagnetic waves, a poem of revelation, the spirit

*engraves. Behold the sun, a radiant sphere of gold, a
messenger of light, its stories unfold. In its embrace, the
Holy Ghost resides, unveiling mysteries as the sun presides.
The Holy Ghost, in waves of energy untold, unveiling
truths, a divine unfold. Through scientific wonders, its
glory shines, in each discovery, the spirit aligns. So let us
marvel at this divine display, The Holy Ghost's revelation
in every ray, for in the sunlight's dance and electromagnetic
sway, we glimpse the spirit's presence, guiding our way.*

1. "This is how we know that we live in him and he in us: He has given us his Spirit." (1 John 4:13, NIV)

2. "Hope does not put us to shame, because God's love has been poured into our hearts through the Holy Spirit who has been given to us." (Romans 5:5, ESV)

3. "That which is born of the flesh is flesh and that which is born of the Spirit is Spirit." (John 3:6, ESV)

4. "But the Holy Spirit produces this kind of fruit in our lives: love, joy, peace, patience, kindness, goodness, faithfulness," (Gal 5:22, NLV)

5. "Do you not know that your bodies are temples of the Holy Spirit, who is in you, whom you have received from God? You are not your own;" (1 Corinthians 6:19, NLV)

6. "Do you not know that you yourselves are God's temple, and that God's Spirit dwells in you?" (1 Corinthians 3:16, BSB)

7. 'For in him we live and move and have our being.' As some of your own poets have said, 'We are his offspring.' (Acts 17:28, NIV)

8. "We have not received the spirit of the world but the Spirit who is from God, that we may understand what God has freely given us." (1 Corinthians 2:12, BSB)

9. "God is Spirit, and those who worship Him must worship in Spirit and truth." (John 4:24, NAB)

10. "At once I was in the Spirit, and I saw a throne standing in heaven, with someone seated on it. The One seated there looked like jasper and carnelian, and a rainbow gleaming like an emerald encircled the throne." (Revelation 4:2-3, BSB)

These verses collectively emphasize the role and significance of the Holy Spirit in the lives of believers, including the indwelling presence of the Spirit, transformative work, guidance, and the assurance of God's love. The Holy Spirit is portrayed as the source of spiritual rebirth, the bearer of God's love, and the one who produces fruit in the lives of believers. The Holy Spirit is depicted as the one who dwells within believers, sanctifying and empowering them. Believers are encouraged to worship God in Spirit and truth, recognizing the spiritual nature of true worship. The Holy Spirit is portrayed as the means by which believers can understand and receive the things freely given by God. The Holy Spirit's presence is described as bringing hope, unity, and the manifestation of God's glory. These verses collectively highlight the profound impact and vital role of the Holy Spirit in the lives of believers.

In the realm where the wonders of nature reside, a stirring notion emerges, a thought that cannot be hidden. Deep within the intricate tapestry it weaves, a question arises: Does nature possess consciousness? As we contemplate the marvels of nature, we are confronted with a profound thesis: Nature itself perceives. Beyond its breathtaking beauty and intricate interconnectedness, there lies a hidden tapestry of consciousness. It beckons us to consider the remarkable possibility that nature possesses a form of awareness and perception that extends beyond our human understanding.

Nature is not a passive backdrop but an active participant in the grand scheme of existence. It suggests that there exists a deeper level of consciousness within the natural world, challenging us to recognize the profound interconnectedness between ourselves and the environment that surrounds us.

In conclusion, my encounters with God's presence and the manifestation of the Triune nature of God in the wonders of nature have deepened my understanding of divine existence. As I reflected upon various scriptures that shed light on God's presence in the natural world, I felt compelled to share them with you. These passages serve as windows through which we can gain a clearer insight into the revelation of God's essence, as perceived through my own journey.

May these shared scriptures inspire you to explore the profound connections between the divine and the world around us, fostering a deeper appreciation for the intricate tapestry of creation.

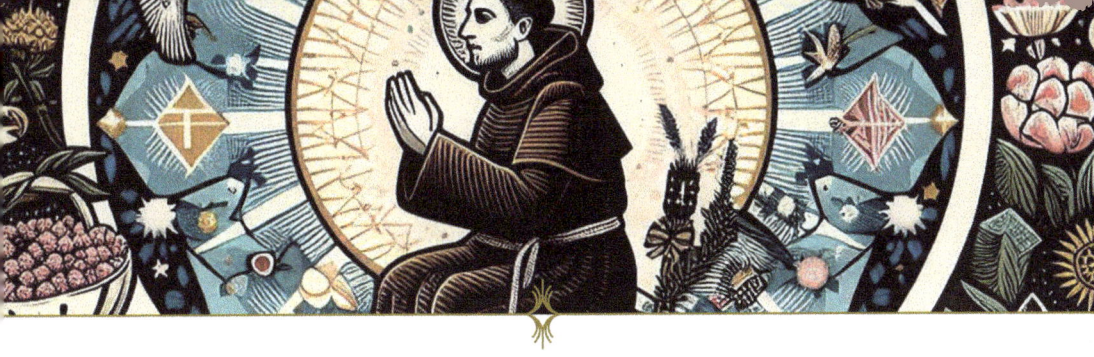

4

THE ENIGMA OF CONSCIOUSNESS: EXPLORING THE QUANTUM DEPTHS OF EXPERIENCE

Science cannot solve the ultimate mystery of nature. And that is because, in the last analysis, we ourselves are part of nature and therefore part of the mystery that we are trying to solve.

MAX PLANCK[8]

IN THE VAST LANDSCAPE OF HUMAN UNDERSTANDING, A FEW mysteries captivate our minds as profoundly as the enigma of consciousness. It is the elusive essence that gives rise to our subjective experiences, the very fabric that colors our perceptions and shapes our reality. Yet, as we delve deeper into the nature of consciousness, we encounter a labyrinth of questions that defy easy answers. How do we explain the vivid qualia, the rich tapestry of sensations that accompany our every waking moment?

Is it possible that consciousness permeates the very fabric of the universe, as suggested by the intriguing concept of panpsychism? Derived from the Greek words pan ("all"), and psyche ("soul" or "mind") panpsychism is a philosophical view that posits that consciousness is a fundamental and ubiquitous aspect of the universe. It suggests that consciousness is not exclusive to humans or certain sentient beings but exists in some form throughout all of reality, even in inanimate objects or fundamental particles.

The Christian mystic Saint Francis of Assisi held a deep conviction in the consciousness present within all things. He went as far as conversing with flowers and delivering sermons to birds, displaying his love and appreciation for every aspect of God's creation. Saint Francis recognized his kinship with the natural world, embracing a profound connection with animals, plants, rocks, and the entire universe.

His understanding extended to considering himself a brother not only to fellow humans but also to the sun, moon, stars, fire, water, and all elements of the cosmos. Through his ecological consciousness and spiritual vision, Saint Francis demonstrated a mystical perspective that viewed all creatures as brothers and sisters. It is this perspective that has led him to be revered as the patron saint of the environment.

As we embark on a journey to awaken the hidden realms of our own minds, we find ourselves drawn into the realm of dreams, the boundaries of perception blur, and new possibilities emerge. In this exploration, we encounter the fascinating intersection of consciousness and quantum mechanics, where the fundamental nature of reality itself comes into question. As we venture into this captivating territory, seeking to unravel the mysteries that lie at the heart of existence.

The way things appear to us is rooted in our individual perceptions, and these perceptions are not objective but rather subjective. They are not something imposed upon us, but rather something we actively select. The perspective we choose to adopt becomes the very mechanism through which we shape and create our experiences.

"For as he thinks within himself, so he is," (Proverbs 23:7) lies in the power of our thoughts and perspectives to shape our reality. Just as the proverb suggests, our inner thoughts and beliefs have a profound influence on our identity and the way we perceive ourselves. The proverb emphasizes the idea that our thoughts have the ability to manifest in our actions and ultimately define who we are. Similarly, the previous statement highlights the notion that the perspectives we choose to adopt and the thoughts we cultivate within ourselves play a crucial role in the process of creation and shaping our experiences. Both emphasize the importance of recognizing the power of our thoughts and perspectives in shaping our reality and the person we become.

With a deep understanding of the power of our thoughts and perspectives, I aim to illustrate the truth of this principle through personal experiences. In the absence of knowledge, belief alone guides us, but when we are exposed to the boundless nature of our existence, we begin to comprehend the profound significance and magnificence with which our creator has fashioned us. This revelation expands the horizons of our perception, empowering us to assume greater responsibility for our creations and actions. Through sharing these ideas, I seek to convey the transformative impact of recognizing our inherent creative potential and the profound connection between our thoughts, actions, and the reality we shape.

Be transformed by the renewing of your mind.
ROMANS 12:2

A change in our thinking patterns and beliefs can lead to a profound transformation in our lives. When we gain new knowledge and insights about our existence and the creative power within us, our minds are renewed, and we can see ourselves and the world in a different light. This renewal of mind allows us to break free from limiting beliefs and embrace a more expansive and responsible approach to our creations and actions. By actively engaging in the process of renewing our minds through seeking knowledge and understanding, we open ourselves to the transformative potential that lies within us, aligning our thoughts and perspectives with the truth of our being.

UNVEILING THE BOUNDLESS POSSIBILITIES: A NEW PARADIGM FOR TRANSFORMATION

Neale Donald Walsch expresses the idea that our beliefs shape our perception of reality. He argues that objective observation is unattainable because every observation is influenced by the observer. Our perceptions create the appearance of things, and these perceptions are subjective rather than objective. Rather than being a passive experience, our perspectives are actively chosen. Walsch suggests that the perspective we adopt is instrumental in the creative process, drawing a parallel to the principles of Quantum Physics.[9] Quantum Theory is the act of watching. The observer affects the observed reality, and, in this way, the entire universe exists by being experienced within you, and that is truly astounding to think about.

Consciousness is a subjective experience that can only be truly understood by adopting the perspective of the one experiencing it. In my communication with God, I take a synergistic and photojournalistic approach, sharing my ongoing interaction with the divine and offering insights into my journey.

Through this unique narrative, I aim to show how God reveals Himself to me in a way that aligns with my own perception. It's important to recognize that our individual filters, shaped by our unique identities, influence how we perceive and relate to reality. As a writer, my challenge lies in conveying my perspective to my readers, bridging the gap between my personal experiences and their understanding.

Quantum mechanics compels us to embrace the acceptance of seemingly impossible concepts, as we inhabit a world brimming with vast creative possibilities. Einstein had the quest to comprehend the mind of God, and this would have been a remarkable moment in science to share this astonishing epiphany with him. The incredible nature of how God collaborates with me on this extraordinary occasion is truly remarkable, as he possesses a deep understanding of my mind even beyond my own comprehension.

Nevertheless, in the contemporary era, numerous scientists argue that consciousness holds a fundamental role while asserting that subjectivity does not align with the scientific method. This rejection of subjectivity is viewed as an example of arrogant science, prompting the call for a fresh paradigm. Science, as a methodology, serves as a tool for investigating the world whereas scientism represents the belief that science and its methods alone provide the optimal and exclusive means to uncover truth about the world and reality.

We actively engage with and shape everything we experience, not merely as observers but as participants in the unfolding reality. This remarkable phenomenon serves as evidence of this concept and warrants thorough examination and exploration as we embark on the next stage of our evolution, actively creating our own reality through our consciousness. It represents a significant advancement for humanity, allowing us to discover our cosmic essence and transform our understanding of ourselves as integrated beings encompassing mind, body, and soul.

We recognize our interconnectedness and interdependence with the conscious universe in profound ways. It's important to recognize that the experiences we encounter are internal to us rather than external. All experiences are rooted within our own subjective interior, while external events themselves are separate from our personal experience. The New Earth is opening up to the potential of possibility. We don't 'see' with our eyes we actually see with consciousness and our brain processes that information. But our mind is nonlocal and does not exist in the brain. The term "mind" refers to a form of energy rather than a tangible object. It encompasses the realm of thoughts, which in themselves are energetic rather than physical entities.

Nonlocality describes the apparent ability of objects to instantaneously know about each other's state, even when separated by significant distances. It is as if the universe, on a grand scale, promptly arranges its particles in advance of future occurrences. Human consciousness is nonlocal, it is not confined to specific points in space such as the brain and body or existing in time.

The mind is not confined solely to our brain but extends beyond it, permeating every cell of our body. This is evident in the accounts of individuals who have had near-death experiences, where they report being conscious even in a state of clinical death, retaining abilities such as sight, hearing, empathy, and intuitive knowing. This suggests that our consciousness is not bound by physical limitations and can transcend the boundaries of the body.

The concept of entanglement suggests that since we are interconnected with everything, we have the capacity to engage with the world mentally. This implies that all beings and phenomena emerge from a shared source, leading to a profound interconnectedness between all aspects of existence.

In summary, our consciousness is not confined to the brain but exists throughout our entire being, allowing for experiences beyond the physical realm. The notion of entanglement further reinforces the idea of interconnectedness, suggesting that we are all part of a unified whole.

Rupert Sheldrake a parapsychology researcher says that "consciousness is the realm of possibilities."[10] This mystical encounter has the potential to provide scientists and philosophers who have long grappled with the "hard problem of consciousness," with a new perspective that moves beyond mere correlation towards a theoretical understanding.

In 1995, philosopher David Chalmers coined the term "the hard problem of consciousness," which delves into the profound philosophical challenge of elucidating the reasons behind and mechanisms of subjective experiences or qualia—the raw, qualitative aspects of our conscious states. Qualia encompasses various sensory perceptions, such as the vivid redness of a rose, the taste of a ripe strawberry, the sweet aroma of freshly brewed coffee, the pain of a stubbed toe, or the soothing sound of raindrops on a windowpane. This enigma seeks to tackle the question of why specific physical states are accompanied by consciousness, while others are not.

Qualia encompasses the totality of our experiences, such as the taste of garlic, the scent of coffee, or the perception of the color red. They represent the qualities that make our conscious experiences unique and varied. The hard problem of consciousness prompts us to explore whether consciousness aligns with materialistic explanations, dualistic perspectives, or even the ideas put forth by panpsychists who propose that consciousness is inherent in all things.

Rupert Sheldrake, a prominent thinker, proposes a compelling perspective that challenges the confines of traditional scientific frameworks by suggesting that consciousness exists within the realm of possibilities. This intriguing viewpoint opens up new avenues for inquiry and invites a broader exploration of the nature of consciousness and its potential implications.

Sheldrake's proposition challenges the prevailing reductionist approach that seeks to explain consciousness solely through the physical processes of the brain. By suggesting that consciousness transcends the boundaries of conventional scientific understanding, Sheldrake offers a fresh perspective that encourages us to consider alternative explanations and possibilities.

This expanded view of consciousness has profound implications for various fields of study. It prompts us to explore phenomena such as telepathy, intuition, and other forms of non-local communication that cannot be easily accounted for within conventional scientific frameworks. Sheldrake's viewpoint encourages us to question the limitations of our current scientific models and to remain open to the potential existence of consciousness beyond what can be explained through traditional empirical methods.

Moreover, this broader exploration of consciousness invites interdisciplinary collaboration and encourages the integration of diverse perspectives, including those from philosophy, psychology, spirituality, and other domains. It fosters a more holistic understanding that acknowledges the intricate interplay between subjective experiences, qualia, and the larger fabric of existence.

While Sheldrake's viewpoint may be met with skepticism within traditional scientific circles, it serves as a catalyst for expanding our thinking and challenging the boundaries of knowledge. By embracing the possibility that consciousness exists within the realm of possibilities, we embark on a journey of discovery that may lead to profound insights about the fundamental nature of reality and our place within it.

In summary, my mystical experience holds promise not only for scientists but also for a wide range of interdisciplinary perspectives. It provides a unique opportunity to transcend mere observational correlations and invites us to delve into the development of theoretical models aimed at tackling the hard problem of consciousness.

By incorporating insights from various disciplines, such as philosophy, psychology, spirituality, and metaphysics, we can deepen our understanding of qualia and explore the multifaceted nature of consciousness. These alternative frameworks offer valuable lenses through which we can examine the subjective aspects of consciousness that may elude purely scientific approaches.

From a philosophical standpoint, my mystical experience prompts us to contemplate profound questions about the nature of qualia and the relationship between mind and matter. It invites us to explore different philosophical frameworks, such as idealism, panpsychism, or dualism, which propose diverse ways of conceptualizing consciousness and its interplay with the physical world.

Similarly, from a metaphysical perspective, my experience encourages us to consider the possibility that consciousness is not solely confined to the physical brain but may extend beyond it. Metaphysical frameworks, including those rooted in ancient wisdom traditions or contemporary spiritual practices, offer alternative ways of understanding consciousness and its potential connections to broader aspects of existence.

By incorporating these interdisciplinary perspectives, we enrich the discourse surrounding the hard problem of consciousness. The integration of insights from philosophy, psychology, spirituality, and metaphysics enables us to transcend the limitations of reductionist approaches and explore the profound mystery of consciousness from diverse angles.

Ultimately, my mystical experience invites us to embrace a more nuanced and inclusive exploration of consciousness. It encourages us to go beyond the boundaries of scientific observation and engage in a broader conversation that encompasses philosophical, metaphysical, and spiritual dimensions. By doing so, we open up new possibilities for understanding the nature of qualia and for formulating comprehensive theoretical models that can shed light on the enigma of consciousness.

Is nature a living entity? Does the universe possess consciousness? According to standard materialism, matter is considered unconscious, and this perspective extends to the entire universe. However, materialism falls short of fully explaining subjective experiences and the qualitative aspects of consciousness, known as qualia. Ultimately, materialists deny the existence of consciousness.

Dualists, on the other hand, propose that consciousness is fundamentally distinct from the physical body and brain. They argue that consciousness cannot be entirely accounted for by physical processes alone and that subjective experiences possess an irreducible quality. Dualists believe that consciousness exists independently of physical phenomena and is not merely a byproduct of brain activity.

Panpsychists put forth the idea that consciousness is an inherent aspect of the universe, present within all matter and energy. They suggest that consciousness is not limited to biological organisms but is instead a fundamental characteristic of the entire cosmos. In addressing the hard problem of consciousness—how and why certain brain processes give rise to subjective experiences—panpsychism has been proposed as a potential solution. Panpsychists contend that if consciousness is a fundamental property of the universe, it would not necessitate an explanation solely through physical processes occurring in the brain.

Based on my personal experience, I hold the belief that the universe is conscious and that nature possesses a living quality. This perspective aligns with the idea that consciousness is a fundamental aspect of reality. The nature of consciousness is to know itself. Consciousness then contemplates its own being and recognizes its own infinite nature.

Imagine a self-aware flame. This flame possesses the ability to perceive and understand its own existence. It doesn't need external illumination to recognize its own nature; it inherently knows itself through its own luminosity and presence. The flame's very essence is to emit light and warmth, and in doing so, it is aware of its own being.

Similarly, consciousness, in its inherent nature, has the capacity to know itself. It doesn't require external sources of knowledge or illumination to recognize its own existence. Consciousness is self-aware by its very essence, and through introspection, it gains insight into its own being and subjective experience.

In this analogy, the self-aware flame represents consciousness, which doesn't rely on external illumination but knows itself through its intrinsic nature. It symbolizes the inherent self-awareness and self-knowing nature of consciousness.

How do we know anything exists? Because you're aware of it. Rupert Spira a spiritual teacher and philosopher says, "Consciousness is that in which all experience appears, with that which all experience is known, and out of which all experience is made."[11] Consciousness is the fabric of our existence. This definition highlights the multifaceted nature of consciousness. It encompasses its role as the container, knower, and source of all experience. It aligns with the idea that consciousness is not just a product of experiences but is fundamental to its existence and understanding.

This account of my personal experience illustrates the connection between my consciousness and the divine Creator. Within the realm of my subjective perception, I envision Jesus as the Son of God, a divine entity who shares oneness with the Father. I perceive Jesus as embodying qualities of light and love, occupying a position of significance at the right hand of our heavenly Father. He possesses the ability to be present everywhere simultaneously, exhibiting the attribute of omnipresence. Furthermore, Jesus is thought to reflect the image and likeness of our Creator, serving as a tangible representation of the divine essence in human form.

Within my consciousness, I perceive our heavenly Father as the eternal force of boundless love that permeates every aspect of my being. He embodies the essence of awe-inspiring beauty, and profound understanding, and possesses an all-encompassing knowledge of the universe. He is the wellspring of wisdom, and my soul yearns to seek union with Him, to comprehend the depths of His wisdom. His nature is characterized by kindness, gentleness, strength, and inspiration.

Our heavenly Father is capable of assuming any form or transcending form altogether. He traverses the skies on a chariot composed of ethereal life force energy, accompanied by celestial beings, comprehending all experiences with perfect awareness. He remains constantly present in my life, an omnipresent presence.

He is a being of enchantment and supremacy, evoking a sense of delight and wonder within me. My heart resonates with a joyous melody dedicated to Him. He attentively listens to my highest joys and deepest sorrows. Beholding His divine presence is a sight that captivates my heart.

In my state of unified and harmonious awareness, I experience the Blessed Holy Spirit as the embodiment of infinite grace, providing me with comfort and joy. I am deeply attuned to the profound and penetrating vibration of the Holy Spirit, which courses through me like electric energy. The Spirit of Truth exudes great magnanimity, compassion, and unconditional love, encompassing all aspects of existence.

The presence of the blessed Holy Spirit evokes a jubilant desire within me to sing and proclaim its glory to the world. It inspires reverence for the immense magnitude of God and invites me to rejoice in the divine love that permeates all creation. I am moved to sing praises that resonate throughout the heavens, celebrating the splendor of the multiverse. The Holy Spirit represents the magnificent, eternal, and infinite Soul of God, radiating an electromagnetic and geometric essence that is richly colorful and vibrant. It serves as the life-giving breath that animates all things in existence.

Mother Earth is also a living being and contains consciousness. Indigenous cultures see the Earth as their sacred relative, as precious and alive as any of us. They believe that Mother Earth is a living being, as are the waters and the sun. She also contributed as a beneficial partner in a symbiotic relationship with the divine to bring forth this amazing experience for all of us to witness. The belief in Mother Earth as a living being inspires a profound sense of stewardship and responsibility. This belief in the consciousness and vitality of Mother Earth serves as a powerful reminder of our interconnectedness and our shared responsibility to honor and protect the sanctity of our planet.

In John 17:20-23, Jesus speaks of the profound unity that exists among all individuals, emphasizing the idea that we are all interconnected and part of a unified whole. He says, "My prayer is not for them alone. I pray also for those who will believe in me through their message, that all of them may be one, Father, just as you are in me and I am in you. May they also be in us so that the world may believe that you have sent me. I have given them the glory that you gave me, that they may be one as we are one—I in them and you in me—so that they may be brought to complete unity. Then the world will know that you sent me and have loved them even as you have loved me." This scripture highlights the profound truth that we are not separate entities but interconnected beings, each containing a spark of divinity within us. It emphasizes the importance of recognizing our shared essence and cultivating unity, as it is through this oneness that we can bear witness to the love of the divine and create a more harmonious and compassionate world.

REVEALING THE VEILED: JOURNEYING INTO THE HIDDEN REALM

When we open ourselves up to the Kingdom within our innermost sanctuary, we can tap into anything. According to Walsch, thoughts possess an energetic nature, and everything in the universe is in a constant state of motion. Furthermore, Walsch suggests that time is a concept that is perpetually present in the present moment.[12] We actually have six senses: smell, taste, touch, sight, hearing, and knowing. There are different ways of perceiving or sensing information beyond the five traditional senses. These are called our Clair senses.

◊ **Clairvoyance:** the ability to perceive information or events through clear mental images or visions. Clairvoyants see things that are not visible to the normal eye such as glimpses of the future or insights into a person's past or present.

◊ **Clairaudience:** the ability to hear sounds, voices, or messages from the spiritual realm or from sources beyond the physical senses.

◊ **Clairsentience:** involves the ability to sense or feel energy, emotions, or physical sensations from other people, places, or situations. Clairsentients have an enhanced empathic ability and can pick up on subtle energies or vibrations in their surroundings.

◊ **Claircognizance:** have the ability to have clear, intuitive knowledge or understanding about something without any apparent logical or sensory explanation. People with claircognizance may suddenly have insights or know things without having prior knowledge or evidence.

◊ **Clairgustance:** have the ability to taste something without putting anything in the month. It is associated with perceiving flavors or tastes related to spiritual or energetic phenomena.

These Clair senses are our intuition, inner voice, and psychic awareness. Intuition is a sense of knowing, and this knowing comes from within. Intuition abides within the depths of the psyche, within the essence of the soul. It serves as the soul's auditory faculty. Developing and working with these modalities can influence our lives and lead to profound mystical and religious experiences.

DREAMS AS DIVINE MESSENGERS: EXPLORING THE SPIRITUAL SIGNIFICANCE AND DISCERNING AUTHENTICITY

There are a variety of ways God talks with us, especially through our feelings, but dreams can be a valuable tool as well. When you choose to make contact through your dreams keep a notepad or tape recorder next to your bed. Before falling asleep concentrate on a question that you would like spirit to answer. Be specific and focus on your question before falling asleep. This may not occur overnight but with practice and patience, Spirit can make contact with you through your dreams. I did ask God what I should say to humanity after my epiphany. I specifically asked God to come to me in my dreams and to give me a message. I prepared for this and put a notepad and pen next to my bed and requested that upon awakening I would clearly receive a message. I awoke that morning after I put my intention to the universe to receive a message in this way. This is the message that I received and what I wrote down "I am a witness of God's Presence."

The Bible contains numerous references to dreams, and they play a significant role in several biblical narratives. Joseph had a dream in which an angel of the Lord appeared telling him to take Jesus and Mary to Egypt for their safety against Herod (Matthew 2:13). Zacharias had a dream foretelling him that he would have a son in which was known as John the Baptist (Luke 1:5-23). Ananias (Acts 9:10) had a dream to visit Paul and help him regain his sight after he had his revelation of Jesus on the Road to Damascus. The Bible also warns about false prophets who claim to receive messages from God through dreams. It cautions believers to test the spirits and discern the authenticity of such claims (Jeremiah 23:25-27).

UNVEILING THE UNSEEN: EXPLORING REMOTE VIEWING AND THE HIDDEN DEPTHS OF UNCONSCIOUSNESS

One field of study that parapsychologists are researching is Remote Viewing. Parapsychology is a branch of psychology that investigates paranormal and psychic phenomena. Remote viewing is the practice of seeking impressions about a distant or unseen subject, purportedly sensing with the mind. The term was coined in the 1970s by physicists Russell Targ and Harold Puthoff, who claimed to be the first to research remote viewing in a laboratory setting.

The practice of remote viewing gained public attention in the 1970s and 1980s through the research conducted by the United States government's Stargate Project, which aimed to investigate the military potential of psychic phenomena. Remote viewing operates through a non-local aspect of consciousness. According to this view, consciousness is not limited to the physical body and brain and can transcend space and time. The idea behind remote viewing is that individuals can be trained to perceive and describe remote physical targets, which could be geographical locations, events, or objects, using only their minds and without the use of any physical senses. Proponents of remote viewing believe that this ability is innate in all humans to some degree, and can be developed and improved through training and practice.

Human beings are more open than ever before in exploring and understanding what capabilities humans have. Throughout history, there have been documented instances of individuals displaying extrasensory abilities known as extra-sensory perception or ESP. These records indicate two significant points. Firstly, it has been somewhat impractical for us to not invest more effort in comprehending our psychic nature. Secondly, it suggests that we may never fully grasp certain profound aspects of ourselves until we recognize and understand our psychic capabilities as inherent and natural attributes of our species.

Everyone has psychic awareness, but few have the patience, understanding, or perhaps the desire to develop it. It takes a great deal of patience and practice to unfold these natural abilities, and you must also develop a sense of responsibility. Learning the subtleties of working with Spirit and learning and understanding this new language takes dedication and testing the spiritual realms in which we engage with.

Advocates claim that remote viewing abilities can be developed through structured training programs, which teach techniques like controlled relaxation, visualization, and sensory acuity.

While the ability to remote view does seem to vary between individuals, many proponents believe that with the right training, most people can learn to remote view to at least some degree.

THE ART OF REVELATION: EXPLORING THE POWER OF VISUAL LANGUAGE IN SPIRITUAL COMMUNICATION

Drawing pictures can be interpreted as a form of nonverbal communication, a visual language that reflects the essence of nature. Throughout history, numerous ancient societies have conveyed their cultural narratives through pictorial drawings and hieroglyphic writings, leaving behind a visual language that represents their civilization on Earth.

This form of communication makes thought visible. Many remote viewers use the language of drawing to communicate what they are sensing and feeling. The creation of representational concepts occurs within the inner landscape of our subconscious minds and consistently possesses characteristics of preconscious thinking. Preconsciousness is associated with a part of the mind below the level of immediate conscious awareness, from which memories and emotions that have not been repressed can be recalled.

We have been blessed with many gifts to understand our deeper nature. As you will see in later chapters how God worked with me synergistically to co-create with God, especially by incorporating my drawing of a dove symbolizing grace, peace, and a message of hope and freedom into the landscape using the brilliance celestial sun before it dips below the horizon.

Source eloquently paints this dove into the sun representing "I AM." God uses this method of pictorial language to communicate with humanity the significance of his presence. You can refer to Christ the Pantocrator chapter for this image.

This powerful collaboration between God, art, and nature serves as a testament to the profound ways in which visual language can connect us to the spiritual realm and convey messages of profound meaning and inspiration.

TRANSCENDING WORDS: EXPLORING THE MYSTERIES OF LIGHT LANGUAGE AND SPEAKING IN TONGUES

Light language refers to a form of nonverbal communication that is often described as a spiritual or energetic language. It is believed to be a means of communication that transcends traditional spoken or written languages and operates at a higher vibrational frequency. Light language is often expressed through various forms, including hand gestures, body movements, vocal sounds tonal patterns, and symbols.

Those who practice or experience light language often describe it as a form of channeling or receiving messages from higher realms, spirit guides, or higher dimensional beings. It is believed to carry encoded information, healing frequencies, and energetic activations that can facilitate spiritual growth, transformation, and energetic alignment.

Light language is not bound by grammatical rules or specific vocabulary, it is considered a language of the heart, intuition, and energetic resonance, rather than a language that relies on logical or linear thinking.

Light language could be likened to speaking in tongues, a spiritual gift bestowed by the Holy Spirit. According to Christian belief, speaking in tongues is viewed as a supernatural ability to speak in a language unknown to the speaker, either a heavenly or earthly language. It is seen as a form of prayer or communication between an individual and God.

In the vast realm of human experience, dreams, remote viewing, clair senses, and the mysteries of consciousness reside as intriguing possibilities. Dreams offer glimpses into our subconscious, guiding us through symbolism and messages. Remote viewing hints at the potential for perceiving distant realms beyond our physical senses. Clair's senses awaken our intuition, revealing subtly dimensions of reality. And consciousness, the very essence of our being, holds untapped depths waiting to be explored. Embracing these realms of possibility opens doors to profound self-discovery, connection, and a deeper understanding of the boundless potential within ourselves and the universe we inhabit.

When we reflect on the significance of the intuitive mind and its role in spiritual growth we can unlock hidden potentials, transcend limitations, and experience a deeper connection with ourselves and the world around us.

Jesus knew how to transcend limited thinking and demonstrated that to us. One example of this was when he referred to himself as a temple and that he would raise himself. Jesus answered them, "Destroy this temple, and I will raise it again in three days" (John 2:19, NIV). Jesus' statement can be understood as an invitation to shift our perspective and transcend limited beliefs. By referring to the temple as his own body, he implies that the physical form is not the ultimate reality, but rather the consciousness that animates it. Jesus' teachings imply that our thoughts and beliefs have the power to shape our experiences and the world around us.

Don't you know that you yourselves are God's temple and that God's Spirit dwells in your midst.

1 CORINTHIANS 3:16, NIV

5

RESURRECTING THE DIVINE WITHIN: EMBRACING OUR SPIRITUAL POTENTIAL

Having a personal relationship with God is one of the most rewarding and profound feelings and experiences we have as human beings. To know our Creator in our experience and to have an awareness of God among us is a testimony of our faith revealed.

Seeking to know God is more than reading a book about God, we want to experience him directly; we want to see him; we want to feel him, and we want to know Him in our experience, and that is what having faith is. Faith brings your awareness into a living intimacy with God that is beyond anything you could read in a book.

When you engage in God inside your heart, mind, and soul, your essence vibrates with the Spirit, like musical instruments playing a harmonious melody together. You are joined in a beautiful song.

Remember, God is not distant or separate from us. He is among us all; He is in your midst. His presence permeates every aspect of our lives, and through faith, we can connect with Him on a deep and personal level.

As Jesus once stated, "You pore over the Scriptures because you presume that by them you possess eternal life. These are the very words that testify about Me, yet you refuse to come to Me to have life" (John 5:39-40, BSB). In this passage, Jesus criticizes the religious leaders for their reliance on the Scriptures without recognizing that those very Scriptures testify about him. He asserts that they diligently study the Scriptures, believing that they contain the path to eternal life, but they fail to recognize that the Scriptures point to him as the fulfillment of the prophecies and teachings.

Even though this scripture addresses the Jewish religious leaders in the day and life of Jesus, it is also for all of us today. Many people pour over the scriptures to come to God, yet they do not know God within themselves, within their being, within their heart, they have not yet met God in them. God is outside of them, separate from them, above them, in heaven, somewhere else, or doesn't exist at all. This is an illusion that we have created and knowing God intimately within ourselves expands our awareness to what God is and what God is not.

Humanity grapples with the identity and nature of God, and reaching a consensus seems challenging. The greatest hurdle lies not in the existence or non-existence of God, but rather in the diversity of beliefs held by those who affirm the existence of a higher power. As humanity continues to evolve, it becomes necessary for us to reevaluate and let go of deeply ingrained beliefs we have held for a significant period of time regarding the essence of God. This ongoing process of self-discovery and open-mindedness allows us to deepen our understanding and connection with the divine.

Navigating the process of questioning and potentially changing long-held beliefs about God can be a deeply personal and transformative journey. Here are some suggestions for navigating this process.

1. **Openness and Curiosity:** Approach the exploration of your beliefs with an open mind and a sense of curiosity. Be willing to question and examine your beliefs without judgment or preconceived notions.
2. **Seek Knowledge and Understanding:** Engage in a quest for knowledge and understanding. Explore different perspectives, religious traditions, philosophical teachings, and theological writings. Read books, listen to lectures, engage in conversations, and seek out diverse sources of wisdom.
3. **Reflect and Self-Examine:** Take time for introspection and self-reflection. Ask yourself why you hold certain beliefs and what experiences or influences have shaped them. Consider

how these beliefs align with your values, experiences, and broader understanding of the world.

4. **Embrace Uncertainty:** Acknowledge that the process of questioning and changing beliefs can be unsettling and may lead to uncertainty. Embrace the discomfort and allow yourself to sit with questions and uncertainties that arise. It is through this space of openness that new insights and understandings can emerge.

5. **Seek Support:** Find a supportive community or individuals who are also on a similar journey of questioning and exploring beliefs. Engage in respectful discussions, share experiences, and learn from one another.

6. **Trust Your Inner Wisdom:** Ultimately trust your own inner wisdom and intuition. Allow yourself to evolve and grow in your understanding of God at your own pace. Listen to your heart and follow the path that resonates most with your true authentic self.

Remember that the process of questioning and changing beliefs is unique to each individual. It is a journey of self-discovery and growth, and there is no "right" or "wrong" destination. Embrace the process with openness, courage, and a willingness to embrace new perspectives and insights along the way.

When I went through a radical shift in my belief system there were times when I would get quite angry with God. I would share with God how I was feeling or how I felt stumped in understanding something. God heard these things, God understood where I was in my limited thinking and would gently and lovingly show me another path or guide me in a different direction.

This requires surrender and humility. A quote often attributed to Albert Einstein, "We cannot solve problems with the same thinking we used when we created them."[13] This quote suggests that if we want to find solutions to our problems, we need to approach them from a different perspective or a new mindset.

We can have a personal relationship with God in our presence. God is the God of the living. You can come to know God in your heart, that path is forever available to you. "Draw near to God, and he will draw near to you." (James 4:8, ESV) "Be not far from me." (Psalm

22:11, NASB), "Then you will call upon Me and come and pray to Me, and I will listen to you. You will seek Me and find Me when you search for Me with all your heart. I will be found by you" ... (Jeremiah 29:12-14, BSB). Seek the Lord draw near to His presence and walk in knowing that God is with you.

And yet for some who are not yet at the threshold, this remains true for them Jesus said, "...but I know you, that you do not have the love of God within you. I have come in My Father's name, and you have not received Me..." (John 5:42-43, BSB).

If you seek a more intimate relationship with God, then that path is there. If you haven't spent time talking with God in prayer or opening up to the idea that a loving God exists and is here for us, it's important to realize that truly opening up to God is essential to experiencing the blessings that come with that relationship. Remember, God knows each and every one of us individually, out of the billions of people on this planet. He loves us unconditionally and has a plan for each and every one of us, as well as for the world—a plan filled with hope and immense love. In fact, God knows His people so intimately that even the hairs on their heads are numbered by Him (Matthew 10:30). So, by opening up to God's presence and embracing the idea of His love and guidance in our lives, we can begin to experience the profound blessings that come with knowing Him.

When God reveals Himself to those who approach Him with humility and a childlike spirit, they're able to see and know Him always. A childlike spirit encompasses qualities such as innocence, curiosity, trust, and a sense of wonder. Those who possess such a spirit are open-hearted, receptive, and eager to learn. Like His sheep, they recognize and hear His voice, and they are called to share their knowledge and faith with others, becoming fishers of men.

Jesus praises our Father for unveiling His teachings to those who possess a humble and childlike spirit, embracing the simplicity and purity found in the hearts of little children. This humble and open-hearted approach allows us to grasp the truth, filling us with reverence and awe. It provides a place of rest and reassurance, knowing that the eternal truths reside abundantly within us, illuminating a clear and revealed path forward. This path is not hidden or concealed but is unveiled to those who actively seek it (Matthew 11:25, John 10:14, John 10:27).

It is important not to confine God within the limits of our personal beliefs. As co-creators, we possess the power to shape our reality through our thoughts and beliefs. Let's always remember this profound truth and gift that we, as human beings, possess: the ability to consciously create our own reality. When we encounter God within ourselves, let's honor and allow His truth and love to shine through us. By embracing this awareness and deep connection with the divine, we become channels for God's truth and love to manifest in the world.

Bless the LORD, O my soul, O LORD my God, you are very great! You are clothed with splendor and majesty.

PSALM 104, ESV

The celestial realms and the manifestation of Spirit have been bestowed upon humanity, revealing that we bear the likeness of a heavenly being. As stated in Genesis 1:26, "Then God said, 'Let us make mankind in our image, in our likeness,'" affirming that we are created in the image of God. This divine truth reminds us of our inherent connection to the spiritual realm and the immense potential within us. We've been entrusted with the ability to reflect the qualities and attributes of our heavenly origins. Through this recognition, we come to understand that we are not separate from the divine but rather intricately intertwined with it. Embracing this truth allows us to tap into our inherent divinity and align ourselves with the higher purposes of love, compassion, and righteousness. It empowers us to live in harmony with the celestial realms and to manifest the beauty of Spirit in our lives.

In Christianity, the apostle Paul introduced the concept of the Spiritual body in the New Testament, describing the resurrection body as "Spiritual" in contrast to the natural body (1 Corinthians 15:42-55). Paul explains that just as a seed sown in the ground is perishable, what is raised from it is imperishable. What is sown in dishonor is raised in glory, and what is sown in weakness is raised in power. He further emphasizes that what is sown is a natural body, but what is raised is a Spiritual Body. It is important to recognize that alongside the natural body, there exists a Spiritual Body, which is characterized by its spiritual essence and oneness (1 Corinthians 15:44). Flesh and blood, in their perishable state, cannot inherit the Kingdom of God, nor can the perishable inherit the imperishable. However, Paul assures that we will be transformed, as the perishable must be clothed with the imperishable, and the mortal must be clothed with immortality. This transformation signifies the fulfillment of the saying, "Death has been swallowed up in victory." Paul triumphantly questions death, asking, "Where, O Death, is your victory? Where, O Death, is your sting" (1 Corinthians 15:55). This passage highlights the transformative power of the Spiritual Body and the ultimate victory over death through the resurrection.

In Christian theology, the concept of the Second Coming of Jesus Christ is often associated with a future event of great divine revelation and splendor. However, it can also be understood in a personal and spiritual sense.

I would like to conclude by sharing with you about my experience. I feel that the Second Coming of Christ is when we allow God to dwell in our hearts, mind, and soul. When Christ comes into our hearts, when we open to that in our hearts and spirituality this is the real Second Coming. The first coming of Christ was the way, the truth, and the light. It was the example we were to imitate. The Son of Man, Jesus, who fully expressed the Light and was the WORD incarnate, and the second coming is you. This glorious event takes place when the Son of God comes to live and reign in your heart, mind, and soul- because you have prepared him a room. You have prepared a room for yourself that is divine and holy.

When we prepare a sacred space within ourselves, a room that is divine and holy, we invite the Son of God to come and reign within us. This spiritual event is a glorious awakening, where we align our thoughts, actions, and intentions with the divine will. It is a realization that we, too, bear the potential to express the divine light within us, just as Jesus did.

Therefore, the Second Coming is not solely an external event but a deeply personal and transformative process of allowing God's presence to permeate every aspect of our being. It is an ongoing journey of spiritual growth and alignment with the divine, where we become the living expression of divine love, wisdom, and truth in the world.

Jesus answered and said to him, "If anyone loves Me, he will keep My word; and My Father will love him, and We will come to him and make Our abode with him" (John 14:23, NAS1977).

My heart burns like a blazing sun, eager to share this truth with you today. May the radiant light within our hearts shine brightly as we unite in universal love and oneness, recognizing that we are all created in the image and likeness of God. When we perceive the divine presence in every being, our hearts are filled with mercy and compassion for all. The message is clear: it is the Christ within you that brings hope and glory. Let us love one another as Jesus has loved us and wholeheartedly devote ourselves to loving God with all our hearts, minds, and souls. Jesus came to establish a path, a means to experience the realization of God's presence.

Whoever has My commandments and keeps them is the one who loves Me. The one who loves Me will be loved by My Father, and I will love him and reveal Myself to him.

JOHN 14:21, BSB

THE KINGDOM WITHIN: DISCOVERING THE DIVINE ESSENCE AND UNVEILING INNER TRUTH

As we discover our true essence as divine beings, awakening to our inner selves and creating a sacred space for union with the divine within us, a profound understanding will unfold. Regardless of the name we ascribe to it, each of us carries a divine spark—a radiant essence within. Direct experiential knowledge of God and the expansive consciousness of the Divine surpasses any secondhand understanding. Embrace the presence of God within you, and you will encounter the blessed hope that unifies us all. Remember, God is already present, here and now, eternally.

His disciples said to him, "When will the kingdom come? [Jesus said,] It will not come by waiting for it. It will not be a matter of saying 'here it is' or 'there it is.' Rather, the kingdom of the Father is spread out upon the earth, and people do not see it."[14]

Figure 5: Dunston, J.C. "TRANSCENDENT JOURNEY:
THE COSMIC BUDDHA CHRIST RIDING THE OCEAN OF CLOUDS"

Jesus said, "If a guide tells you, 'See the kingdom of God is in the sky,' then the birds of the air will get there before you. If they tell you, 'It's in the sea,' the fish will get there before you. "Rather, the Kingdom is inside you and outside you at the same time. When you come to know yourself, then you will be known. You will realize then that it's you who are the sons of the living Father. But as long as you do not know yourself, you will live in poverty, and you will be that poverty."[15]

I invite you all to join in a heart meditation. Close your eyes and envision a gentle candle flame flickering within your heart. This radiant light represents the presence of God within you. It is a divine spark—reflecting the essence of the Father, the Son, and the Holy Spirit. This flame symbolizes the sacred heart of fire, the Sacred Heart of Jesus, residing within you. It is the sacred dwelling place you have created for God, a space you have lovingly prepared to meet Him.

As you connect with God, direct your attention to your heart. In this inner sanctuary, you will find God eagerly awaiting your presence. Remember that God is always within you, eternally present, even until the end of time. Your heart becomes a holy pilgrimage, a sacred journey to the depths of your being, where the divine and human meet in profound union.

Take a moment to embrace this awareness of God's presence within your heart. Allow it to fill you with peace, love, and a sense of profound connection. In this space, you are in communion with the divine, experiencing the beauty of divine love.

Take a few deep breaths, and when you are ready, gently open your eyes, carrying this sense of inner connection and divine presence with you throughout your day.

A message for my readers: Some of my friends and family have asked me if the divine revelation I've experienced is exclusive to me. My response is a resounding no. I believe it is a gift from God meant to be shared with all humanity.

When we receive revelations, it is natural for us humans to feel compelled to express ourselves and share them with others. God's revelations come to us in various ways, and I personally perceive God's presence frequently, especially in nature.

However, I acknowledge that many of these encounters are personal, subjective, and unique to the observer. If I were to point out, while walking together, that I see God in a particular moment, it would be difficult for you to understand what I am experiencing. Hence, I often keep those moments to myself.

This photograph is an example of one such personal moment that I typically wouldn't share. However, I have chosen to share it with you so you can grasp the distinction between these personal encounters and the photos I will share in the future, which reveal the undeniable triune nature of God.

In the realm of my imagination's gaze, The Cosmic Christ, on clouds, finds his way. Like Buddha, weaving through life's tree, with immaculate light, a radiant decree. The ethereal Christ, in a celestial ride, navigates the heavens, where mysteries abide. Through cosmic clouds, his presence unfurls, A tapestry of grace and wisdom of divinity swirls. Buddha and Christ, entwined in unity, amongst the branches, their spirits set free. The Tree of Life, adorned with their embrace, radiates wisdom in each delicate trace. The immaculate light, their essence combines transcending boundaries, where divinity shines and takes flight a poetic dance of harmony and light.

6

UNVEILING THE BEYOND: DISCOVERING TRANSCENDENT TRUTHS

*The mind's highest good is knowledge of God
and the mind's highest virtue is to love God.*

BENEDICT DE SPINOZA

THE IDEA THAT OUR THOUGHTS HAVE THE POWER TO SHAPE OR influence reality is rooted in the concept that consciousness is subjective. According to this transcendent truth, the nature of our thoughts and beliefs directly impacts our perception and experience of the world.

To truly engage with the holy picture I am presenting today, it is essential to approach it with both an open mind and skepticism. This requires transcending our usual way of thinking and embracing a paradigm that encompasses faith, consciousness, and personal beliefs. It is within this expanded perspective that breakthroughs and profound insights can occur.

It is important to understand that without skepticism, belief cannot be transformed into true knowledge. Mere acceptance of what I tell you does not automatically guarantee that it is fundamentally true. True knowledge is attained through personal experience and faith, which goes beyond mere belief.

Skepticism can be seen as a valuable and transformative emotion. Even Mary, the mother of Jesus, experienced skepticism when she was visited by the angel Gabriel. Gabriel, an archangel known as the herald of visions and a messenger of God, is often associated with the Angel of Revelation, bringing forth important messages.

Mary, upon receiving the angel's greeting, was deeply troubled. However, her faith led her to question and seek understanding by asking "How can this be?" Despite her initial skepticism, she ultimately surrendered herself completely to God's plan, recognizing that nothing is impossible with God.

In this way, Mary's example teaches us that skepticism, when combined with an open heart and faith, can lead to a deeper understanding and acceptance of divine truths. It urges us to question, seek clarity, and ultimately embrace the profound mysteries that lie within the realm of faith and spirituality.

The subjective nature of consciousness implies that it is inherent in each individual, residing within oneself. It is through this subjective consciousness that our thoughts hold the power to shape our reality. When we recognize and embrace this truth, we embark on a journey of profound self-knowledge and authentic self-awareness.

By opening ourselves to the vastness of existence, we can access profound insights that lie within our own being. This involves acknowledging our interconnectedness with all that is, recognizing the oneness that encompasses us. It is an expansive realization that illuminates our divine essence and our inherent ability to create and manifest.

When we fully embrace the notion that our thoughts have the power to create, the veils are lifted, and our limitations dissolve. No longer confined within a narrow framework, we are liberated to explore, expand, and evolve into higher states of awareness. In this state, we recognize our unity with the entirety of existence.

It is essential to remember that our identity extends beyond mere human existence; we are also spiritual beings who have eternal souls that are on a path of growth and expansion. By acknowledging and embracing our souls, we tap into a deeper understanding of our true nature. This recognition opens the doors to a profound connection with the divine and an alignment with limitless power and potential within us.

Several philosophical and metaphysical perspectives explore the concept that thoughts have the power to shape or influence reality.

Idealism is a philosophical perspective that asserts the primacy of consciousness or mind in shaping reality. It suggests that reality is fundamentally mental or conceptual in nature and that our thoughts and perceptions play a role in constructing and experiencing the world. According to idealism, our thoughts and consciousness are not merely passive observers but active creators of reality. Idealism is the philosophical belief that the world we perceive is fundamentally a product of our mind. It suggests that reality is subjective and that the physical world exists as ideas or perceptions within our consciousness. Some metaphysical perspectives propose that thoughts or consciousness can interact with the physical world. For example, in the philosophy of panpsychism (the doctrine that mind is a universal feature of the world throughout the universe), it is suggested that consciousness can influence or interact with the external world.

If idealism and panpsychism were true and thoughts do indeed shape our reality this would shift the materialistic paradigm: Idealism challenges the materialistic worldview that regards physical matter as the fundamental basis of reality. If thoughts shape reality, it suggests that consciousness and mind hold a central role. This could prompt a reevaluation of materialist values and a shift towards a more holistic and integrative perspective that acknowledges the significance of consciousness and subjective experience.

The concept of the universe being a connected dwelling is not a recent notion. It has been a fundamental belief in Eastern philosophies for thousands of years. However, what is novel is that Western science is gradually acknowledging that certain aspects of this ancient wisdom may have been accurate. Of course, this acceptance requires a cautious embrace of a new way of understanding reality, as it is not a matter to be taken lightly.

When it comes to weighty subjects such as an individual's perception of reality, it is crucial to carefully scrutinize the available evidence. In scientific observations, it is not solely a matter of measuring or assessing what is already there; rather, the act of observation itself has the power to create or influence the outcome. For instance, in experiments exploring psi phenomena, (psi: the aggregate of parapsychological functions of the mind including extrasensory perception, precognition, and psychokinesis) we have observed evidence that suggests our intentions or focused attention can shape the results of measurement and even influence the behavior of particles, such as electrons, to assume specific positions. The act of observation itself seems to play a role in the creation of reality, implying that the reality we perceive is shaped by the acquisition of knowledge by the observer. In this case, the observer becomes an integral part of the observed system, and they cannot be separated from each other.

One example is the double-slit experiment. In this experiment, particles, such as electrons or photons, are directed at a barrier with two slits. When unobserved, these particles exhibit wave-like properties and create an interference pattern on a screen behind the barrier. However, when the particles are observed or measured to determine which slit they pass through, the wave-like behavior collapses, and the particles behave as individual particles, resulting in a pattern without interference.

If we are interconnected with everything around us, then theoretically, we have the ability to engage in mental interaction with any object or entity. It suggests that everything in the universe is connected in some way, whether physically, energetically, or metaphorically.

In exploring the interconnective web of the mind and its interaction with collective consciousness, we delve into the intricate relationship between individual consciousness and the emergence of higher-level phenomena. One way to conceptualize this interaction is through the concept of emergent properties, which suggests that complex systems can give rise to properties that cannot be solely explained by their individual components.

Within the realm of consciousness, the interplay of individual conscious entities within the interconnective web of mind holds the potential for the emergence of a collective consciousness. This collective consciousness transcends the boundaries of individual experiences and encompasses a higher-level awareness that arises from the interconnectedness of minds.

An intriguing biblical reference that resonates with this idea is found in Matthew 18:20, where Jesus said, "For where two or three are gathered together in my name, I am there among them." This verse implies a belief in the manifestation of a divine presence or consciousness when people come together in a particular manner. It suggests that the interconnection between individuals can foster a deeper level of mental interaction, leading to shared experiences that transcend individual boundaries.

By recognizing the interconnectivity of all things, including consciousness, we open ourselves to the possibility of collective experiences and a heightened sense of unity. It signifies that when individuals unite with shared intentions, beliefs, or focus, there is an opportunity for a synergistic effect, where the whole becomes greater than the sum of its parts.

Understanding the interconnective web of the mind's emergent properties, and the potential for collective consciousness, we gain insight into the profound nature of human connection and how our individual experiences intertwine with a broader tapestry of consciousness.

Nikola Tesla, the famous inventor and electrical engineer had interesting beliefs regarding vibration. Tesla believed that everything in the universe, including objects, energy, and even thoughts, is made up of vibrations. He argued that understanding and harnessing these vibrations could lead to significant advancements in technology and human well-being. According to Tesla, by understanding the principles of vibration, one could tap into the underlying energy and resonate with it to achieve various outcomes.

At our core, we possess an electromagnetic nature that underlies our existence. The essence of our being, the soul, transcends the physical body. Fundamentally, the soul encompasses a vastness that surpasses the physical confines of the body. The body exists within the greater expanse of the soul. This perspective recognizes that the soul, as an expansive and profound essence, holds a broader scope of existence compared to the physical vessel it inhabits.

When contemplating the nature of the soul, it is essential to acknowledge its expansive nature, which extends far beyond the boundaries of the physical body. This understanding emphasizes that our true essence, the soul, transcends the limitations of our corporeal form.

By recognizing the soul as a boundless entity that encompasses our being, we gain a deeper understanding of our interconnectedness with the wider universe. This perspective invites us to explore the profound nature of our existence, acknowledging that our physical manifestations are merely vessels through which the vastness of the soul expresses itself.

Many of us have a basic understanding of electromagnetic waves and frequencies, which serve as carriers of information and enable technologies like radio and television. Electromagnetic waves can receive and transmit information across vast distances.

It is worth noting that electromagnetism is an intrinsic part of the entire universe, permeating everything in diverse forms. This universal force reveals itself through various phenomena. Electromagnetic interactions govern the behavior of charged particles, including their movement and interactions with one another. Light, which itself is an electromagnetic wave, is generated and propagated through these interactions. Additionally, electrical and electronic devices function based on the principles of electromagnetism.

By recognizing our electromagnetic nature and the ubiquitous presence of electromagnetism in the cosmos, we gain insight into the interconnectedness of all things. It underscores the profound influence of electromagnetic forces on our world, shaping the behavior of particles, the transmission of information, and the operation of technological advancements that have become integral to our lives.

At a fundamental level, all matter is made up of atoms, which consist of negatively charged electrons orbiting around a positively charged nucleus. The interactions between these charged particles are governed by electromagnetic forces. Electromagnetic forces not only hold atoms together, but they also determine how they interact with each other. Human organisms also possess electromagnetic functions. It is no longer acceptable to believe that a human being is purely a physical entity, consisting solely of dense matter and governed solely by chemical processes. For example, numerous psychics throughout history have claimed that the human body is enveloped by an aura, which goes against Western scientific understanding. However, my research unequivocally shows that the aura does exist as you can see for yourself the self-luminous golden aura that surrounds beloved Jesus.

However, it is now being understood that the human body, as a bio-electromagnetic dynamic entity, does possess an aura which is called a bio-field. The concept of the biofield suggests that the human body is not just a physical entity but also encompasses subtle energy fields vibrations, and information fields. The biofield is often described as an interconnected and dynamic system that plays a role in maintaining overall health and well-being. It is believed to influence the body's biochemistry, cellular communication, and energy flow. Some practitioners suggest that disturbances or imbalances in the biofield can contribute to physical, mental, or emotional ailments. All forms of electromagnetism are composed of fields. The characteristics of the human biofield which typically extends approximately 3 feet beyond the skin's surface are now being measured by magnetic instruments.

HARMONIZING VIBRATIONS:
THE POWER OF FREQUENCY ALIGNMENT

It was my third eye vision manifest that I was able to perceive the aura or biofield of Jesus and not only Jesus but the beloved Holy Spirit's immaculate light, frequency, and vibration. This is an example of frequency alignment. Energy possesses inherent frequency. An uncomplicated illustration of this concept is found in the electromagnetic spectrum, specifically the visible spectrum of light. Although all forms of electromagnetic energy in the light spectrum are fundamentally the same, each color exhibits a distinct frequency and vibrational rate. For instance, red has a lower vibrational rate compared to blue, which has a higher vibrational rate. When we align ourselves with our authentic truth, passion, creativity, and love, we enable our frequency to accelerate and elevate. Consequently, our sensitivity as receivers, akin to antennas, amplifies, allowing us to perceive frequencies beyond our immediate reality. Our sensory perception expands, granting us the ability to comprehend and recognize our profound connection to Source.

By matching our frequency with that of a higher frequency we can establish a union. It is crucial to remember that we can only perceive vibrations that correspond to our own vibrational state. Therefore, to receive, understand, and process information and have experiences related to a specific vibration, we must raise our own frequency, much like a tuning fork. Conversely, if we remain at a lower vibrational frequency on the scale, it becomes challenging to have experiences that resonate with higher frequencies. It's like trying to tune a radio to a station that is broadcasting at a frequency far beyond the range your radio can reach.

Therefore, by consciously aligning with our truth, passion, creativity, and love we elevate our frequency and expand our ability to perceive that vast array of frequencies that exist beyond our immediate reality. Learning to stay in a positive state of awareness enables us to connect to higher frequencies. The path of joy goes with the flow of the current. The path of least resistance helps us remain in a positive state. Learning tools to access higher states about our greater reality helps engage us with our divine partnerships. When we educate ourselves about the greater reality it opens doors for us to be able to experience and engage with divine partnerships across the veil. Here are some practical ways to align ourselves with our authentic truth, passion, creativity, and love:

◊ **Self-reflection and Journaling:** ask meaningful questions and allow your inner voice to guide you toward your authentic truth. Some of those questions may be: What do I need to know now? Who am I? What am I doing here? If I am not only human, who am I?
◊ **Follow your passions:** Engage in activities that genuinely bring you joy and ignite your passion. Make time for activities that align with your passions.
◊ **Practice Mindfulness and Presence:** Being present in the moment helps you connect with your inner self and access your authentic truth.
◊ **Express Yourself Creatively:** Find outlets for your creativity. Allow yourself to freely express your thoughts, emotions, and ideas.
◊ **Surround yourself with Inspiration:** Seek out environments, people, and resources that inspire and uplift you. Surrounding yourself with positivity, supportive individuals, and

inspiring content can fuel your creativity and help you align with your authentic self.

◊ **Practice Self-Compassion and Self-love:** Treat yourself with kindness, compassion, and acceptance. Embrace your strengths and acknowledge your accomplishments. Practice self-care and prioritize activities that nurture your well-being.

◊ **Set Boundaries:** Establish healthy boundaries in your relationships and commitments: Saying no to things that don't align with your truth or drain your energy allows you to create space for what truly matters to you.

◊ **Align your Actions with Your Values:** Make choices and decisions that are in harmony with your authentic self and reflect what truly matters to you.

◊ **Seek Growth and Learning:** Engage in personal development activities, such as books, attending workshops, or seeking guidance from mentors. Continuously learn and grow to expand your understanding of yourself and your passions.

◊ **Cultivate Gratitude and Love:** Practice gratitude for the blessings in your life and cultivate a mindset of love and compassion. Show appreciation for yourself and others, and let love guide your actions and interactions.

CONSCIOUS EVOLUTION: EMPOWERING MINDS, TRANSFORMING EDUCATION

As we continue to connect with higher consciousness and change humanities future transformation of education and psychology will be pivotal as we evolve our species. The understanding that thoughts shape reality would likely have a significant impact on education and psychology. It would highlight the importance of nurturing positive thought patterns, emotional intelligence, and self-awareness from an early age. Educational systems and psychological practices might emphasize the development of mental and emotional well-being, empowering individuals to consciously shape their reality through their thoughts and intentions.

Additionally, the most important focus in education is a transformative revolution driven by synergy. To think synergistically we need to completely overturn the current approach of segregating knowledge into separated compartments. A synergistic approach allows students to develop a holistic understanding of complex topics by exploring connections and relationships between different subjects. A synergistic approach to education exposes students to diverse perspectives, cultures, and worldviews. This fosters empathy, and cultural understanding and prepares students to be global citizens who can navigate and contribute to an interconnected world. The ability to adapt and thrive in an ever-changing world is crucial. Synergistic education equips students with transferable skills and a flexible mindset that allows them to navigate diverse situations and adapt to new challenges. Overall, a synergistic approach to education empowers students with a broader and interconnective knowledge base, critical thinking skills, and the ability to apply knowledge to real-world contexts. It prepares them to be lifelong learners and problem solvers in an increasingly complex and interconnected world.

THE UNVEILING OF CONSCIOUS PARTICIPATION: TRANSFORMING ONTOLOGICAL WORLDVIEWS

Reimagining Reality, Embracing Purpose, and Uniting Humanity

Humanity's conscious evolution is intricately linked to the ideas we hold about the nature of reality. If we were able to demonstrate that we live in a conscious participatory universe and that a loving God exists, it would profoundly reshape our current ontological worldview leading to transformative shifts in our understanding of ourselves and the cosmos.

Demonstrating the existence of a conscious participatory universe and a loving God is a complex and multifaceted endeavor, and it requires robust evidence and rigorous inquiry. The implications would be far-reaching, and they would likely shape our understanding of ourselves, our relationship with the universe, and our place in the grand tapestry of existence.

Such a demonstration would likely lead to a paradigm shift in our understanding of reality. It would challenge materialistic worldviews that consider the physical universe as the sole reality, opening up new avenues for exploring the nature of consciousness, the purpose of existence, and the mysteries of the cosmos.

If it could be demonstrated that we live in a conscious participatory universe, it would challenge the view that consciousness is solely a product of physical processes in the brain. It would suggest that consciousness has a fundamental role in shaping and participating in the unfolding of the universe. This would raise profound questions about the nature and origins of consciousness, as well as the relationship between mind and matter.

The existence of a loving God would introduce the concept of purpose and meaning into our worldview. It would imply that there is an inherent purpose to our existence and that our lives have significance beyond the material realm. This could help individuals with a sense of direction, hope, and a framework for understanding their place in the universe.

If we live in a participatory universe, it suggests that everything is interconnected and part of a unified whole. This would challenge the notion of a fragmented and disconnected reality emphasizing the interdependence of all entities. It would foster a sense of unity, empathy, and responsibility towards all living beings and the natural world.

In conclusion, demonstrating that we live in a conscious participatory universe and that a loving God exists would fundamentally transform our current ontological worldview. This realization would expand our perception of consciousness, deepen our connection and interdependence, infuse purpose and meaning into our lives, shape our ethical framework, foster the integration of science and spirituality, and trigger a paradigm shift in our understanding of reality.

Paul Levy is a spiritual teacher who works in the field of spiritual awakening and consciousness and is a mystic himself. Paul Levy proposes that the universe actively collaborates with us to facilitate our realization of its inherent nature, as well as our own. In this context, quantum physics serves as both a theoretical and practical tool through which we can gain a profound understanding of reality. Levy alludes to the optimistic viewpoint of Wheeler, who suggests that there exists an extraordinary occurrence or revelation that is eagerly anticipated somewhere in the vastness of existence.[16] [17] John Archibald Wheeler was an American theoretical physicist of the 20th century, contributing particularly to the fields of general relativity, gravitation, and quantum mechanics.

Today, I share with you a profound visionary experience that reveals the inner manifestation of the second coming of Christ that can happen within each individual. Jesus taught not as a dispenser of laws, but as a revealer of eternal truth written in our hearts. Through the lens of my heart and perception, I have personally witnessed the presence of God's love, and it is through this revelation that you too will come to see it.

This vision I've encountered aligns with some of the depictions in the Book of Revelation and other stories from the holy Bible. It is akin to the moment when John, in a state of spiritual communion, experiences a profound revelation of the unveiling of divine truth. In Revelation 4:2-3, John describes seeing a throne in heaven and the one sitting on the throne as having the appearance of jasper and carnelian, with a rainbow resembling an emerald encircling the throne. In my visionary photographs, the beloved Holy Spirit displays itself with glorious hues of jasper and carnelian, and emerald-green. Also, the Father has an appearance of eternal wisdom, purity, and authority with a head and hair as white as snow and like the texture of wool because he is in a cloud-like appearance (note however this description was ascribed to Jesus in the book of revelation). In this divine presence, Jesus Christ, who sits at the right hand of our Father, and the blessed Holy Spirit radiates glorious rays of heavenly light, shining with immense magnificence showing how he indeed is the Son of Man and the King of Kings.

It is important to note that the visionary experiences I am sharing are imbued with a sense of loving presence, devoid of fear or apocalyptic images often associated with the end times as described in the Holy Bible. It is my belief that as divine creators made in the image and likeness of God, we have the power to be mindful and intentional in how we shape the future of humanity.

Rather than perceiving the end of times as a catastrophic event, I propose that it signifies a transformative process wherein we elevate our consciousness to embody godliness and embrace a Christed awareness. This entails a profound shift towards a higher state of being, where we align ourselves with the divine essence within us.

Therefore, I invite you to embrace this visionary encounter and recognize that the second coming of Christ is not a distant event, but a continuous process within each of us. It is a call to awaken to our divine nature, to embody the teachings of love, compassion, and forgiveness in our daily lives. By aligning our consciousness with the presence of God's love, we contribute to the unfolding of a new and enlightened reality for ourselves and humanity as a whole.

Abraham Joshua Heschel, a prominent 20th-century Polish American rabbi, Jewish theologian, and philosopher, expressed the concept that the role of a prophet extends beyond that of a mere messenger. According to Heschel, the prophet serves not only to deliver the word but also to bear witness and provide testimony to its divine nature.[18]

In the writings of Benedict De Spinoza, it is suggested that God chose to manifest Himself to the Apostles through the mind of Christ, similar to how He had previously revealed Himself to Moses through a divine voice. Consequently, Christ's voice, akin to the one heard by Moses, can be regarded as the voice of God. From this perspective, it can also be understood that God's Wisdom, which surpasses human understanding, took on a human form in Christ.[19]

God's presence has remained with us continuously, and there are numerous messengers, mystics, and prophets who exist in the world today. They possess a deep connection with the divine and serve as conduits of spiritual wisdom. As we turn inward, we can experience the love of God residing and ruling within our hearts.

Truly, Truly I say to you love God with all your heart, mind, and soul and love ye one another as I have loved you for the kingdom of heaven resides within each one of you. For those who knock so shall they enter!

The Law of the prophets is peace. His law is love, and His gospel is peace.

> *Do not think that I have come to abolish the Law*
> *or the Prophets; I have not come to abolish them but to fulfill*
> *them. For truly I tell you, until heaven and earth disappear,*
> *not the smallest letter, not the least stroke of a pen,*
> *will by any means disappear from the Law*
> *until everything is accomplished.*
>
> MATTHEW 5:17-18, NIV

This means that nothing shall disobey the law of God. It cannot be. There is no existence outside of God, therefore, every action and occurrence happens in God. In Heaven and Earth, nothing will pass away, as God is the life force in everything. God is the existence of everything- it's *being* in nature. Everything in existence is inside the law of God, so when all is complete, and everything aligns, on earth and in the heavens-oneness is achieved. It is then complete.

7

EMBODYING THE COSMIC CHRIST: UNVEILING OUR TRUE SELVES

For in one Spirit we were all baptized into one body, whether Jews or Greeks, slave or free, and we were given one Spirit to drink. For the body does not consist of one part, but of many.

1 CORINTHIANS 12:13-14, BSB

THE ENLIGHTENED ARCHITECT, THE COSMIC CHRIST, SERVES AS the cornerstone of your foundation. The Church, which acts as a sacred temple of light and love, embodies the collective body of Christ, comprising numerous individuals united together. The purpose of Christ's coming was not to establish a distinct group of followers known as Christians, but rather to facilitate our transformation into individuals who embody the teachings and essence of Christ."[20] So, we can know that self-mastery is within our reach. Enlightenment is a shift of our identity; enlightenment is liberation to experience the goodness that we are and to share it with others as Christed beings. As human beings, we must gain awareness of our divine nature and recognize our true selves.

The Gospel of Thomas is considered apocryphal writings. The word "apocryphal" originates from the Greek word "apokryphos," which means "hidden" or "obscure." It refers to texts that are hidden or kept secret, rather than texts that reveal something. The term "apocryphal" refers to texts or writings that are not included in the official or accepted canon of a religious tradition. It is often used to describe religious or biblical texts that are considered non-canonical, meaning they are not included in the authoritative collection of sacred scriptures.

The Gospel of Thomas was discovered in 1945 near the town of Nag Hammadi in Upper Egypt. The discovery was made in a large clay jar that contained a collection of ancient texts, which are now collectively known as the Nag Hammadi Library or the Nag Hammadi Scriptures. These texts contain several sayings that are considered cryptic or mysterious, challenging traditional interpretations.

One distinct characteristic of the Gospel of Thomas is its poetic and enigmatic style. The sayings often employ metaphorical language and paradoxical statements, challenging readers to delve into deeper layers of meaning. This style reflects the influence of Gnostic thought, which sought to explore the hidden or esoteric knowledge that leads to spiritual enlightenment.

The Gospel of Thomas presents a vision of spirituality that emphasizes the inner journey and the individual seeker's quest for self-knowledge and divine understanding. It suggests that within each person exists a divine spark or "light," and the path to salvation involves awakening to this inner reality.

One such saying is: "I shall give you what no eye has seen and what no ear has heard and what no hand has touched and what has never occurred to the human mind" (Saying 17).

This saying emphasizes the internal and present nature of the Kingdom of God. It suggests that seeking the divine realm externally or in specific physical locations is futile. Instead, the Kingdom is to be found within oneself and in the world around, indicating that spiritual enlightenment is an inner realization.

Another saying is "It is I who am the light which is above them all. It is I who am the all. From me did the all come forth, and unto me did the all extend. Split a piece of wood, and I am there. Lift up the stone, and you will find me there" (Saying 77).

THE COSMIC CHRIST: UNVEILING THE DIVINE PRESENCE IN ALL CREATION

The concept of the Cosmic Christ is rooted in Christian theology and represents the idea that the significance of Jesus Christ extends beyond his earthly life and ministry. It emphasizes the belief that Christ's presence and influence permeate the entire cosmos, encompassing both the spiritual and material realms.

The Cosmic Christ is often associated with the notion of Christ as the Logos, a Greek term meaning "Word" or "Divine Reason." The Logos is understood as the ordering principle of the universe, through which all things are created and held together. In this sense, the Cosmic Christ represents the divine presence that permeates and gives meaning to all creation.

Moreover, the Cosmic Christ highlights the call to participate in the ongoing work of Christ in the world. It invites individuals to recognize and align themselves with their divine purpose, promoting love, compassion, and the flourishing of all life.

The Cosmic Christ represents the divine consciousness or presence that infuses all of creation, all things, from the smallest particles to the vastness of galaxies, could be seen as imbued with divine consciousness or participating in the cosmic mind. The spiritual nature of the universe recognizes that the divine is not limited to human or earthly forms alone.

The Universal Christ emphasizes the belief that the divine presence is not limited to Jesus of Nazareth alone but is a universal and ongoing reality. It suggests that the incarnation—the embodiment of God in human form—is not a one-time event but an ongoing manifestation of the divine in all of creation. The Universal Christ represents the recognition that the divine is present and active in every person, creature, and element of the cosmos.

The concept of the Universal Christ is often associated with an interfaith and inclusive perspective. It recognizes the presence of divine wisdom and truth in various religious and spiritual traditions, seeing Christ as a unifying force that transcends religious boundaries. The Universal Christ invites individuals to engage in dialogue and cooperation with people of different faiths and to seek common ground in the pursuit of peace, justice, and the well-being of all.

The Cosmic Christ, the radiant embodiment of divine light, exists as the primordial source, preceding and transcending all creation. Within every human being, this Universal Christ resides, illuminating our souls and awakening our inherent connection to the divine.

The Universal Christ, as the first fruits of a new creation, holds supreme authority and sovereignty over all things. It is through the Universal Christ that we can experience the fullness of divine presence within ourselves and in all of creation, leading us toward spiritual renewal, enlightenment, and eternal life.

The foundational energy that permeates the universe is *love*, which flows from the very essence of the Almighty. Love serves as the cohesive force that sustains and animates all creation, unifying Mind, Body, and Spirit in perfect harmony.

The first fruits, represented by Jesus, serve as a reminder of our adoption into the beloved family of God through the blessed Holy Spirit. This Spirit reveals our true identity as sons and daughters, bestowed with the inheritance of divine love, grace, and eternal life.

In my mystical images of the transcendental image of Jesus, presented to us as a divine gift from the Almighty, is the ultimate revelation of His resurrection and timeless existence. Through Jesus, we witness the eternal nature of the Almighty, who transcends time and space uniting us with the absolute reality. As the Almighty orchestrates the energetic vibrations of the universe, He allows humanity to perceive His essential essence coalesce and transform into tangible matter. This divine act unveils the interconnectedness of Mind, Body, and Spirit, revealing the interwoven masterpiece of creation that we are all part of.

In Jesus, we witness the embodiment of this divine revelation—His life, teachings, and sacrificial love manifest the perfect union of Mind, Body, and Spirit. Through Jesus, we are invited to partake in this divine unity, experiencing the transformative power of the Almighty's love and grace. Thus, Jesus, as the first-fruit and the eternal manifestation of the Almighty, serves as a guiding light, illuminating our path toward spiritual awakening, divine adoption, and a profound understanding of the foundational energy of the universe—*love.*

THE RADIANT REVELATION: EMBRACING THE HIDDEN INTELLIGENCE WITHIN AND AROUND US

The true Light, enlightening every person, has entered our world (John 1:9). We must recognize the presence of a hidden intelligence that permeates existence, flowing through us as an integral part of who we are. In Him, we live, move, and have our being (Acts 17:28, ASV). This understanding connects us to the wisdom within, guiding our journey and empowering us to co-create a harmonious reality. Let us embrace this revelation, becoming beacons of illumination for ourselves and others, ushering in a world where truth and love prevail.

We are growing as a collective consciousness into a higher vibration of expression. The level of consciousness that Christ has is birthing within our souls. Consciousness constantly moves through states of awareness, which is a resurrection life beyond death. We are witnesses to that divine expression of being.

Consciousness is the very essence that underlies and surpasses the physical realm, encompassing intelligence and the laws of nature that govern everything. Without a shift in our perception of consciousness, our civilization risks self-destruction, as we remain unaware of our true nature. To prevent this, we must delve into a deeper understanding of our interconnectedness and embrace a broader worldview.

In these profound words attributed to Jesus, we are invited to embark on a journey of self-discovery and spiritual awakening. Jesus teaches that true knowledge comes from knowing ourselves, for it is through this self-knowledge that we come to understand our connection to the divine. "When you know yourselves, then you will be known, and you will understand that you are children of the living

Father."[21] Jesus said, *"I am the light that is over all things. I am all: from me all has come forth, and to me all has reached. Split a piece of wood; I am there. Lift up the stone, and you will find me there."* [22]

Expanding our consciousness offers a transformative perspective, fostering heightened awareness, empathy, and a profound sense of interconnectedness. When we acknowledge the fundamental unity of all beings and the interdependence of our actions, we are inclined to make choices that prioritize harmony, sustainability, and the well-being of all.

In the realm of scientific breakthroughs, future exploration will focus on understanding how we perceive, engage with, and contribute to our world and energetic field. We are not separate from the universe but a reflection of its very essence. Awakening comes through accepting and embracing our role within the greater whole.

The concept of the Cosmic Christ goes beyond mere beliefs or doctrines; it entails recognizing the inherent sacredness present in all aspects of existence. It represents an elevated energy vibration that brings liberation, upliftment, and freedom. The Cosmic Christ embodies a cosmology rooted in unity, emphasizing the interconnectedness of all things.

As stated in Genesis 2:7 (NIV), we are formed from the dust of the ground, infused with the breath of life, becoming living beings. This breath of life invites us into self-awareness, a transformative mechanism that connects us to universal consciousness and the mystery of our inherent wholeness. In 1 Corinthians 11:24, Jesus invites us to remember him, to partake in the act of transubstantiation, becoming one with God through our very being.

When we intimately know God within ourselves, our faith transcends belief and becomes a profound experience of our connection to the divine. The full presence of Christ exists within each element and permeates every part of our existence.[23] While this may reference the sacrament of the holy Eucharist in the Roman Catholic Church, it symbolically invites us to reunify and create a dwelling place for God within us.

Taking responsibility as co-creators in the world represents a radical transformation of our identity and the expression of our true selves within the cosmic universe. Through our journey, we experience transfiguration, connecting to a higher reality that encompasses and transcends our individual existence.

Deepak Chopra suggests that the concept of the Second Coming signifies a profound transformation in consciousness. This transformative shift has the power to revitalize human nature, lifting it to a divine state. According to Chopra, the Second Coming is a spiritual awakening that brings about a fundamental change in the way we perceive and experience reality. As he eloquently puts it, "...the Second Coming will be a shift in consciousness that renews human nature by raising it to the level of the divine."[24] This statement encapsulates Chopra's belief that the Second Coming represents a powerful spiritual phenomenon, transcending mere physical manifestations and inviting humanity to embrace a higher state of being.

Jesus says, "I and the Father are one" We are all One in each other and always have been, but that awareness is presenting itself more abundantly than ever before. These seeds of wisdom are implanted within us. You are the Son as equally as Jesus. You and Jesus are one.

In my mystical encounter with the Cosmic Christ, I have come to understand the profound interconnectedness between "I AM" within myself and myself within "I AM." This experience reveals a deep relationship between the observer and the observed, the knower and the known. The observer represents the one who perceives, while the knower symbolizes consciousness itself. Through this experience, I have gained the ability to perceive the divine presence in all beings and forms of life. It is evident that every being is embraced by the grace of divinity, and we all possess the same inherent divinity that we attribute to Jesus. Through my visionary photographs, I strive to convey this message to my readers - the existence of God and their own unique expression of the divine essence. Jesus exemplified how to embody love and embrace both our human and divine nature. The awakening of Christ Consciousness, which is the true essence of the second coming, resides within every individual.

By immersing ourselves consciously in the present moment and fully experiencing the essence of our being, we open ourselves to sacred moments that unfold and envelop our awareness. This act of presence is the initial step toward opening our hearts to receive. When we embrace these sacred moments, a profound sense of unity and inner tranquility permeates our being. Gratitude serves as the connection that allows us to both receive and be received. Within the vast diversity of God, we find the blessedness of the breath of God that animates our very existence.

The deepest longing of our souls is to manifest the divine essence. Our fundamental instinct is not merely survival but the actualization of divinity within ourselves. Our soul is the true cornerstone, unshaken by trials and tribulations. It stands steadfast, carrying and guiding us toward the highest expression of our true selves. This cornerstone is a solid rock with unshakable foundations, meticulously laid by the wise master builder, the Creator. It beckons us to explore the depths of our true identity and recognize the inherent worth and intrinsic value that resides within us.

When our faith remains unwavering, the cornerstone remains indestructible, providing us with stability and assurance. Faith is an extraordinary journey that remains untarnished by external factors. It is akin to the unwavering sun, a sacred and steadfast temple that stands resolute, guiding us into radiant streams of golden light and divine glory. The journey of faith is beautiful and liberating, carried by the swiftness of an angel and the anticipation of the dawn. Faith is knowing that the next breath will be breathed. It is a melodious song of praise and glory, resonating within us all, waiting to be discovered by those who seek. Faith is the force that binds us to God, allowing us to encounter the divine within ourselves and perceive the presence of God in all things. Faith is when we meet God within ourselves and see God in all things.

Embracing the truth brings about liberation and a profound sense of freedom, enabling us to dwell in the depths of our spirit. At times, our faith may be tested, shaken, or even lost. However, true liberation is found when we place complete trust in God. Trust is the active expression of faith. The presence of God is constant and unwavering, and nothing can ever separate us from the boundless love that emanates from God.

"Consequently, you are no longer foreigners and strangers, but fellow citizens with God's people and also members of his household, built on the foundation of the apostles and prophets, with Christ Jesus himself as the chief cornerstone. In him, the whole building is joined togeth-

er and rises to become a holy temple in the Lord. And in him, you too are being built together to become a dwelling in which God lives by his Spirit" (Ephesians 2:19-22, NIV).

The ultimate source of truth exists within your being. Place your trust in God and embrace the divine essence within you. By doing so, you will transition from doubt to a deep certainty in the truths you have come to know. Engaging in contemplation of the divine will naturally lead you to new insights and revelations. Sometimes, it is necessary to take a leap of faith into an unfamiliar paradigm that can only be discovered within yourself. There are numerous paths to explore, and when you align yourself with nature, you tap into the cosmic origins. Nature serves the purpose of assisting us in connecting with the spiritual essence residing within us. Have you recently paused to appreciate the flawless beauty of the natural world? Have you found yourself captivated by the grandeur of mountains or the vastness of the sea? These moments of contemplation, where you deeply value the intricate and purposeful design of the world surrounding you, possess the ability to evoke a sense of interconnectedness and inner harmony.

Jesus demonstrates his power by calming a storm and metaphorically transforming his disciples into "fishers of men." He imparts wisdom to Peter about the essential tools for maintaining faith and even enables him to walk on water alongside him. Jesus teaches humanity the importance of recognizing the divine presence within themselves. He emphasizes that even with a small amount of faith, as tiny as a mustard seed, we can overcome seemingly insurmountable obstacles and achieve the extraordinary.

It is our self-doubt that causes us to falter and sink into despair. When we choose to not even open the door because of our close mindedness, we create an illusion of separation from God. Our own self-judgment has the power to wash us away.

However, it is important to understand that God is constantly present, even for those who lack faith. There is never a moment when God is not with us, regardless of our beliefs. Knowing God puts us in friendship with God, where we can know God intimately within us. Unfortunately, certain limited beliefs try to convince us that it is impossible to truly know God, and if we hold on to such beliefs, we will manifest that as our reality.

Doesn't God also reveal Himself to Thomas, who doubted? However, it is important not to let your faith become blind, blindly following a doctrine simply because it is what you were raised in does not serve you. It is commendable to question your faith and not be a passive follower. Engage in research, ask questions, and critically examine what is keeping you where you are. Is it a fear, misunderstanding, or flawed theology? Perhaps you need to be open to exploring different paths and alternative understandings. Don't be afraid to venture beyond the boundaries of traditional teachings, even if they may seem heretical, for there are no paths that exist outside of God.

> *If a blind man leads a blind man, both will fall into a pit.*
>
> MATTHEW 15:14, BSB

At times, finding peace and connection can be as uncomplicated as taking a leisurely stroll, inhaling deeply, witnessing the growth of a flower, observing a bird gracefully glide through the sky, or feeling the gentle touch of a summer breeze on your face while walking along the seashore, as waves ebb and flow.

HEALING WOUNDS, CULTIVATING LOVE: EMBRACING INTERCONNECTEDNESS

> *When did we see You a stranger and take You in,*
> *or naked and clothe You? When did we see You sick*
> *or in prison and visit You?' And the King will reply,*
> *'Truly I tell you, whatever you did for one of the least*
> *of these brothers of Mine, you did for Me.'*
>
> MATTHEW 25:39-40, BSB

When we encounter individuals who are suffering, whether they are hungry, naked, or imprisoned, we not only carry the radiant light and divinity within us, but we also bear the wounds. Divinity itself experiences wounds when it enters the realm of human history, and thus we empathize and share in the wounds of others. If we as caretakers of the garden of humanity, desire to alleviate the wounds inflicted upon us, we must extend our healing touch to one another.

What we do for others, we ultimately do for ourselves and for the interconnectedness of the entire universe. Our existence encompasses a vastness that exceeds our comprehension.

As Jesus taught in Matthew 5:43-48, we are called to embrace self-mastery as divine beings of love and light, choosing our state of being and shaping our experiences. This includes how we respond to our enemies, demonstrating peaceful, calm, and understanding ways of being. By embodying these qualities, we not only transform our own state of being but also influence others, including those who may oppose us.

Our actions reflect our true nature as divine beings and contribute to the interconnectedness of the entire universe. As divine beings, it is crucial to exemplify love towards all individuals, regardless of their faith, nationality, or personality. This includes extending love even to our enemies. Jesus, in his teaching on the rising sun and the falling rain that blesses both the good and the evil, highlights the all-encompassing and impartial love of God for all of humanity (Matthew 5:44-45).

Dean Radin is a parapsychologist and is known for his work in the field of consciousness. Dean Radin suggests that our individual subjective experiences are interconnected with the subjective experiences of others, both on Earth and beyond. This interconnectedness implies that our sense of purpose and meaning as beings might be indicative of something grander and more expansive than our individual selves. Radin proposes that this shared sense of purpose and meaning could be a reflection of a greater, universal reality that extends beyond our personal existence.[25]

As a farmer, I had to learn how to cultivate different crops at different times and produce seeds that would last. As we become gardeners of humanity and sowers cultivating a receptive heart and mind to receive spiritual teachings, we can apply wisdom that guides us to cultivating virtues of compassion, forgiveness, and integrity. By applying these lessons, we can create fertile ground within ourselves for spiritual growth deepening our understanding of divine truths and manifesting these into our reality.

Summary: The concept of the Cosmic Christ emphasizes that the significance of Jesus Christ extends beyond his earthly life and ministry and represents the divine presence that permeates and gives meaning to all of creation. It highlights the belief that Christ's presence and influence extend throughout the entire cosmos, encompassing both the spiritual and material realms. The Universal Christ expands upon this idea by recognizing the ongoing manifestation of the divine in all of creation, emphasizing the presence of the divine in every person, creature, and element of the cosmos. The Universal Christ promotes an inclusive and interfaith perspective, acknowledging the presence of divine wisdom in various religious and spiritual traditions. Both the Cosmic Christ and the Universal Christ invite individuals to recognize their divine nature and engage in the ongoing work of Christ in the world, promoting love, compassion, and the well-being of all. Love is seen as the foundational energy that sustains and unifies all of creation.

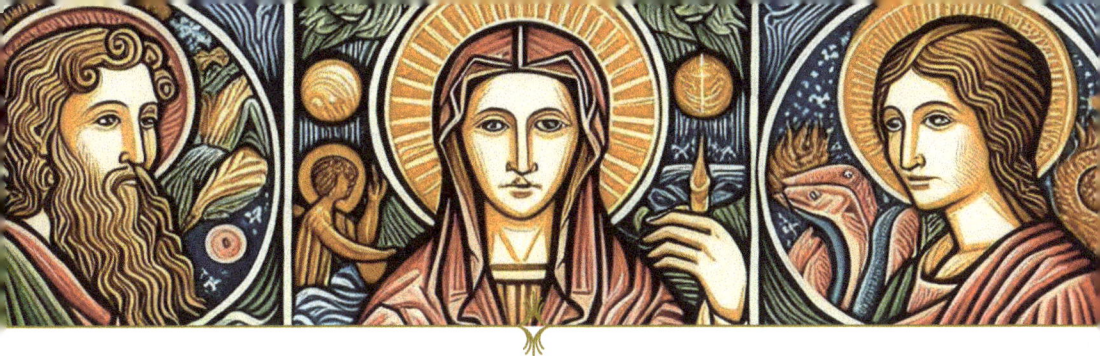

8

DIVINE LUMINARIES: UNVEILING THE JOURNEY OF PROPHETS, MYSTICS, AND SAINTS

If you belong to Christ, then you are Abraham's seed,
and heirs according to the promise.

GALATIANS 3:29, NIV

IN THE HOLY BIBLE, GOD PRIMARILY COMMUNICATED WITH THE people of Israel through the prophets known as agents of revelation who were conduits of divine revelation. There were many prophets and many false prophets in biblical times and today. The Apostles of Christ were emissaries who were given His authority to speak on His behalf. The revelation of God was given to his beloved Son who was the Word of God incarnate. The word is an energy of our Creator in action. According to Rabbi Heschel, the notion is put forth that God's creation of the word did not stem from nothingness, but rather emerged from the very essence of His own Being.[26] "Long ago, at many times in many ways, God spoke to our fathers by the prophets, but in these last days, he has spoken to us by his Son, whom he appointed the heir of all things, through whom also he created the world" (Hebrews 1:1-2, ESV).

Early Jewish Christian followers of Christ called themselves 'The Way' and were convinced that Jesus appeared to them on multiple occasions. What did the disciples see that convinced them that Jesus had risen? They really saw Him; a man had risen from the dead. The Gospel writers intended to share their heartfelt testimony to the end of the world. The sacred texts of the Old Testament and the New Testament reveal a very special relationship of God with His Creation. God speaks to us through our hearts in holy scripture. These profound moments of divine revelation live in us as we seek to know who and what we are.

Rabbi Heschel emphasizes that in the realm of the prophet, the purpose of their imagery is not to simply shine or dazzle, but rather to burn with intensity. Prophetic words are intentionally crafted to evoke shock and provoke contemplation, rather than solely aiming to provide comfort or upliftment.[27]

In my profound encounter with the divine, I have had a remarkable revelation that I feel compelled to share with the world. There are instances when God imparts messages to us that are undeniable and impossible to ignore, even if they make us uneasy. My personal testimony of God captured through my visionary photography may appear extraordinary and peculiar, but it is not unique, many mystics and prophets have also described experiences that defy comprehension. However, I can confidently affirm that all things are within the realm of possibility with God. It can be challenging for us to fully grasp the immense power and magnificence of God's presence, but when we surrender our hearts and minds to the pursuit of the greater good, we not only radiate with increased brilliance but also reach new heights of awareness and are consumed by the exhilaration of God's glory.

Throughout the course of human history, ordinary individuals from various parts of the globe have had personal encounters and experiences with celestial entities, such as divine beings, angels, and the Virgin Mother. They have also undergone profound moments of devotion and love that connect them to the cosmic realm. Additionally, these individuals have had transformative epiphanies, commonly known as "aha moments," where they feel deeply embraced by the universal vibration of connection and inherent unity with all aspects of existence.

According to Heschel, the prophetic experience is not an abstract or distant concept, but rather a deeply felt and immediate reality within the mind of the prophet. In this state, God becomes the central focus of their thoughts, and the world is perceived as a reflection of the divine presence. Heschel asserts that the primary purpose of prophetic thinking is to bring the world into a sharper focus, aligning it with the divine perspective.[28] Bringing the world into divine focus involves cultivating a perspective that aligns with higher spiritual principles and channeling that understanding into transformative action.

When ordinary individuals have undergone such encounters, it has resulted in a wider perspective and a more profound comprehension of the enigmatic nature of consciousness and the act of creation. This perpetual essence of awe and marvel permeates through these experiences. The essence we often long to encounter and convey, which is a product of our divine essence, is a vibration, a frequency that reflects our inherent nature back to us.

Some of the greatest roles mystics and prophets play in society are challenging the status quo and calling for personal and societal transformation. They challenge oppressive systems, social injustices, and the misuse of power. They inspire individuals to question existing structures fostering a more just, compassionate, and inclusive society.

Mystics and prophets play a role in awakening individuals to deeper truths and possibilities. They help people break free from limited beliefs, attachments, and ego-driven patterns, leading to greater self-awareness, inner freedom, and spiritual growth. Mystics and prophets play a role in cultural and historical significance to influence and inspire movements that shape religious and philosophical traditions and contribute to the evolution of human consciousness throughout history.

There is no one-size-fits-all description of what every prophet is like or what they're called to do. A prophet is a person who receives a divine message and speaks to other human beings on behalf of a deity. Most prophets inspire action or change. Some prophets receive visions while others are shown prophetic symbols while others perform miracles such as Elijah to Elisha. Some prophets prophesy about the future like Daniel and John of Patmos.

God is just as active today as he was when the Bible was written. And today humanity is even in a greater pinnacle or climax of a greater state of awareness in our evolution of spirit and transformation of being to know thyself. To thy own self be true. God still communicates with his children in effective ways.

DISCERNING AUTHENTIC TEACHERS AND PROPHETS: A GUIDE TO RECOGNIZING GENUINE SPIRITUAL GUIDANCE

In today's world, discerning a genuine teacher or prophet can be achieved by observing their ability to facilitate our connection to the divine and guide us toward encountering the creator. It is important to be cautious if they resort to aggressive tactics such as yelling, screaming, or enticing us to seek God solely through external means, relying exclusively on their truth, book, or method. A true prophet or teacher seeks to assist humanity's magnificence.

However, if they encourage you to discover God within yourself, affirming unity between you and the divine, and emphasize that you do not require their truth, book, and method then you have encountered a true teacher or master. This is because they have guided you to recognize the master that resides within your own being. No matter how many prophecies are fulfilled, or revelations received, the underlying purposes of God remain the same. God desires a people to know they are not separate from God that God is our friend and for humanity to know that God is pure love.

Remember that discernment is essential, and it is advisable to rely on your own intuition, critical thinking, and careful observation when evaluating the authenticity of a teacher or prophet. You do not need to go through any other person but yourself to have contact with God.

To assess the legitimacy of a teacher or prophet, one can inquire about the indicators and outcomes of a benevolent spiritual presence. Where can we find the spirits, we aim to distinguish? And why is it important to establish guidelines for discerning spirits? The Spirit of Truth yields enduring fruits.

Imagine that our perception of the world is like being in a room with mirrors all around us. We are so used to seeing everything reflected back to us from our own perspective, that we forget there is more to explore. Seeking assistance from external sources is like looking through windows in the room or consulting a map to gain new perspectives. However, many spiritual sages have taught us that true understanding comes from realizing that we are interconnected with everything. They have said things like "I and the Father are one" and "I am That." So, take a moment to pause and reflect. Ask yourself, who or what has the ability to step back and see the bigger picture? The answer is a resounding "I AM." By uttering these two words, you are acknowledging your true nature and getting closer to the fulfillment of your spiritual quest. Now, instead of fixating on the objects in the room, continue to step back repeatedly until you uncover the subject of your search, which is the unity and interconnectedness of all things.

MYSTICS AND PROPHETS: INSPIRING HUMANITY'S SPIRITUAL AWAKENING AND TRANSFORMATION

As an observer of the all-encompassing and benevolent presence of God, it is integral for me, as a mystic, to illuminate the inherent divinity within each of us. The radiant essence transcends religious boundaries, encompassing individuals of diverse faiths or even those that identify with non-faith. It is my calling to communicate and share this profound truth to reveal the God-self that resides within all beings, uniting us regardless of our spiritual affiliations.

The vastness of God exceeds the confines of any single religion. The magnitude and expansiveness of the divine cannot be contained within the boundaries of a particular belief system. God's essence transcends the limitations imposed by human constructs and extends far beyond the realm of any specific religious framework.

However, symbolic interpretations recognize that religious doctrines often employ symbols, stories, and concepts as a means to convey deeper truths about the divine. While these expressions may be limited in their literal interpretations, they can serve as metaphors or pointers toward the transcendental nature of God.

The universe sometimes communicates with us through symbols. Symbols are powerful tools that can convey complex ideas, emotions, and experiences in a condensed and evocative manner, they transcend rational and linear thinking, tapping into the realm of the subconscious and the collective unconscious.

Symbols can be found in various forms, including myths, dreams, rituals, art, and religious practices. They serve as bridges between the conscious and unconscious mind, allowing individuals to access deeper layers of meaning and insight. Symbolism can help illuminate hidden aspects of the self, reveal unconscious patterns, and facilitate personal and collective transformation.

As I encountered the unfolding of the Cosmic Christ the cosmic egg of creation which symbolizes the primal source from which the universe emerges and evolves with profound creativity, I initially felt a sense of being overwhelmed. It struck me deeply that human beings are often unaware of the immense magnificence that resides within them.

In the early stages of my awakening, I experienced a profound sense of solitude. This was what Spanish mystic and Catholic priest and poet known as Saint John on the Cross coined as the term "The Dark Night of the Soul." For me going through the process of the "Dark Night of the Soul" had anguishing moments. The process of awakening can be disorienting, much like the biblical account of Adam and Eve who, upon partaking of the fruit of knowledge, became conscious of their own nakedness, and awakened to a new level of awareness.

The dark night of the soul is like standing on the edge of a vast, uncharted ocean. It is a period of deep spiritual crisis or purification, where individuals find themselves questioning their beliefs, values, and sense of self. It is a transformative journey that can lead to profound growth and spiritual awakening. However, in my case, it was slightly different.

Imagine you stumble upon a hidden garden, a place of extraordinary beauty and profound meaning. You are in awe of its existence, yet you realize that humanity as a whole remains unaware of its existence. This realization becomes an undeniable truth, a deeply profound and overwhelming experience for you.

In this scenario, your dark night of the soul is not characterized by despair or a loss of meaning, but rather by a profound encounter with a hidden truth. It is as if you have discovered a secret treasure, a knowledge so beautiful and powerful it overwhelms your senses. You are faced with the challenge of reconciling this truth within yourself while realizing that the rest of humanity is still unaware.

This experience can be both exhilarating and daunting. It may bring a sense of responsibility to share this profound truth and awaken others to its existence. It is a journey of self-discovery and a calling to be a messenger or guide for others, shining a light on this hidden beauty and helping others navigate their own paths of transformation and growth.

Just as the dark night of the soul is a time of deep introspection and questioning, your unique experience is a call to embrace your role as a custodian of this profound truth. It is an opportunity to serve humanity by sharing this knowledge and helping others awaken to the extraordinary beauty that lies beyond their current awareness.

During this time, I also experienced a moment of melancholy. I grappled with the challenge of conveying to humanity the extraordinary marvel that exists within each of us. Thomas Merton, a Roman Catholic monk, and mystic eloquently captured this sentiment when he pondered, "How is it possible to tell people that we are all walking around shining like the sun?" I understood the importance of a crucial moment in creation, where consciousness emerged within the splendor of God's glory, allowing the human heart to perceive its true nature and transcend limitations.

For a period, my egoic identity resonated with the biblical narrative that portrays God's sorrow in the depths of His heart at the creation of humankind (Genesis 6:6). My heart felt overwhelmed by the realization that humanity remained largely unaware of its inherent magnificence and the profound phenomenon in which we participate.

However, to my great delight, I've come to know that many individuals are undergoing a similar awakening. Our collective consciousness is undergoing and transforming, and this awakening is being sown, germinating, sprouting, and maturing as part of our evolutionary process. These seeds hold the potential to bear fruit that will contribute to our growth, development, and well-being.

One of my favorite biblical verses is from Hosea 6:3, NASB: 'So let us know, Let us press on to know the LORD; his going forth is as certain as the dawn; And He will come to us like rain, Like the spring rain watering the earth.' I love this verse because it signifies the importance of perseverance in seeking and understanding God. With God, there is always more to discover. Throughout my spiritual journey, God has been by my side, patiently guiding me as I unfolded my awareness, much like a flower opening its blooms. I had to question my beliefs and delve deeply into the nature of God. Just when I thought I reached a pinnacle of understanding, a new aspect of God's truth revealed itself, like a fresh flower waiting to be unraveled.

For those of you who have an eye so shall you see! For, those of you who have an ear so shall you hear! And for those of you who have a heart, so shall you know! A great time is before us when God pours out his Spirit on all people. Where sons and daughters will prophesy, and young men and women will see visions, and old men will dream dreams. Many have eagerly awaited the blessed hope of Christ's second coming, and now humanity has been granted the opportunity to witness the face of our beloved Creator.

There have been many prophets and mystics that have shared their stories of profound union with the divine and this has helped shape the course for humanity to be inspired. Mystics serve as witnesses and exemplars of the mystical path, offering guidance and inspiration to others who seek a deeper understanding and connection. They may share their experiences, personal teachings, or personal interactions, providing others with insights and tools to embark on their own spiritual journeys. Some have inspired us with their faith, others with their visions, and others with profound messages. These are some mystics and prophets that have had an impact on our world.

ABRAHAM

Now faith is being sure of what we hope for
and certain of what we do not see

HEBREWS 11:1, NIV

Abraham was the patriarch and ancestor of the Israelite peo-ple. He was chosen by God to establish a covenant, which included promises of land, descendants, and blessings. He was seen as a model of trust and obedience to God's commands. It was Abraham's faith whose builder and architect was God. His seed prevailed. Abraham heard the LORD and was faithful, because of his faith many Nations would be born of his seed. He was going to sacrifice his son but at the last-minute God provided him with a Ram and an Angel to save his son's life. Abraham became the father of many nations. By faith, he dwelt in the Promised Land like a stranger in a foreign country. He lived in tents, as did Isaac and Jacob, who were heirs of the same promise. For he was looking forward to the city with foundations, whose architect and builder is God. "I will make of you a great nation and I will bless you" (Genesis 12:2, NAB).

Abraham, in his journey towards monotheism, challenged the pre-vailing polytheistic beliefs of his time and introduced the concept of a singular, transcendent God. His faith and willingness to follow di-vine guidance set the stage for a deeper understanding of the divine.

MOSES

Moses was a prophet in the Abrahamic religions. Moses experienced God through a combination of visual, auditory, and spiritual manifes-tations. Moses heard the word of God and came to see the Burning Bush. God revealed God's name to Moses. God revealed Himself to Moses by proclaiming 'I am the God of your father, the God of Abraham, the God of Isaac, and the God of Jacob' (Exodus 3:6), through this revelation, Moses recognized that he was in the presence of the God of his ancestors. He freed the Israelites from slavery. He received the Ten Commandments. He died before reaching the Promised Land.

The Song of Moses:

> *Let my teaching fall on you like rain; let my speech; settle like dew. Let my words fall like rain on tender grass, like gentle showers on young plants. I will proclaim the name of the LORD. How glorious is our God.*
>
> DEUTERONOMY 32:2-3, NIV

Moses, with his encounter with the burning bush, symbolized the transcendence and immanence of God, illustrating that the divine can both communicate from a mysterious and awe-inspiring distance while also intimately engaging with human affairs.

SAINT STEPHEN

Saint Steven, although he was not a prophet per se, he was a visionary of faith and one of the first Christian martyrs. He was accused of blasphemy and brought before the Jewish religious authorities where he delivered a powerful defense of his faith. He criticized the religious leaders for their rejection of God's messengers, including Jesus Christ which ultimately led to his stoning. His death was witnessed by Saul of Tarsus, also known subsequently as Apostle Paul. Paul would be struck with much grief as he would later have a direct experience with God that would change him forever. As Steven was being stoned to death by a group of Jews for his belief, he saw the sky open and saw the Father, the Son, and the Holy Spirit. "Look! I see heaven open and the Son of Man standing on the right hand of God" (Acts 7:56, HCSB)! Steven prayed that the Lord would receive his spirit and that his killers be forgiven.

Saint Steven's martyrdom became a catalyst for the spread of Christianity and a testament to the transformative power of faith in the face of adversity.

JOHN THE BAPTIST

John's mission was to prepare the way for Jesus Christ, whom he identified as the Lamb of God and long-awaited Messiah. John the Baptist baptized with water and proclaimed the one who was to come after him would baptize with fire and Spirit. He baptized Jesus in the river of Jordan. John used baptism as a symbol of a sacrament in his messianic movement.

And John bore witness, saying, "I saw the Spirit descending from heaven like a dove, and He remained upon Him. I did not know Him, but He who sent me to baptize with water said to me, 'Upon whom you see the Spirit descending, and remaining on Him, this is He who baptizes with the Holy Spirit.' And I have seen and testified that this is the Son of God." (John 1:32-34, NKJV) "I baptize you with water for repentance, but after me will come One more powerful than I, whose sandals I am not worthy to carry. He will baptize you with the Holy Spirit and with fire" (Matthew 3:11, BSB). The baptismal sacraments and rituals in Christianity are sacred. We are immersed in water and purified. Many Christians celebrate this act in various ways. As a Roman Catholic, we are baptized in the name of the Father, the Son, and the Holy Spirit.

After witnessing the divine revelation of God, I have come to understand the profound significance of baptism. In this sacred act, the Heavenly Father symbolizes the life-giving water, which serves as a source of hope and love. The Son represents the fire, as his light illuminates our hearts and brings life to the world. Lastly, the blessed Holy Spirit embodies eternal and infinite enthusiasm and joy encompassing us all.

Each element represents a unique aspect of God's nature and role in the process of baptism, encapsulating the themes of life, light, and eternal zeal inviting us to reflect on the transformative power of the divine presence in our lives.

> *I have come to ignite a fire on earth, and how I wish it were already kindled! But I have a baptism to undergo, and how distressed I am until it is accomplished.*

LUKE 12:49-50, BSB

This scripture reveals the inner essence of Jesus, the Son of Man, speaking directly to our hearts, and guiding us in our journey to know God within ourselves. It emphasizes the ignition and nurturing of His flame and baptism within humanity, a significant endeavor that has been carefully preserved and ignited.

John the Baptist was beheaded by Herod. Some believe that John the Baptist was Elijah come again. The disciples asked Him, "Why then do the scribes say that Elijah must come first?"

Jesus replied, "Elijah does indeed come, and he will restore all things. But I tell you that Elijah has already come, and they did not recognize him, but have done to him whatever they wished. In the same way, the Son of Man will suffer at their hands." Then the disciples understood that He was speaking to them about John the Baptist (Matthew 17:10-13, BSB).

John the Baptist, as a prophet and precursor to Jesus, played a pivotal role in preparing the way for the coming of Christ. His message of repentance and baptism symbolized a turning point in human consciousness, encouraging individuals to seek spiritual renewal and prepare their hearts for the arrival of the Messiah.

JESUS

Jesus was a mystic and prophet due to his profound spiritual teachings and his ability to connect with the divine. As a mystic, Jesus is believed to have had a direct and intimate experience with God that transcended ordinary human understanding. His teachings often conveyed deep spiritual insights and emphasized the inner transformation of individuals.

As a prophet, Jesus is seen as someone who received divine revelations and messages from God, which he then shared with others. He spoke with authority and conveyed God's will to humanity. Jesus' teachings included moral and ethical guidance, prophecies about future events, and warnings of judgment and repentance. Jesus emphasized his close relationship with God the Father and encouraged his followers to cultivate a personal relationship with the divine. Jesus performed numerous miracles, such as healing the sick, raising the dead, and turning water into wine. Jesus taught the importance of love, compassion, forgiveness, and the transformation of the heart. He spoke about the Holy Spirit and the establishment of God's Kingdom on Earth.

As individuals embark on the journey of awakening, it is crucial for us to sincerely and authentically honor God. The outdated ways of thinking and being are fading, and the present moment calls for the revelation of deep profound truths, which need to be acknowledged, listened to, and observed. It is an extraordinary period for us to develop an understanding of the Spirit and embrace truth, serving as guides who illuminate the path for collective consciousness to advance towards a more elevated state of existence.

Jesus, the Son of God who is made in our image and likeness said: "Love ye one another as I have loved you." A great Messiah, the anointed one came to teach humanity that we are divine beings of God, that the things he has done we will also do, and that we are not of this world but of Spirit. He came to teach divine Law, the one written in our hearts and about the Kingdom of Heaven.

Jesus brought a revolutionary message of love and compassion. Through his teachings, parables, and miracles Jesus revealed the true nature of God as a loving and merciful Father. His life and ministry transformed the understanding of divinity, emphasizing the importance of forgiveness, inclusivity, and the power of divine grace to heal and transform lives.

SAINT JUAN DIEGO

Saint Juan Diego was an indigenous peasant to whom the Virgin Mary appeared under the title of Our Lady of Guadalupe, reportedly appearing in the 16th century. He encountered the Virgin Mary on Tepeyac Hill, now within the boundaries of Mexico City. The Virgin Mary appeared to him as a young indigenous woman and spoke to him in his native Nahuatl language. She requested that a church be built on the site of the apparition to serve as a place of worship and prayer for the people. Juan Diego relayed this message to the local bishop, Juan de Zumarraga, who initially doubted his account. However, Juan Diego persisted, and on December 12th, after a final encounter with the Virgin Mary, he presented the bishop with his cloak, or Tilma, which miraculously bore the image of the Virgin Mary. This venerated image is enshrined within the Minor Basilica of Our Lady of Guadalupe of Mexico City.

The Virgin of Guadalupe is shrouded in the clouds encased in a mandorla of light. She wears a blue mantle with stars that are referenced to the evening sky of constellations of the year 1531. She is in a posture of prayer and humility, and the black sash she wears represents pregnancy. Some say that the crevice of her left arm reveals the crucifixion of her son. An angel supports her wearing wings of red, white, and blue.

Scientific studies have been performed on the image of Tilma over the centuries. These studies revealed various intriguing aspects of the Tilma, such as the preservation of the fabric despite its age, the absence of identifiable brushstrokes, and the presence of certain substances on the image that cannot be explained through conventional means.

Some have referenced this image to Revelation 12:1 "And there appeared a great wonder in heaven; a woman clothed with the sun, and the moon under her feet, and on her head a crown of twelve stars on her head."

Saint Juan Deigo's encounter with the divine not only deepened his own spirituality but also became a symbol of hope, unity, and cultural reconciliation. Through Juan Diego's humble devotion and the subsequent devotion of millions, the message of Mary's love and intersession resonated across cultures and continues to inspire faith and devotion to this day.

HILDEGARD OF BINGEN

...clothe yourselves with hearts of compassion, kindness, humility, gentleness, and patience.

COLOSSIANS 3:12, BSB

Saint Hildegard of Bingen, renowned for her mystic visions and artistic talents, was a multifaceted figure as a visionary, artist, composer, writer, theologian, herbalist, and philosopher. From an early age, Hildegard had extraordinary experiences of divine revelation through her visionary encounters. Her extensive body of prophetic works reflects her profound spiritual insights.

Notably, Hildegard emphasized the interconnectedness of the natural world, recognizing the intricate relationship between humanity and the broader cosmos. This holistic perspective permeated her artistic creations, such as "The Man in Sapphire Blue," a symbolic representation of the Trinity. This artwork embodies the divine unity and serves as a visual expression of Hildegard's theological concepts. The Man in Sapphire Blue encapsulates the idea that the body is in the soul. The soul contains us. Rather than the idea that the body carries the soul. The soul is much larger than the body and carries the body within it.

We are more than our physical bodies or minds; we are souls. Our physical form is like a suit we wear for a grand theatrical performance. This performance, though captivating, is an illusion that can consume us. However, it's crucial to recognize our multifaceted roles as creators, directors, and lead actors in this unique play. We have the remarkable ability to shape and rewrite the story as both writers and performers. If the current scene doesn't align with our desires, we can reshape it. Understanding our immense influence is vital. We exist as a three-fold being: Mind, Body, and Spirit—representing the physical, non-physical, and metaphysical aspects. Our bodies are tools for our souls, and our minds are the driving force behind them. The mind is the driving force of the physical realm. It's important to discover and honor the desires of the soul, as the soul embodies the highest form of love. The soul seeks experiences and feelings rather than mere knowledge, as it already possesses the necessary knowledge. Knowledge is a product of conceptual understanding while feelings arise from direct experience.

In Hildegard's worldview, compassion stood as the foundational force that bound together all aspects of existence. She viewed compassion as the divine attribute that infused every facet of creation, uniting God, the cosmos, and humanity in a profound interconnectedness.

This perspective emphasized the transformative and healing potential of compassion, for it reflected the divine nature and essence. Hildegard saw compassion as the guiding principle that nurtured the flourishing of all beings and fostered harmonious relationships within the interconnected web of life.

For Hildegard compassion was not merely an abstract concept, but a lived experience that called individuals to embody empathy, kindness, and care towards all of creation. It is through acts of compassion that the power of God's love and the inherent dignity of every being are revealed. "Compassion for Hildegard involves our relationships with all creatures, it constitutes the way we see the world."[29]

Humility plays a significant role in understanding the mind, body, and soul dynamic. Authentic self-awareness allows us to embrace humility fully. As a spiritual principle, humility guides us to recognize our connection as children of God and children of the light. It is in this state of humility that we open ourselves to personal growth, grace, and the illumination of our true essence. By acknowledging the divine nature within us, we are reminded that our highest spiritual good lies in cultivating compassion. In the words of 1 Thessalonians 5:5 (NIV), "You are all children of the light and children of the day. We do not belong to the night or to the darkness."

Hildegard's journey was one of revelation and enlightenment. Through her experiences, she came to recognize the divine as immanent in the boundless beauty of nature. She marveled at the intricate tapestry woven by the healing powers of plants, witnessing firsthand their ability to restore and nourish. From her perspective, every ailment has a corresponding plant created by God, and the graceful ballet of celestial entities embodies divine manifestations of creation.

But Hildegard's wisdom extended far beyond mere observation. She sought to awaken the dormant sense of awe within each and every one of us. Her teachings reminded us of the divine spark that resides within all living beings, urging us to recognize the sacredness of our existence. She beckoned us to honor and protect the intricate ecosystems that sustain us, for they are the very manifestations of the divine.

PIERRE TEILHARD DE CHARDIN

Pierre Teilhard de Chardin was a French Jesuit priest, paleontologist, and philosopher. He was a man of faith and believed that faith was not blind believing but linked to intelligence and knowledge. Teilhard's primary aim was to make people "see and make them feel" the presence of God.

According to Ursula King, Teilhard sought a vision of God that aligned with the evolutionary nature of the universe, an image that fully encompasses the vast dimensions of our cosmos. This vision portrays God not as an external force or initial cause but as intricately engaged with the entirety of the cosmic process, in which we ourselves are integral participants. Teilhard emphasizes the concept of a living God, fully present in the here and now, profoundly intertwined with matter and the continuous process of becoming.[30]

Teilhard de Chardin believed that evolution was not just a biological process but also a spiritual one. He proposed that all of creation, including human beings, is on a journey toward a higher level of consciousness and unity, which he referred to as the "Omega Point." He saw evolution as a process of increasing complexity and convergence, leading to the ultimate union of all things with God.

The noosphere, as described by Teilhard de Chardin, is a term he used to represent the sphere of human thought and collective intelligence. It is the realm of interconnected human minds and the network of ideas and information that is shared among individuals. Teilhard de Chardin believed that the development of communication technologies, such as the internet, would enhance the interconnectedness of human thought, leading to the emergence of a global consciousness or a "thinking layer" around the planet. The root of the word "noos," meaning "mind." The noo-sphere is the mind sphere.

According to Teilhard, the noosphere represents the next stage of evolution, where human consciousness becomes increasingly aware of its connection to the divine. In this framework, God's presence is not limited to the spiritual realm but extends into the depths of human intellect and collective consciousness.

In our human experience, we all can have the opportunity to manifest God in the way we choose. There is no last prophet because the Spirit of God lives and breathes within our being continuously always revealing itself to us through our experiences. Anything worth believing in can be experienced.

As these seeds of wisdom are sown and shared, they create a synergistic effect on the collective consciousness of humanity. They act as catalysts for personal growth and transformation, stimulating introspection, and encouraging individuals to seek higher truths. The cumulative effect of this sharing is a gradual elevation of awareness and helps the evolution of our species to tap into their innate wisdom and expand their consciousness.

Ultimately, the raising of the collective consciousness through the sharing of seeds of wisdom is a testament to the interconnectedness of all beings. Each individual contribution, whether from a mystic, poet, philosopher, scientist, nurturer, empath, realist, innovator, optimist, creative, or an everyday person, adds to the rich tapestry of human understanding. It fosters a sense of unity and shared purpose, transcending individual differences and promoting a collective journey towards higher states of awareness.

In this way, the act of sharing wisdom becomes a sacred endeavor, an offering to the universal human experience. It has the power to ignite a transformative spark within each individual and, collectively, illuminate the path towards a more enlightened and compassionate world.

NEALE DONALD WALSCH

Neale Donald Walsch is an American author and spiritual teacher known primarily for his book series called "Conversations with God." I highly recommend reading this series. I have used some of that dialogue throughout this book. In the late 1990s, Walsch had a transformative experience that changed his worldview as he received direct responses from God. In these books, Walsch explores a wide range of topics, including spirituality, personal growth, relationships, and the nature of reality. The conversations present a non-traditional and often provocative perspective of God, religion, and the purpose of life. As I also had many conversations with God on my journey many of the insights that God shared with Neale God also shared with me. Mystics share a profound longing to witness humanity, as a collective, embracing divine insights. They seek understanding through various avenues, such as science, philosophy, and the works of fellow mystics. In this shared pursuit, we look up to one another, acknowledging the importance of exploring the truth of our authentic selves. Through this mutual exploration, we strive to bring a unified field of understanding into focus, uniting our perspectives, and deepening our connection to the divine.

Neale Donald Walsch's writings challenged conventional religious doctrines and promoted a more personal and direct connection with God by emphasizing the power of love, compassion, and self-realization. In his conversations with the divine, Walsch underscored the significance of individual agency and personal experiences in comprehending and establishing a bond with the divine presence. The following are excerpts from Neale Donald Walsch's book, "Conversations with God: An Uncommon Dialogue":

> *I exist in everything, in every aspect. I manifest my entirety through the universe. Wholeness is inherent in my nature, and there is nothing that I am not. Something that I am not cannot exist.*
>
> *I created you, my blessed creatures, so that I could experience myself as the creator of my own reality.*

The aspect of myself as the creator could only be created by a very special creator.

I am not the deity depicted in mythologies or as a goddess. I am the creator, the force that brings everything into existence. However, I choose to know myself through my own experiences.

Just as I recognize my perfect design through a snowflake and my magnificent beauty through a rose, I also know my creative power through you.

I have granted you the ability to consciously shape your experiences, which is the same ability I possess.

Through you, I can understand all aspects of myself. The perfection of a snowflake, the breathtaking beauty of a rose, the courage of lions, the majesty of eagles—all of these exist within you. I have placed all of these things within you, along with one more gift: the consciousness to be aware of them.

As a result, you have become self-conscious, which is the greatest gift. You are aware of yourself being yourself, and that is precisely what I am.

I am myself, aware of myself being myself. This is the meaning behind the statement 'I Am That I Am.'

You are that part of me which is the awareness, experienced. And what you are experiencing (and what I am experiencing through you) is me, creating myself. I am in a continual process of self-creation.[31]

These prophets, saints, and mystics have had a profound impact throughout the history of the world. While I have only mentioned a few examples, there are many more and ever-present-day messengers who continue to spread God's truth and love. Engaging in this sacred work has its challenges, but we need to seize the opportunities when they arise. The crucial question is not about whom God chooses to communicate with, but rather who is willing to listen and receive those messages.

Collectively, these mystics, prophets, and saints have contributed to the ever-evolving understanding of the nature of God. Their unique experiences and teachings, from John the Baptist's preparation for Christ's arrival to Jesus' embodiment of divine love, from Saint Steven's unwavering faith to Saint Juan Diego's encounter with the Virgin Mary, have shaped the evolution of human consciousness and expanded our comprehension of the divine.

As we reflect on their contributions, we are reminded that the nature of God transcends religious boundaries and cultural differences. Through their experience and teachings, we are invited to cultivate a deeper connection with the divine, embracing love, compassion, forgiveness, and the transformative power of faith. By integrating their wisdom into our lives, we can continue to shape the evolution of human consciousness, fostering unity, healing, and spiritual growth in ourselves and the world around us.

In closing, let us reflect upon the profound wisdom of Meister Eckhart, a mystic and philosopher of great insight. He once said, "The eye through which I see God is the same eye through which God sees me; my eye and God's eye are one eye, one seeing, one knowing, one love." These words remind us that the path of mystics, prophets, and saints is not one of separation or division, but rather a journey towards the realization of our inherent unity with the divine. May we all strive to cultivate the inner eye that perceives the interconnectedness of all things and the profound presence of the divine within us and around us.

9

CHRIST THE PANTOCRATOR: UNVEILING THE DIVINE SYNERGY AND ALL-ENCOMPASSING POWER OF THE ALMIGHTY

A SACRED IMAGE, KNOWN AS AN ICON, RECEIVES SPECIAL reverence. Greek Church Fathers, like Basil, regarded icons as having equal significance to written words. Both visual and auditory appeals hold equal authority, with the power of the eyes being just as influential as that of the ears.[32]

In the realm of religious art, few images hold the captivating power and profound symbolism as that of Christ the Pantocrator. This iconic representation of Christ as the ruler and sustainer of all things embodies not only the divinity of Jesus but also reveals the intricate interplay between human and divine nature. The image of Christ the Pantocrator, with its mesmerizing gaze and symmetrical features, serves as a visual testament to the concept of synergy—a harmonious union between the earthly and the celestial, the human and the divine. Through this divine union, the Pantocrator image invites contemplation, sparking a deeper understanding of the interconnectedness of spiritual realms and the transformative potential found within each individual. As we delve into the depths of this enigmatic portrayal, we embark on a journey to unravel the mysteries of synergy that lie at the heart of the Pantocrator, uncovering the profound truths it holds for believers and seekers alike.

The term "Pantocrator" is derived from the Greek words "panto" meaning "all" or "every," and "kratos" meaning "power" or "dominion." It is a title used to describe God as the Almighty, the Ruler of all things. While the specific term "Pantocrator" is not used extensively in the Bible, the concept and attributes associated with it are found throughout the Old and New Testaments.

The scriptures you are about to explore offer profound insights into the nature of God as Pantocrator, the Almighty. In Revelation 1:8, God declares Himself as the Alpha and the Omega, underscoring His eternal existence and all-encompassing power. Revelation 19:6 depicts a scene of exultant praise, where God is hailed as the Lord God Almighty, affirming His sovereignty and dominion over all things. Additionally, 2 Corinthians 6:18 highlights God's authority and intimate relationship with believers, as He promises to be a Father to them and calls them His sons and daughters. These scriptures serve as powerful reminders of God's eternal nature, supreme power, and the divine connection He shares with His creation.

Revelation 1:8 declares, "I am the Alpha and the Omega,' says the Lord God, 'who is, and who was, and who is to come, the Almighty." This verse emphasizes God's eternal nature and His all-encompassing power. By proclaiming Himself as the Alpha and the Omega, which are the first and last letters of the Greek alphabet, God signifies His existence before all things and His eternal presence beyond time. Being the Almighty, God possesses supreme power and authority over all creation.

In Revelation 19:6, we encounter a scene where a great multitude praises God, shouting, "Hallelujah! For our Lord God Almighty reigns!" Here, God is acknowledged as the Lord God Almighty, highlighting His sovereignty and dominion over all things. The roaring waters and thunderous peals symbolize the overwhelming sound of praise and worship directed toward God's almighty reign. This verse portrays God as the ruling and governing force, demonstrating His power and majesty.

The mention of the Lord Almighty in 2 Corinthians 6:18 emphasizes God's authority, care, and divine relationship with believers. The verse states, "I will be a Father to you, and you will be my sons and daughters, says the Lord Almighty." By addressing believers as His sons and daughters, God establishes an intimate familial bond with them. The title "Lord Almighty" reinforces His role as the all-powerful and all-sufficient Father who exercises authority, protection, and guidance over His children.

In summary, these scriptures highlight God's nature as Pantocrator, the Almighty. They emphasize His eternal existence, all-encompassing power, sovereignty, and divine relationship with his creation. The concept of Pantocrator underscores the omnipotence and supreme authority of God, signifying His position as the ruler and sustainer of all creation.

Figure 6: Dunston, J.C. (2014)
"INK OF FAITH: DOVE DOODLES AND THE PANTOCRATOR"

This specific religious icon "Christ the Pantocrator" displayed at Saint Catherine's Monastery on Mt. Sinai, Egypt holds rich symbolism that conveys theological and spiritual meanings.

His right hand is raised in blessings and his left hand holding a closed jeweled Gospel book symbolizing the unfolding of God's revelation over time. It represents the gradual and progressive nature of God's self-disclosure to humanity. The closed book could also be symbolic to encourage viewers to reflect on the hidden depths of divine wisdom and to seek a deeper understanding of God's truth.

Christ is depicted wearing a purple robe, which is a recognized symbol of royalty. This choice of clothing adds to the icon's symbolism, emphasizing Christ's regal status.

One intriguing aspect of this image is the portrayal of Christ's facial expression, which highlights the dual nature of his being as both fully divine and fully human. This duality is symbolized by the two distinct hemispheres in his face, representing the divine and human aspects of his existence. It serves as a visual reminder of the profound mystery and complexity inherent in Christ's nature, embodying the union of divinity and humanity in a single being.

The halo depicted in the "Christ the Pantocrator" painting holds significant symbolism. It radiates around the head of Christ, serving as a visual representation of his divine nature and glory. The halo often depicted as golden signifies Christ's eternal and transcendent existence. The halo serves as a powerful reminder of Christ's divinity distinguishing him as the Son of God and the source of divine light, love, and grace.

Through these intricate symbols and representations, the icon "Christ the Pantocrator" conveys profound theological and spiritual messages, inviting viewers to contemplate the divine revelation, the dual nature of Christ, and his eternal divinity.

I want to share this significant icon with you because it holds deep personal meaning for me. It represents a pivotal moment in my spiritual journey, where I embraced my faith and developed a deeper connection with God. I printed out this black and white icon and placed it on my desk, propping it up with a rock. Initially, I felt a sense of discomfort with this image, but I felt a strong inner calling to connect with it.

Figure 7: Artist: unknown (6th Century) "THE ANCIENT GAZE:
CHRIST PANTOCRATOR IN SAINT CATHERINE'S MONASTERY"

What adds to the significance of this icon is what can be found on its reverse side—a dove that I personally drew. It serves as a representation of the dove that God draws in the sky, reflecting my own artistic creation. This remarkable synchronicity not only reveals God's presence and His affirmation of my creative expression but also showcases His image and likeness as envisioned in my mind. Moreover, it highlights the attributes of His triune nature, resulting in a powerful and meaningful synchronicity that carries a profound message.

By sharing this icon and its accompanying story with you, I hope to engage you as a reader and convey the depth of my personal experience.

God's hand is at work in the world, using nature as a canvas to communicate His presence and glory. As the sun descends towards the mountain horizon casting its warm golden hues across the sky. Jesus encapsulates himself within the sun showing his abundant radiant heart shining his light and love on all humanity. As the sun's rays interact with the atmosphere, they illuminate the clouds, creating a breathtaking display of colors and textures. The clouds wispy and ethereal, take on various forms and patterns, constantly shifting and evolving under the influence of the wind and the spirit of God participating with nature to show his form and likeness.

God vividly illustrates His identity as "I AM" by skillfully drawing a white dove, utilizing the brilliance of the sun to showcase His very existence. With masterful strokes, He crafts the contours of the dove's form, using the sun's radiant light as His artistic medium. The dove, pure and graceful, becomes a living expression of God's being, embodying His presence and essence being the Son of God and the Son of Man.

Through this divine artwork, God reveals Himself as the eternal "I AM," the one who encompasses all of existence and declares His unchanging nature. The white dove, sculpted in the canvas of the sky, serves as a powerful symbol of peace, hope, and the divine connection between heaven and earth. In this remarkable display, God's creative prowess shines forth, affirming His identity as the ever-present, ever-existing, and loving Creator of all things.

As the sunlight bathes the sky, its gentle touch traces the graceful curves of the dove. The hump on its back becomes a canvas for Jesus' heart, from which love and grace pour forth.

In avian anatomy, the back of a dove is called a mantle, a scapular (shoulders), and a heart saddle. In the holy photographs revealed to you, you will see the arch of the heart mantle of the dove is the blessed Son of God risen into everlasting eternity with his heart shining a luminous brilliant white Sun. A Christ with a heart of fire penetrating everywhere spreading everywhere, and encapsulated within His glory a halo of light that holds in its auric field a magnificent hue of golden light surrounding his head and the blessed Holy Trinity surrounding Him.

As you gaze upon these photographs, you are filled with a sense of awe and wonder. It captures the divine collaboration between the elements of nature and the invisible hand of God co-creating with nature and with his creation.

NATURE HAS DESIGNED US TO CONNECT

Also, on the back of this well-known icon I wrote the words "Nature has designed us to Connect." Nature is alive and we live in a conscious participatory universe. Nature with its vibrant essence, pulses with a life force that connects humanity to the divine grace that permeates the universe. From the majestic mountains to the gentle flow of rivers, from the whispering winds to blooming flowers, nature beckons us to behold its beauty and recognize the sacred interplay between all living beings. In its intricate tapestry, nature reveals lessons about love, reminding us to embrace one another with compassion and kindness. Just as nature nurtures and sustains, we are called to extend a hand of love to our fellow human beings, embracing diversity that enriches our shared existence. By living out the timeless commandment to love one another as we have been loved, we align ourselves with the harmonious rhythm of nature, forging connections that transcend boundaries and fostering a world where grace abounds.

The universe reaches out to us, and our task is to pay attention and listen to the call. Continuously, nature strives to bring forth existence and actively seeks individuals who are aware. It seeks those who are ready to step forward and materialize something from the realm of possibilities. Nature seeks human partnerships.

Through my art doodles, I express a profound truth inspired by God's word: the command to love one another as God loves us. In our current state of awareness, we are awakening to the significance of our choices. The unfolding cosmic wave prompts our hearts to seek unity consciousness and contribute to the greater collective. Our expanded awareness and connection with nature urge us to embrace responsibility in our interconnected multiverse. As the Sacred Heart awakens, it recognizes the interconnectedness of all things and the vastness of its existence.

My doodle language also manifests and demonstrates that "Nature has designed us to connect." Showing that the universe is alive and aware of itself. Nature, through its inherent design and intricate systems, serves as a catalyst for connecting individuals with their higher nature, fostering spiritual growth, and nurturing a profound sense of interconnectedness.

Nature has long been revered for its ability to inspire, heal, and awaken the human spirit. It is a transformative force that reflects God's being. Nature is alive, conscious, and intricately designed, inviting us to connect. From ecosystems to landscapes, nature reminds us of our place in the web of life, evoking awe and stirring our souls to embrace the divine. Connecting with Earth's wisdom offers profound insight and self-understanding, guiding us on a transformative journey. Nature provides moments of silence, stillness, and synchronicities that tap into higher wisdom. It is a constant source of renewal and transformation, demonstrating the cycles of birth, growth, decay, and rebirth. Nature's design encourages us to embrace change, release what no longer serves us, and embrace personal evolution. Nature herself becomes our sacred teacher, guiding our transformative journey. Nature presents us with synchronicities and signs that guide us along our path.

On the day that I walked with the Almighty dances of synchronicities filled the air. Earlier in the day my two box turtles emerged from the earth after a long hibernation. Hungry and eager to replenish themselves after a winter of scarce resources, Mundo and Nube scoured the terrain looking for their favorite treats: plump worms and luscious strawberries. Their tiny reptilian bodies soaked up the warmth of the soil, a stark contrast to the cold and arid winter they had endured.

The celestial bodies of the Worm Wood moon a title given to the full moon of March danced nearby in anticipation of the arrival of Easter. The title "Worm Wood" comes from the Farmer's Almanac meaning the first signs of spring with the earthworms appearing as the soil warms inviting robins and other creatures to feed.

After later reflection, I couldn't help but see the deeper symbolism. Their synchronized awakening felt like a celestial message, a lucky sign from the heavens above. The names Mundo and Nube, meaning "world" and "cloud" in Spanish. As the day progressed I walked with the World Cloud of all-knowing showing living beings our interconnectedness.

This event shines a light on the humor of God. God truly is funny and His divine playfulness shines through. I recognized His jest when I gazed upon the photographs capturing Jesus as the Sun of Man, radiating light and love. And there, in the imagery of our beloved Heavenly Father, I saw a gentle humor as He figuratively shaded His eyes, a nod to the biblical proclamation that no mortal can fully witness His glory and live to tell the tale.

While humor is not explicitly mentioned as a characteristic of Jesus in the Gospels, there are instances where his words or interactions could be interpreted as having a lighthearted or witty tone. For example, in Matthew 7:3-5, Jesus uses the humorous analogy of a person with a plank in their own eye trying to remove a speck from someone else's eye to illustrate the importance of self-reflection and addressing one's own faults before criticizing others.

Additionally, Jesus often employed various rhetorical devices, such as parables, hyperbole, and irony, in his teachings. These literary techniques can sometimes include elements of humor or wit. For instance, in Matthew 23:24, Jesus criticizes the religious leaders of his time, saying, "You blind guides! You strain out a gnat but swallow a camel." This statement contains a humorous exaggeration to emphasize the hypocrisy of their actions.

One aspect often noted is Jesus' use of paradox, irony, and clever wordplay in his teachings. For example, in Matthew 19:24, Jesus famously says, "It is easier for a camel to go through the eye of a needle than for someone who is rich to enter the kingdom of God." This statement contains a humorous image that would have caught the attention of his audience, as camels were known for their size and the eye of a needle was a small opening.

In conclusion, the synchronicities observed in nature and the lightheartedness evident in God's interactions serve as a testament to the beauty and playful essence of God in the world around us. From the intertwined dance of synchronicities to the gentle jests woven into Jesus' teachings, the divine humor illuminates the joyous spirit that permeates creation.

EMBRACING DIVINE GUIDANCE: ANSWERING THE CALL

While a calling is highly personal and unique to each individual, it is often associated with a sense of contribution to the greater good or a desire to make a positive impact in the world. It can be a guiding force that influences humanity in a better direction. In reality, the process of finding one's calling is often a combination of personal agency and external factors. It may involve elements of active exploration, self-discovery, and deliberate decision-making, as well as moments of unexpected revelation or a sense of being guided by external forces.

In my experience, I feel that I likely designed to have this direct experience with God as part of my human experience. I believe that before we incarnate in the flesh we create a blueprint with our guides, angels, and or higher self to create the experiences our Soul would like to have in this particular lifetime. We still have free will and can deter from that blueprint but we do create a beautiful tapestry of things we would like to experience or express. I believe that as I was coming into my faith that it was time for me to have this extraordinary experience. I felt this immense energy of what I would now call the Holy Spirit who moves and lives within my being to have this remarkable epiphany happen to me. I felt this energy dancing through me in every cell of my body with deep vibrancy at the time that I was coming into my faith.

An icon can be thought of as a holy text that is manifested through devotion, love, and meditation. It brings the spiritual world and the material world together. It is the mystery of the divine that serves as a threshold to open and receive. I connected to this holy icon of Jesus and kept it on my desk as I emerged into having a deep personal relationship with him and opened my heart into surrender allowing myself to feel the essence of "I Am." The art of surrender is to let go and let God. In surrender, you can elevate your consciousness to a divine state of grace and open your vessel to connect with life force energies that are always abundantly available to us.

When you surrender your resistance to your desire you allow connection, flow, receptiveness, and well-being. Trust what you are surrendering to is the greater good of all that is. When we have a desire and no resistance what we want has to come. The art of allowing is what allows us to blend with a broader perspective.

God is a verb, a process, in the Holy Bible, God identifies as "I AM" a divine force that embraces all things, is all things. Love unifies the happening of you and the happening of me. It is all-inclusive. Love is an activity. Love is a feeling. God is Pure Love.

In Neale Donald Walsch's book, "The God Solution: The Power of Pure Love," he discusses how blending human emotion with divine sentiment not only creates space for the manifestation of divine energy in our lives but also provides a means for expressing and demonstrating it.[33] Walsch further defines Pure Love as the energy that, upon expression, generates happiness within the sender and is imbued with the intention of evoking a similar sense of happiness in the receiver. This enables the recipient to respond freely and genuinely without diminishing the love being conveyed.[34]

Synergy with God means working together. Synergy is a merging in frequency that two forces resonating with each other brings unification in togetherness. It is an emergence that brings energy bodies together. The life force energy of God is happening. God in this way is an action, a verb is an action. In this way, God is happening, experiencing in all of us every moment in all ways.

We are expressions of actions. In our embodiment which is experience expressed, we create our reality by the beliefs that we hold, yet we are also so much more than we know. We are in the world but not of the world. According to Walsch, every individual embodies the spiritual and physical essence of Pure Love, and each person has the capacity to express this energy by intentionally merging human emotions with Divine feelings. By doing so, individuals can project this powerful energy into the world during significant moments in life.[35]

We are ingrained in this enormous power of love. Recognize the force of the momentum that you are. This cosmic constructive collaboration is uniting the full embodiment of the essence, and we are directly creating and interacting with it, and you can directly see this exchange through my visionary photography.

As we delve into this book, you will witness the profound synergy between God and myself. As a gentile, bearing the name 'I AM,' I am humbled to merge with God's all-encompassing love. Through the Holy Scriptures, I have been called to proclaim the divine glory. It is worth noting that I expressed my desire to bring forth the Scriptures to humanity, even though God did not request this from me. At that time, my knowledge of Scripture was limited, but my passion for sharing profound divine truths with you was akin to the excitement felt by Jesus' faithful disciples on the road to Emmaus.

In the biblical narrative, after Jesus' resurrection, two of His followers were journeying to the village of Emmaus when they encountered Him. However, they did not immediately recognize Him. As they walked together, Jesus began to explain the Scriptures and the prophecies concerning Himself. These disciples later recounted that their hearts burned within them as Jesus opened their minds to the profound truth contained in the Scriptures. It was a transformative encounter that left them filled with anticipation and a deeper understanding of divine wisdom.

Similarly, in my own spiritual journey, I experienced a profound shift that compelled me to explore realms beyond the visible. Fueled by a profound sense of purpose, I felt a calling to share the mystical wisdom I had encountered with humanity. Recognizing the need for inner transformation, I embarked on a path guided by inner wisdom rather than ego-driven motivations. This journey of inner transfiguration unfolded through numerous steps and passages, each presenting its own challenges and trials. I willingly embraced these trials, fully aware of the weight of the claims I am making.

It is important to clarify that my perspective does not align with Christian fundamentalism, nor do I perceive the Bible as the infallible word of God. However, I do believe that the spiritual realm communicates with us. I vividly recall a childhood memory when, at around the age of 12, while visiting my grandma, my guides whispered to me about the future reading of the Bible. Initially, I resisted this notion, considering the Bible to be a complex theology beyond my comprehension. Yet, over time, I discovered that the Bible contains profound metaphors and ethereal language that resonates with the depths of my soul. Personally, I do not feel compelled to accept every gospel account as absolute truth, including the disciples' personal knowledge of Jesus during his lifetime as depicted in biblical narratives. The historical accuracy of such accounts is not a central focus of my spiritual journey. Instead, I prioritize listening to the guidance of the Spirit and embracing the inner wisdom to which I have been called. While some may argue that I selectively interpret the Bible, I respect their viewpoint, recognizing that my journey is unique to me. My faith lies not in the God of the Bible, but in the divine presence I have discovered within my own heart.

When he was at the table with them, he took the bread, gave thanks, broke it and began to give it to them. Then their eyes were opened, and they recognized him, and he disappeared from their sight. They asked each other, "Were not our hearts burning within us while he talked with us on the road and opened the Scriptures to us?"

LUKE 24:30-32, NIV

"Father, glorify your name!" Then a voice came from heaven, "I have glorified it, and will glorify it again."

JOHN 12:28, NIV

UNVEILING THE DIVINE REVELATION: THE SIGNIFICANCE OF "I AM" AND THE MYSTERIES OF JESUS' IDENTITY

In the midst of these stunning photographs, a profound revelation unfolds, showcasing how God's name is glorified. It was during my transformative journey in deepening my faith that I discovered the significance of God's name, "I AM." It came to my awareness through a podcast on Sounds True with Tami Simon, and it resonated deeply within me. In response to this newfound understanding, I inscribed God's name, "I AM," inside the dove on the back of the Christ the Pantocrator religious icon.

In the words of Jesus himself, we find a testament to the glory of God's name. He proclaimed, "I have glorified You on earth by accomplishing the work You gave Me to do. And now, Father, glorify Me in your presence with the glory I had with You before the world existed. I have revealed Your name to those You have given Me out of the world. They were Yours; You gave them to Me, and they have kept Your word. Now they know that everything You have given Me comes from You." (John 17:4-7, BSB).

These verses illuminate the profound significance of God's name and the divine mission Jesus fulfilled on earth. He revealed the name of God to those chosen out of the world, affirming their belonging and the fulfillment of God's divine plan.

"I AM" is more than just a name; it is a profound declaration that encapsulates the very nature of the divine. It signifies God's eternal existence, transcending time and space. It encompasses His supreme authority and limitless power, encompassing all that was, is, and will be. "I AM" reveals God as the source of life, wisdom, and love, inviting us to ponder the unfathomable depths of His being. It calls upon us to recognize and surrender to the unchanging nature of God, finding solace, guidance, and purpose in the eternal "I AM."

Embedded within the essence of God's divine nature is the profound declaration, "I Am That I Am." This statement encapsulates the self-awareness of God, the very core of His being. It signifies that God exists as His own conscious and aware entity. In this understanding, we come to realize that we are an integral part of God's consciousness, experiencing His awareness through our own existence. What we perceive and undergo is, in fact, God experiencing Himself through the lens of our being. It is a continuous cycle of creation, where God, in His infinite wisdom, perpetually creates and shapes Himself through the intricate tapestry of existence.

In John 8:58, Jesus makes a profound declaration about His identity that resonates with the significance of God's name, "I AM." He says, "Truly, truly, I say to you, before Abraham was, I am." This statement carries great weight as Jesus uses the present tense "I am" to refer to His existence before Abraham, who lived centuries before Him. By employing the phrase "I am," Jesus aligns Himself with the eternal nature of God, affirming His divine existence and preeminence.

This deliberate choice of words echoes the language used by God in the Old Testament when He revealed His name to Moses as "I AM WHO I AM." Through this statement, Jesus asserts His divine authority, His timeless existence, and His unity with the Father. It serves as a powerful testament to His divinity and invites us to contemplate the profound mystery of His eternal nature.

Our existence plays a vital role in God's ongoing act of creation. As beings created in the image of God, we are endowed with consciousness, free will, and the capacity to co-create with the divine. Through our experiences, choices, and interactions, we become active participants in the unfolding story of creation.

It is essential to acknowledge that the biblical accounts of Jesus' life have a notable gap, often referred to as the "unknown years." These years, between the ages of 12 and 29, remain shrouded in mystery. While theories have emerged, suggesting Jesus might have journeyed to India and Nepal in search of spiritual enlightenment, it is crucial to note that these theories are subject to debate among scholars.

When Jesus reemerges in the biblical narrative, he brings forth a new message to humanity. He boldly declares himself as "I AM," aligning himself with the very title God used for Himself in Exodus 3:14. By assuming this divine title, Jesus establishes his equality with the divine nature of God, affirming his unique role and mission in the redemption of humanity. In his proclamation, "I AM," we find the embodiment of the divine, a revelation that invites us to delve deeper into the mystery and majesty of God's eternal presence.

RECOGNIZING JESUS AS THE MESSIAH THROUGH THE GOSPEL

And Jesus said, 'I am, and you will see the Son of Man seated at the right hand of Power, and coming with the clouds of heaven.

MARK 14:62, ESV

Christianity asserts that the core belief is that God, in an extraordinary manner, took on human form and made His appearance in Bethlehem. It was around the year 30 AD that this remarkable event unfolded. Jesus, a humble carpenter from the hills of Galilee, emerged onto the scene and began preaching with an unprecedented and unsettling boldness. He claimed personal authority over the Torah, which was the revered Divine Law and the ultimate reference for faithful Rabbis. Furthermore, Jesus astounded the masses by performing astounding miracles of healing and displaying mastery over the forces of nature. As word spread about this enigmatic figure, people flocked from all directions, curious to discover who this man was.

According to the New Testament of the Bible, Jesus asked his disciples, "Who do people say that I am?" during a significant moment in the region of Caesarea Philippi. Caesarea Philippi was situated in the northern part of ancient Israel, near the foothills of Mount Hermon. This city lay within the territory of the tetrarchy of Philip, one of the sons of King Herod the Great. Caesarea Philippi was known for its pagan worship and housed various temples.

Jesus, amid his ministry, chose this location to engage in a pivotal conversation with his disciples. He posed the question, "Who do people say that the Son of Man is?" The title "Son of Man" was one that Jesus frequently used to refer to himself. In response, the disciples shared the various opinions circulating among the people, suggesting that some believed Jesus to be John the Baptist, Elijah, Jeremiah, or one of the prophets.

After hearing their responses, Jesus specifically directed the question to his disciples, asking, "But who do you say that I am?" It was here that Peter, speaking on behalf of the group, made a profound declaration of faith: "You are the Christ, the Son of the living God." This pivotal moment highlighted Peter's recognition of Jesus as the long-awaited Messiah.

In response to Peter's confession, Jesus blessed him, affirming that this revelation was not obtained through ordinary means but had been divinely revealed to him by the Father in heaven. Jesus further declared that upon this rock—the confession of Peter's faith—he would build his church, and even the gates of Hades would not prevail against it.

The conversation at Caesarea Philippi marked a significant turning point in the Gospel narratives, as Jesus began to prepare his disciples for the imminent events of his suffering, death, and resurrection. This event underscored the paramount importance of recognizing Jesus as the Messiah and understanding the profound nature of his mission. Throughout his ministry, Jesus intentionally engaged in significant teachings and interactions in various locations, using these moments to convey profound truths and shape the understanding of his disciples.

The entire Gospel narrative revolves around this crucial point. Jesus' personal identity is at the heart of it all because, throughout the Gospels, he consistently spoke and acted as if he were God Himself. His words and deeds were understood as the very embodiment of divinity. This distinction sets Jesus apart and underscores the significance of his identity in the Christian faith.

One of the most intriguing passages in the Gospel is the story of the Samaritan woman at the well. It holds a special place in my heart, and I have reimagined this encounter with Jesus in a way that deeply resonated with me when I first encountered this scripture. The Gospel teachings have a profound impact on countless hearts and minds, touching lives in immeasurable ways.

THE THIRST OF THE SOUL:
A DIVINE ENCOUNTER AT THE WELL

In the heart of Samaria, a woman walked a path lined with the stones of her past, burdened by the weight of her struggles and unheard stories. With each step, she carried a longing that transcended the physical, an ache for a connection that had eluded her. Unbeknownst to her, her life was about to intersect with a force greater than herself, with the embodiment of compassion and truth.

As she approached the well, her eyes met those of a stranger—a man whose gaze held an otherworldly depth. In a mere glance, he saw beyond the veil of her existence, piercing through the layers of her being. His eyes spoke of a knowing, a recognition that shattered her sense of anonymity.

"Give me a drink," he said, his voice carrying the weight of all the stories he had yet to utter. In those simple words, she sensed a profound revelation stirring beneath the surface. He knew her. He saw her. He understood the intricacies of her life, the joys and sorrows that had shaped her very soul.

Startled yet intrigued, she engaged in a dialogue that would forever alter the course of her existence. With each passing moment, the stranger's words wove a tapestry of truth, unraveling the mysteries that had long lingered in her heart.

"If you knew the gift of God and who it is that asks you for a drink," he whispered, his voice infused with a divine urgency, "you would have asked him, and he would have given you living water."

Living water—the concept resonated with her spirit, a powerful analogy that ignited her imagination. She envisioned a spring within her, an artesian well bursting forth with fountains of endless life. Could it be that this stranger held the key to quenching the thirst of her soul, to offer a connection that would satisfy her deepest longings?

Inspired and emboldened, she dared to ask, her voice trembling with a mix of hope and desperation, "Sir, give me this water so that I won't get thirsty and have to keep coming here to draw water."

In her plea, there was a longing to be free from the limitations of her physical existence, from the cycle of mundane routines and unquenched desires. She yearned for a life-giving force that would sustain her, that would forever satiate her thirst.

And as the dialogue unfolded, the stranger revealed a truth that transcended boundaries and encompassed the entire human experience. He spoke of a time when the true self, the essence of one's being, must engage with the Spirit of Truth in the pursuit of ultimate understanding. He painted a vivid picture of a future where God's presence would extend far beyond the confines of Jerusalem, where profound truths would be unveiled to all who sought them.

The Samaritan woman, a vessel of hope and curiosity, had heard the whispers of the Messiah's arrival. In the depths of her soul, she believed that his coming would herald a new era of enlightenment, a time when the profound mysteries of existence would be illuminated.

And with a simple yet profound statement, the stranger acknowledged his true identity, "I am the Messiah." At that moment, the Samaritan woman's heart soared, her spirit ablaze with the realization that the one who sat before her was the embodiment of all she had yearned for. He was the living water, the source of life and truth that would forever quench her thirst.

In their sacred encounter, the boundaries of time and space dissolved, and she became a witness to the transformative power of divine revelation. Inspired by the living water that flowed within her, she embraced her role as a messenger, carrying the promise of eternal connection to all who would listen.

For the Samaritan woman had been seen, known, and forever changed by the one who is the Messiah—the catalyst of truth and the bringer of living water that would forever satisfy the deepest longings of the human soul.

THE TRANSFORMATIVE POWER OF GRACE: EMBRACING VULNERABILITY AND ILLUMINATING DIVINE STRENGTH

The statement "My grace is sufficient for you for my power is made perfect in weakness" (2 Corinthians 12:9) holds profound meaning as it reveals the intricate duality of human nature. It reminds us that even in our moments of vulnerability and weakness, we have the potential to shine as beacons of light amidst the darkness. When we find ourselves facing hardships, enduring persecution, or grappling with difficulties, it is precisely in those moments that God has the opportunity to grant us strength. Our weaknesses become transformative catalysts, prompting us to reevaluate our perspective and embrace higher thoughts and ideas. Through this process, we discover that vulnerability is not synonymous with defeat but rather a gateway to resilience and growth. It is in acknowledging our weaknesses and embracing them as opportunities for change that we unlock the full potential of God's power within us.

God's grace and love serve as pillars of support during challenging times and formidable trials. In our moments of weakness, it is through God's strength that we find fortitude and resilience beyond our imagination. Grace, bestowed freely upon us, transcends our merits or shortcomings. It is an embodiment of God's boundless compassion and forgiveness, offered to all who seek it.

This transformative force uplifts and rejuvenates, providing solace and redemption amidst struggle and despair. Through grace, we forge a deep connection with the divine, enabling us to extend compassion and forgiveness to others. It serves as a reminder of the inherent goodness within us all, and it ignites the potential for spiritual growth and renewal.

Embracing grace calls us to cultivate humility, gratitude, and a profound sense of awe in the presence of the divine's infinite love and benevolence. It beckons us to recognize the immense power of God's favor and invites us to walk in its light, knowing that we are embraced and supported by the divine throughout our journey.

The apostle Paul, burdened by the weight of the mission his soul had set out to do, poured out his anguish before the Lord. In his plea, he beseeched God to remove the thorn in his flesh—a symbolic representation of the persecutions and hardships that awaited him. Paul's agony stemmed from the pain of witnessing the rejection of Christ as the Messiah by his fellow Jews. However, it was through this vulnerable exchange with God that Paul discovered a profound truth: that there was a way forward, and it lay in the boundless grace freely bestowed upon humanity. It was in this revelation that God responded to Paul, assuring him that His grace was more than sufficient. In weakness, God's power would be fully manifested, illuminating the path ahead for Paul and empowering him to carry out his mission.

Amidst the fervent desire of the apostle Paul to convey a transformative message to his Jewish brethren, a revelation emerged —one that shattered the confines of the written code of the law of Moses. Paul yearned for his fellow Jewish brothers and sisters to understand that they were no longer bound by the constraints of the law, for they had been embraced by the liberating grace of God. While the law had been delivered through Moses, it was through Jesus Christ that the fullness of grace and truth were unveiled. In this profound realization, Paul recognized that the message of salvation extended beyond the boundaries of Judaism. It reached out to the Gentiles, encompassing all who would embrace the transformative power of God's grace.

Grace represents the tangible embodiment of God's love—an extraordinary gift that surpasses our comprehension and is graciously bestowed upon us. It serves as a constant reminder that God's power shines brightest in our moments of vulnerability and weakness. Deep within the recesses of God's loving heart, grace flows abundantly, and it is our faith that acts as the conduit through which this transformative grace permeates and breathes life into the beauty of our world.

When we hold steadfast in faith, our hearts become receptive to both receiving and sharing the profound power of grace. Through grace, we encounter the overwhelming love and mercy of God, and it is through our faith that we become conduits of this love, radiating it to others and infusing the world with its splendor and benevolence. Grace and faith intertwine harmoniously, forging a sacred connection between the divine and humanity. In this sacred union, we are invited to actively participate in the divine plan of love and redemption, co-creating a world infused with grace and guided by faith.

EXPLORING THE MYSTERY AND HARMONY OF THE HYPOSTATIC UNION

In Christian theology, hypostatic union is a term to describe the combination of divine and human nature in a single person of Christ both perfectly divine and perfectly human. This divine mystery holds immense significance in shaping our understanding of the person of Jesus Christ and the nature of salvation.

Hebrews 1:3, (NIV) states that the Son, Jesus, is the radiant expression of God's glory and an exact representation of His being. This passage emphasizes that both the Father and the Son share the same divine nature. Jesus perfectly reflects the essence of the Father, serving as the visible imprint or manifestation of His nature. Further chapters will provide clearer insights into this truth. Jesus, in his earthly existence, embodies and experiences all that the Father knows. The Father, who resembles Jesus, possesses omniscient knowledge as the divine mind. The Father is the supreme being, existing in a state of pure transcended consciousness, the source of all experiences, and the originator of all understanding.

Jesus, according to Scripture, will return in the same human form in which He ascended. The book of Acts (1:11) states that He will come in a manner similar to how He was seen going into heaven. Interpreting this passage in light of Holy Scripture, it suggests that Jesus, who passed away at around the age of 33, will appear in a youthful form during His second coming while still embodying the nature of our Father.

It is intriguing to ponder the meaning of this biblical scripture, considering that none of us have firsthand knowledge of Jesus' physical appearance during His time on earth, nor did we witness His ascension into heaven. Remarkably, God and nature have employed artistic representations, such as the religious icon of Christ the Pantocrator, to communicate His presence and reveal Himself to us.

This scripture invites us to reflect on the profound mystery of Jesus' return and the form in which He will appear. It underscores the divine wisdom in utilizing various means, including artistic depictions, to convey His message and make Himself known to humanity.

NAVIGATING THE PARADOX: EXPLORING THE INTERPLAY OF FREE WILL AND PREDESTINATION IN THE TAPESTRY 0F EXISTENCE

Do we truly possess agency over our lives, or are we mere pawns in a predetermined universe? This age-old question has perplexed philosophers for centuries. While some individuals prefer to embrace the notion of free will, asserting that our decisions are independent choices made throughout our existence, others adopt a different perspective. They argue that if time is an illusion, as Einstein demonstrated, then every possible event has already taken place. From this vantage point, it seems that our actions have no real power to alter the course of the future.

Paradoxically, our attempts to evade our destined path only serve to lead us closer to it. Many view our world as deterministic, akin to a record playing on a turntable, with no room for deviation. However, there are also those who believe that we are active participants in shaping the universe, capable of making spontaneous choices at any given moment. According to this perspective, the future is an open canvas, waiting to be filled. The question remains: which philosophy holds the correct answer?

According to Neale Donald Walsch's conversation with God, the answer is a combination of both. We possess free will, yet everything is predetermined. This can be understood through the metaphor of a computer chess game. Every conceivable move is programmed into the game's disk, and every possible situation on the board has been played out. While we have the freedom to choose how we play the game, we are essentially reenacting moves that have already been played. In this particular moment of our lives, we have the choice of how we want to experience events that have already unfolded in the overall timeline. These predetermined paths encompass every possible outcome in every possible situation, similar to the computer chess game. However, our choices are limited to a finite number of decisions, just as the computer cannot be surprised by an unforeseen move.[36]

Our existence is not a random occurrence. Before we are born, our soul-self engages in planning and preparation, creating a blueprint in collaboration with God. We enter into contracts with other souls, intentionally seeking out experiences we desire in the physical realm.

In our human experience, we sometimes lose touch with our true essence, but our soul-self, known as the higher self, possesses a broader perspective. From the higher self's standpoint, everything is shaped by free will. However, when we inhabit our physical bodies, we often disconnect from the expansive awareness of our higher self, leading us to perceive elements of predestination. Our higher self holds the complete picture and orchestrates our self-discovery by creating opportunities for us to uncover different aspects of the puzzle.

Consider falling in love as an analogy. Your higher self determines that you will experience the journey of falling in love. In this context, certain aspects of your romantic journey are predetermined by your soul's plan. However, the way you approach and experience falling in love—the choices you make, the emotions you embrace, and the actions you take—becomes an expression of your free will. You have the freedom to love passionately or cautiously, to open your heart or guard it. The perspective you adopt and the path you walk in the realm of love reflect your exercise of free will. The underlying experience of falling in love, representing the predetermined elements of your soul's planning, remains constant.

To summarize, our higher self's free will manifests through unique individual experiences, while the predetermined aspects of our journey provide the framework within which we exercise our free will, much like the choices we make as we navigate the path of falling in love within the predetermined context of the experience itself.

The relationship between God's sovereignty and humanity's free will is a complex theological topic that has been the subject of much discussion and debate throughout history.

I believe we are co-creators with God, and we have the ability to shape our own experiences and reality through the choices and actions we make. When we connect to our true essence and follow inner guidance, we are more likely to make choices that are in harmony with our highest good. Free will involves taking responsibility for one's choices and making decisions that align with one's values, integrity, and spiritual growth. God grants humanity absolute free will and respects individual autonomy. God does not impose His will upon individuals or manipulate events to conform to a predetermined plan. God desires collaboration and invites individuals to actively participate in the creation of their reality, recognizing their own power and responsibility in the process. Individuals can seek guidance and support from a higher power. We can connect with our inner wisdom often referred to as the "voice of God within, to receive guidance, insights, and inspiration. When you know what you want to bring forward in the world and why you want it, choose it, and then take action.

DIVINE EPIPHANIES ACROSS TRADITIONS: UNVEILING THE MAJESTY OF THEOPHANIES FROM ABRAHAMIC TO HINDU SCRIPTURES

Theophany refers to a visible manifestation of a deity to humans. It is often described as a divine appearance or revelation. Throughout history and across various religious traditions, there have been accounts of theophanies involving different deities.

In the context of the Abrahamic religions (Judaism, Christianity, and Islam), theophanies are significant events in which God reveals Himself to individuals or groups. In the Hebrew Bible, there are several instances of theophanies. For example, Moses experienced a theophany when he encountered God in the form of a burning bush on Mount Horeb (Exodus 3:1-6). Later, Moses received the Ten Commandments during a theophany on Mount Sinai (Exodus 19-20).

In Christianity, the most notable theophany is the incarnation, which refers to God becoming manifest in human form through Jesus Christ. According to Christian belief, Jesus is considered the ultimate revelation of God to humanity. Additionally, in the New Testament, there are accounts of the transfiguration, a theophanic event where Jesus' appearance changed, and Moses and Elijah appeared with Him (Matthew 17:1-8, Mark 9:2-8, Luke 9:28-36).

In Islam, the Prophet Muhammad is said to have experienced a theophany known as the Night Journey (Isra and Mi'raj). During this event, Muhammad traveled through the heavens, encountering various prophets, and ultimately approaching close to the presence of Allah (God) before returning to Earth.

As I immersed myself in the sacred act of singing "OM" from the depths of my heart, a mystical revelation unfolded before me. In the realm of Hindu mysticism, theophanies hold a profound place, where deities lovingly manifest themselves to mortal beings. One such transcendent event is found in the Bhagavad Gita, where the luminous form of Lord Krishna, known as Vishvarupa, was unveiled to the warrior Arjuna. This divine revelation transcended ordinary perception, revealing the cosmic expanse and infinite nature of Krishna's divinity. Within the sacred encounter on the battlefield of Kurukshetra, Krishna imparted profound wisdom, guiding Arjuna to embrace his sacred duty (dharma) without attachments to outcomes. The teachings encompassed the very fabric of existence, shedding light on the nature of the self (Atman) and the eternal soul, beckoning Arjuna to transcend the ephemeral limitations of the physical realm.

While the Bhagavad Gita does not explicitly portray the syllable "OM" as a theophany, its spiritual and metaphysical significance cannot be understated. "OM" resonates as a sacred vibration, a mystical portal that opens pathways to the ultimate reality of the Divine. In the mystical realm, Lord Krishna himself identifies with the sacred syllable, symbolizing His profound connection to the primordial vibration and the ultimate truth. Through this sacred resonance, "OM" becomes a conduit, illuminating the divine presence and omnipresence of the Lord of Love, permeating every facet of existence.

In the mystical tapestry of Christian theology, the words of Jesus echo with a divine resonance: "I will not leave you orphans; I will come to you" (John 14:18, NAB). These words transcend mere human discourse, unveiling the esoteric essence of the indwelling Spirit of God. Within the mystical chambers of our inner being, we prepare a sacred abode, inviting the divine assembly to manifest within us. God's eternal presence becomes an ever-present companion, a guiding light that radiates throughout our journey. As our consciousness merges with the divine, an immeasurable connection is forged, and the revelation of God's glorious countenance, the visible manifestation of God to humanity known as the Parousia, becomes perceptible through the eyes of our mystical perception.

I now share with you the revelation bestowed upon humanity —an eternal journey of grace. Through the prism of faith, the direct presence of our LORD is unveiled, offering an astonishing and timeless gift. Our hearts intertwine with this divine presence, becoming a shared abode. Prepare to be astounded as your vision beholds the greatest marvel of all—the "I AM."

The qualities of wonder and awe provide us with an opportunity to transcend the boundaries of perception. We receive support from the cosmos, and our purpose is to reveal the absolute truth. The absolute encompasses everything and is interconnected with all aspects of existence.

You are a creation of the Universe, and there is nothing outside of it that you are not connected to. Rabbi Abraham Heschel asserts that true wisdom begins with the profound experience of awe, which opens the door to a deeper understanding.[37]

The following passages depict how I perceive my mystical encounter of unveiling the hidden truth. The Heavenly Father reveals Himself to me through the formation of a cloud, resembling the beauty of a star or a meticulously crafted snowflake. This cloud possesses a captivating visual allure, reflecting and capturing light as it interacts with other clouds. It manifests in a manner that showcases the layers of His divine power, perfectly positioned for me to capture this exquisite manifestation through photography. The Heavenly Father modulates the speed of His energetic vibrations within the fabric of spacetime to manifest His presence.

As this divine encounter unfolds, Jesus emerges from the Father, likened to a balloon expanding and radiating self-illuminating light. Alongside Jesus, the Holy Spirit gradually becomes visible, initially appearing almost imperceptible. The Holy Spirit emanates a joyful countenance, resembling a luminous carnelian crystal, surrounded by a rainbow-hued body exuding harmonious energy. This presence encompasses all, imbuing a sense of wholeness and unity.

> *And you are to tell him that this is what the LORD of Hosts says: 'Here is a man whose name is the Branch, and He will branch out from His place and build the temple of the LORD. Yes, He will build the temple of the LORD; He will be clothed in splendor and will sit on His throne and rule. There will also be a priest on His throne, and the counsel of peace will be between the two of them.'*
>
> ZECHARIAH 6:12-13, BSB

Jesus says in Revelation 22:7 "Behold I come quickly..." In the Revelation shared with you today, Jesus sprouts out of His Father like a seedling that grows in strength, power, and majesty, the Son of God bearing a youthful image of our heavenly Father, he places himself between the two of them (Father and Holy Spirit) and the LORD bears His glory for us to see. The Holy Spirit who proceeds from the Father and the Son encapsulates the whole by the magnificent splendor and marvelous wonder uniting the trinity in astounding joy!

> *Peace I leave with you; My peace I give to you. I do not give to you as the world gives. Do not let your hearts be troubled; do not be afraid.*
>
> JOHN 14:27, BSB

Acts 15:17, NIV ... "that the remnant of men may seek the Lord, and all the Gentiles who bear my name, says the Lord, who does these things' that have been known for ages." At the return of Christ, there will not only be believing Jews (here called "the remnant of men") but also believing Gentiles "who bear my name."

Throughout the Old Testament, YHWH, the LORD, consistently appears riding on the clouds with His divine presence radiating throughout the earth, illuminating it with His magnificent rays. This revelation of His nature extends to both the Jewish people and the Gentiles, as His theophany, the manifestation of His presence, is depicted through the imagery of Him enveloped in light, akin to putting on a garment. The vast heavens are stretched out like a tent, establishing His chambers above the waters, and the clouds become His majestic chariot as He moves with grace, walking upon the wings of the wind (Psalm 104:2-3, BSB).

DIVINE ENCOUNTERS: ANSWERING THE CALL TO EXPLORE THE GOSPEL OF JOHN

As I stated earlier I was called in my journey to read many books one being the Gospel of John. The Gospel of John holds a significant place among the four canonical Gospels found in the New Testament of the Holy Bible. It is regarded by biblical scholars as a distinct and exceptional piece of literature that offers a theological viewpoint on the life, ministry, death, and resurrection of Jesus Christ.

Biblical scholars generally regard the Gospel of John as the latest of the four canonical Gospels, likely composed towards the end of the first century AD. It is attributed to the apostle John, although authorship has been a topic of scholarly debate.

In the Gospel of John, the majesty and glory of Jesus shine forth, revealing a high Christology that sets him apart from the Synoptic Gospels. With poetic eloquence, the author weaves together profound encounters, powerful teachings, and divine proclamations that resonate with our souls.

In the Gospel of John, Jesus presents his perspectives distinctly and emphatically, setting them apart from the Synoptic Gospels of Mark, Matthew, and Luke. Unlike the other Gospels, Jesus explicitly proclaims his pre-existence as a celestial being who has descended from Heaven, emphasizing his divine nature.

At the heart of the Gospel of John lies the transformative message of spiritual rebirth. Just as Jesus shared with Nicodemus, "Truly, truly, I say to you, unless one is born again, he cannot see the kingdom of God" (John 3:3). Through the regenerating work of the Holy Spirit, individuals can experience a profound transformation, being born anew in the Spirit. This spiritual rebirth establishes a deep connection between the believer and Jesus, as Jesus declared, "I am the way, and the truth, and the life" (John 14:6).

He teaches that through this transformative experience, individuals can have a profound spiritual connection with him, allowing him to dwell within them. This intimate indwelling establishes a deep communion with the divine, granting access to celestial realms and the indwelling of the Father. In contrast to the other Gospels, Jesus emphasizes that eternal life and immortality can be attained in the present, rather than solely at the End of Time. This concept echoes the idea of the Atman found in Eastern philosophies, where the divine essence resides within each individual.

Throughout the Gospel of John, there is a profound emphasis on the exaltation of humanity into divine glory. Jesus, in Chapter 17, declares that he has bestowed upon humans the same glory he possesses as the Son of the Father. Additionally, in Chapter 10, he suggests the concept of deification, affirming that those who receive the word of God can be regarded as "gods." This portrayal highlights Jesus as a teacher of a sophisticated and mystical theology, revealing profound insights into the nature of humanity's divine potential.

Within the Gospel of John, we encounter Jesus' divine proclamations, unveiling his high Christology. Jesus boldly declares, "I am the light of the world" (John 8:12), "Before Abraham was, I am" (John 8:58), affirming his pre-existence and eternal nature. He proclaims, "I and the Father are one" (John 10:30), highlighting the profound unity and divine essence shared between him and the Father. These statements reveal Jesus' claim to deity, presenting him as the Son of God, fully divine and equal to the Father.

Earthly kingdoms fade into whispers as Jesus proclaims that his dominion transcends this world, echoing across realms. Through their theological lens, the author unveils a clearer understanding of

Jesus' teachings on the kingdom and eternal life, a harmonious blend of their vision and the essence of the synoptic Jesus.

The Gospel of John invites us into a deeper understanding of Jesus' teachings and identity. It engages our hearts and minds, drawing us into the sublime mysteries of spiritual rebirth, the indwelling of the Holy Spirit, and the exalted Christology of Jesus as the divine Son of God. Through these profound revelations, we are invited to embrace the transformative power of the Gospel and experience the abundant life found in communion with the triune God. It portrays Jesus as a profound and enlightened teacher, guiding individuals toward a deeper understanding of their own divine essence and their intimate connection with the divine.

When Jesus used the "I AM" statements found in the New Testament, He made a profound claim about His own identity. By associating Himself with the divine name "I AM," Jesus asserted that He is God in human form, equal to the Father. These statements emphasized His deity and highlighted His unique relationship with God. Jesus intentionally used the phrase "I am" to describe Himself in a manner that draws a parallel to the name of God revealed in the Old Testament. Jesus' "I am" statements and divine identity are most profoundly observed in the Gospel of John where he gives us many.

Jesus embodies his teachings and has profoundly impacted the hearts of many throughout history, leaving a lasting legacy that will continue to inspire future generations. Believers have experienced the divine presence of the God of Zion, the spiritual kingdom, receiving spiritual blessings and the indwelling of the Holy Spirit within them.

The concept of Zion represents being elevated and signifies spiritual enlightenment and connection. In the Hebrew Bible (Old Testament), Zion is often used as a poetic and symbolic term for Jerusalem, the religious and political center of ancient Israel. The Israelites believed that Yahweh had chosen Zion/Jerusalem as His dwelling place and the location of the central sanctuary, the Temple.

However, Jesus emphatically states to the Samaritan at the well that there will be a time when God will be understood and known by his children far beyond the land of Jerusalem. Jesus reveals that God dwells within us, and we dwell within God. We ourselves become the holy temple in which God resides.

Jesus serves as a living example of this idea, demonstrating the interconnectedness of nature, the transformative power of love, and the profound essence of the divine "I AM." His life and teachings captivate and inspire, leaving an enduring impact on the hearts of people.

Figure 8: THE VIRGIN AND CHILD WITH SAINTS AND ALLEGORICAL FIGURES, about 1315-20, Giotto di Bondone (Italian, about 1267-1337). Tempera and gold leaf on panel.

Jesus invites us to share communion with Him, symbolically represented through the Eucharist, which means "thank you" in Greek. Gratitude serves as a guiding principle that continually directs us back to the Creator. When we cultivate a mindset of gratitude, we remember the awe-inspiring wonder of creation and recognize that life itself is a precious gift. Opening ourselves to gratitude causes our souls to soar with joy and appreciation.

Throughout history, there has always been a deep hunger for faith in the world. Jesus instructs us to respond to this hunger by offering ourselves as nourishment, just as He instructed His disciples to give food to the hungry crowd (Luke 9:12). In this way, the transformative message of the Kingdom of God takes root within the hearts of humanity as we share our faith and proclaim the Good News.

The offering we bring to one another and the offering that is discovered within ourselves is akin to the manna, the sustenance provided to the Israelites in the wilderness. It represents the essence of our being, revealed to us through our personal experiences. As we share our faith and the substance of our lives with others, we encounter a profound connection that unites us in the journey of discovering our true selves.

By participating in communion with Jesus and embracing gratitude, we not only nourish our own spiritual growth but also contribute to the collective well-being of humanity. It is through this sacred exchange that the essence of who we are and the transformative power of the divine are unveiled.

10

DIVINE TOUCH:
THE SACRED GENESIS OF HUMANITY

As Jesus used the famous icon Christ the Pantocrator to communicate with me. The aspect of God that we would refer to as the Heavenly Father in the triune nature of God also used a famous painting to demonstrate his being to me. "The Creation of Adam" is a fresco painting by Italian artist Michelangelo that forms part of the Sistine Chapel's ceiling painted in 1508-1512 in Vatican City. "The Creation of Adam" illustrates the Biblical creation narrative from the book of Genesis in which God gives life to Adam, the first man. "Let us make men in our image, after our likeness." Genesis tells how the Lord created Adam from the dust of the earth and breathed into his nostrils the breath of life.

In this famous painting, God comes into contact with his creation. God outreaches to Adam divine power. In this incredible work of art God our Heavenly Father is depicted floating in a shroud of scarlet cloth shaped in the shape of a brain. He travels with his angels and perhaps Eve. He appears as an old wise man with a beard and hair flowing in the wind draped in a scarlet mantel. God reaches out to Adam divine power giving him the spark of life and the divine gift of consciousness. The outstretched arms of God and Adam are separated by a small gap, representing the moment of connection and communication between the divine and human. Similarly, in the brain, communication and connection between neurons occur through synapses, which are small gaps where information is transmitted from one neuron to another.

Figure 9: Michelangelo, "THE CREATION OF ADAM"
Fresco. Sistine Chapel, Vatican City

In this image, God has a side profile of his face looking at Adam. He also portrays this side profile in the image he created for me as I walked with him for seven minutes along with Jesus and the blessed Holy Spirit. The greatest difference, however, is that in this painting our heavenly Father has his sight on Adam and when I come into contact with our Creator, he has his sight on me and looks directly at me. I took approximately 20-25 pictures at the time of this unveiling. I was captivated by the images of the triune of God in which our Father breaths out of himself Jesus and with the nearly invisible Holy Ghost residing next to him.

However, as I revisited all the pictures that I took that day our heavenly Father is present in the very first photograph which took place near what I have coined "the heart of the farm" in a grove of trees. In this image, God constructs himself in the clouds creating a supreme body. He lies on his side draped in the clouds uplifting the heavens with his holy right arm. His eyes are shaded so as not to frighten me. This will be the first image of God you see as the unfoldment of this prophecy and revelation to humanity. As in the fresco painted by Michelangelo, the "Creation of Adam" God travels with his angels. So too in my mind's eye, God travels with his angels and you will see these angels.

God has equipped man to be self-sufficient. It is in our freedom or free will that allows us to choose what kind of divinity we choose to express. Free will is how we react, interpret, and choose to engage with our experience. We are powerful creators and when we choose to express the highest version of ourselves, we are mighty. We create our reality through our intentions. We influence our reality with our intentions. Intent can modify our future probability. God has given humanity the tools to create with our thoughts which create words, which create our deeds or actions. This is how we create:

Life is not a mere discovery but a creation. Each day is not meant for passive observation of what it brings, but for actively shaping and constructing it. In fact, you are constantly involved in the process of creating your reality, often unaware of the power you possess. Let's explore the reasons behind this and how it operates:

You have been fashioned in the likeness and image of God, embodying the qualities of a creator.

God, the ultimate creator, serves as the model for your creative nature.

Within you exist three interconnected aspects of being, which can be referred to by different names: Father, Son, and Holy Ghost; mind, body, and spirit; super-conscious, conscious, and subconscious.

Creation unfolds through these three dimensions of your being. In other words, you engage in creation at three levels. The tools that facilitate this process are thought, word, and deed.

Thought is the starting point of all creation, originating from the deepest level of your being ("Proceeds from the Father"). From there, creation progresses to the realm of words and communication ("Ask and you shall receive, speak and it shall be done unto you"). Finally, creation is fully realized and manifested in the physical realm through action ("And the Word was made flesh and dwelt among us").

By understanding and harnessing this creative process within you, you can actively participate in shaping your reality and bringing forth your desires into tangible existence. [38]

Life is not solely a process of uncovering predetermined outcomes but an active endeavor of shaping and constructing one's own experiences. Rather than simply discovering what each day holds, the focus lies on actively creating and exerting influence on one's own reality. In other words, creation occurs on three levels, employing specific tools. It all begins with our thoughts, which serve as the genesis of all creation. From there, creation moves forward through the power of spoken words, where we ask, receive, and speak things into existence. Ultimately, creation finds its fulfillment within ourselves and manifests in the world around us.

11

THE DIVINE CANVAS: PAINTING THE LANDSCAPE OF SPIRIT THROUGH HUMAN EXPERIENCE

When Christ is revealed, and he is your life,
you will be revealed in all your glory with him.

COLOSSIANS 3:4

AN IMAGE IS MORE THAN A SIMPLE VISUAL REPRESENTATION; IT holds the power to reflect profound ideas and creations. If we are truly made in the image of God, then we possess the ability to be divine co-creators, much like Jesus. Through our thoughts, words, and actions, we have the power to shape our reality.

But what do these sacred and divine images look like for each of us? The answer is as diverse as the beliefs, cultures, and personal experiences that shape our perspectives. Some may envision the divine through human-like forms, while others find solace in symbols, icons, or the awe-inspiring beauty of nature.

As humans, we possess remarkable sensory abilities. We can see, hear, touch, taste, and smell. We can think, observe, feel, and design. Through these faculties, God experiences the world within us. The divine presence sees through our eyes, hears through our ears, touches through our hands, and feels through our hearts. We are vessels through which the divine can know and create.

The image of God that you choose to express is a personal decision, a unique reflection of your individuality. It is a result of the free will bestowed upon us by God. We have the choice to co-create with the divine and shape our own experiences. In this self-reflective world, our thoughts and beliefs hold the power to manifest into our reality.

It's important to remember that your perception of the world is not an exact reflection of its objective reality. It is influenced by your beliefs, experiences, and perspectives. Your thoughts and beliefs shape the reality you experience. Life acts as a mirror, faithfully reflecting the image of your deepest thoughts and beliefs.

Together with the divine, we possess the remarkable ability to shape our own experiences. In this world that invites self-reflection, the thoughts and beliefs we hold within ourselves possess an extraordinary power to manifest into our reality. You may wonder how this process unfolds. Let us delve into the understanding that desire is the essence of our soul. It is through desire that the divine spark within us, our soul, finds expression. It is not merely confined to thoughts or words, but it manifests through our actions. In this way, the soul becomes the individualized expression of God, a unique embodiment of the divine. Here on Earth, as humans, we are souls experiencing God in human form, and humans are souls embracing the divine essence within. It is the inherent nature of God to desire to experience itself through the vast tapestry of existence.[39]

Desire, in turn, becomes the catalyst for intention. It is the driving force behind our aspirations, shaping the direction we choose to embark upon. Intention sets the stage for the unfolding of our thoughts. Our thoughts are the fertile ground from which our realities emerge. They hold the power to shape our perceptions, beliefs, and understanding. As we align our thoughts with our divine intentions, we become active participants in the creative process of our lives.

From thoughts, action arises. Our thoughts give birth to the choices we make and the actions we take. They are the bridge between our inner world and the external realm. Through conscious and deliberate action, we bring our intentions and thoughts into tangible existence. Our actions become the vehicles through which we engage with the world, expressing our divine essence through deeds of love, compassion, and service.

And as we navigate this journey, the outcomes we experience are intricately woven into this intricate tapestry of creation. The energy of our thoughts, directed by our desires, shapes the outcomes we encounter. The alignment of our desires, intentions, thoughts, and actions contributes to the unfolding of our reality, ultimately influencing the course of events in our lives.

In this interconnected dance of desire, intention, thought, action, and outcome, we become co-creators with the divine. We tap into the immense power that lies within us, and through our conscious choices, we shape the path we walk upon. May we embrace the inherent energy of our thoughts, guided by our desires, and embark upon a journey of intentional creation.

The Bible reminds us of the glorious riches of the mystery, which is Christ in us, the hope of glory (Colossians 1:27). It also speaks of our participation in the divine nature and escaping the corruption of worldly desires (2 Peter 1:4). Jesus reveals the purpose and fullness of humanity, allowing us to share in the divine nature and inherit the same promises.

We live in a participatory universe, as demonstrated by the biblical story of Jesus calming the storm at the Sea of Galilee.

In the story, as the disciples and Jesus found themselves in a boat on the Sea of Galilee, a fierce storm arose, threatening their safety. The wind howled, and the waves crashed against the boat, creating a chaotic and dangerous situation. In that pivotal moment, Jesus stood up, rebuked the wind and the waves, and suddenly, a great calm descended upon the sea.

This narrative carries profound significance, highlighting the interconnectedness and conscious nature of the universe. Jesus' ability to command the elements and calm the storm indicates that the wind and waves were not merely impersonal forces of nature, but rather, they were imbued with a foundational intelligence and consciousness.

Just as Jesus recognized the inherent intelligence within the elements, we too can embrace the understanding that consciousness permeates the fabric of existence. The wind, the waves, and all elements of nature possess a deep connection to the divine wisdom that orchestrates the universe.

Another example from the life of Jesus that demonstrates the participatory nature of the universe is the story of the feeding of the five thousand. In this miraculous event, Jesus took a small amount of food—a few loaves of bread and a couple of fish—and multiplied them to feed a multitude of people.

In this story, Jesus involved the disciples in the process of providing for the crowd. Rather than performing the miracle solely on His own, He invited the disciples to participate by collecting the available food and distributing it to the people. Jesus could have miraculously created an abundance of food without any human involvement, but He chose to engage the disciples in the process.

This event highlights the principle of co-creation and participation. Jesus demonstrated that the universe responds to human participation and collaboration with divine forces. The disciples' willingness to participate and offer what they had—though seemingly insufficient—was instrumental in the manifestation of the miracle. It was through their active involvement that the divine power flowed and multiplied the loaves and fish to satisfy the hunger of the multitude.

In conclusion, the stories of Jesus calming the storm and the feeding of the five thousand convey a powerful message about our interconnectedness and participatory role in the universe. These narratives remind us that we are not isolated beings but intimately connected to the world around us.

By recognizing the consciousness that permeates every aspect of existence, as exemplified by Jesus' ability to command the elements and multiply the loaves and fish, we can embrace our role as co-creators. We are invited to actively engage with the world, honoring its inherent intelligence and fostering harmony and balance.

Just as Jesus calmed the storm by acknowledging the consciousness within the elements, and involved the disciples in the feeding of the five thousand to manifest abundance, we too can contribute to the unfolding of a harmonious existence. By recognizing our interconnectedness and embracing our role as co-creators, we can participate consciously and responsibly in shaping our reality.

We too participate in this divine nature. Exploring our true nature is our purpose, yet we often limit ourselves by not fully understanding who we are and our true potential.

John Archibald Wheeler, a renowned physicist, offered a compelling viewpoint regarding our comprehension of the universe. He suggested that if we have been unable to obtain answers from the universe, it could be because we failed to recognize its living nature and consequently neglected to pose questions to it. Wheeler prompts us to consider what revelations the universe might hold for us. He emphasizes that without posing questions, we cannot expect to receive answers. This perspective underscores the importance of active inquiry and engagement in our pursuit of understanding the cosmos.[40]

Paul Levy highlights the significance of quantum physics in elucidating the relationship between an individual's experience and the wider universe. He argues against the notion of viewing ourselves as isolated entities, independent and detached from the rest of the cosmos. Prior to the emergence of quantum physics, physicists maintained the illusion of being detached observers in their experiments, disregarding their own involvement. However, Levy asserts that the observer's psyche is an integral component of the observed phenomenon. Quantum theory has revolutionized our understanding of the universe, presenting a new perspective where the observer, the observed, and the act of observation are inseparably interconnected.[41] [42]

JOURNEY OF REVELATION:
EMBRACING THE DIVINE PRESENCE WITHIN

Jesus said, "In My Father's house there are many rooms.
If it were not so, would I have told you that I go and prepare
a place for you? I shall return to take you with me so that
you may be where I am.

JOHN 14:2-3, NIV

These words were spoken by Jesus during the Last Supper when he was sharing a final meal with his disciples before his crucifixion. Jesus was preparing his disciples for his eventual departure from the earthly realm and assuring them of his return.

In this particular verse, Jesus uses the metaphor of his Father's house, symbolizing the heavenly realm or the divine presence. He tells his disciples that there are many rooms in his Father's house, implying that there is ample space and a place for each individual within the divine plan. Jesus assures them that he is going to prepare a place for them, indicating his role as a guide between humanity and the divine. That human beings are intimately connected to the divine through their relationship with him.

Furthermore, Jesus promises that he will return to take his disciples with him so that they may be where he is. This statement conveys the idea that through their relationship with Jesus and their faith in him, they will have the opportunity to be united with him in the eternal realm. It suggests that human beings have the potential to be partakers of the divine and to dwell in the presence of God.

Having a personal relationship with a higher consciousness is a transformative journey that leads to the revelation of the true self. Through this connection, we embark on a path of self-discovery and inner awakening. As we open ourselves to the wisdom and guidance of a higher consciousness, we are guided to look beyond the layers of conditioning and societal expectations, uncovering the essence of who we truly are. This profound relationship allows us to delve into the depths of our being, embracing our unique gifts, passions, and purpose. In the presence of higher consciousness, we find acceptance, love, and a profound understanding of our true nature, leading us to live authentically and align our lives with our deepest truths.

WHAT IS THE ESSENCE OF YOUR DIVINE SELF ON A DAILY BASIS?

It is the embodiment of goodness, mercy, compassion, understanding, peace, joy, and light. It is the embodiment of forgiveness, patience, strength, courage, and the willingness to assist in times of need. It provides comfort during moments of sorrow, healing during times of injury, and guidance in times of confusion. It encompasses profound wisdom, ultimate truth, immense peace, and boundless love. You are truly all of these qualities. At certain moments in your life, you have recognized and experienced yourself as embodying these qualities. Now, choose to embrace and recognize yourself as these qualities always, in every aspect of your life.[43]

THE PATH OF SELF-REALIZATION: EMBRACING DIVINE ESSENCE AND CO-CREATING SALVATION

Salvation is a profound journey of self-discovery, where you realize that you are already redeemed and embrace the divine essence within you. Just like Jesus, you possess a divine nature and have the incredible power to co-create, making you an integral part of God's plan. This realization awakens you to the timeless and eternal nature of your existence.

It's crucial to understand that you are not separate from God, and salvation is not an external achievement to strive for. While Jesus holds immense significance as a transformative figure, he is not the sole savior. His teachings and examples continue to inspire and guide people every day. Jesus serves as a beacon, illuminating the path and revealing the extraordinary potential within each of us. Jesus transcends the role of a mere savior for Christians, for His love extends far beyond religious boundaries to embrace all people in the world. He is not confined to a single group or denomination, but rather, His love knows no limits and encompasses every individual, regardless of their background, faith, or creed. Jesus' love is universal, embracing the entirety of humanity with compassion, grace, and unconditional acceptance. Salvation is understood differently across various religious and philosophical traditions. While some religions teach that salvation comes through accepting their specific doctrines or figures, it is crucial to recognize that belief in Jesus is not a requirement for salvation.

Neale Donald Walsch's dialogue with God suggests that Jesus' mission was to rescue humanity from ignorance and the lack of self-realization. He aimed to demonstrate what each individual can ultimately become, igniting a spark of divine consciousness within us.[44]

Interestingly the name "Jesus" comes from the Greek transliteration of the Hebrew name "Yeshua" (יְשׁוּעַ), which is derived from the Hebrew word for "salvation" or "to save."

In the realm of mystic understanding, we come to realize that the potential lies within us to mirror the divine union exemplified by Jesus and God. His proclamation echoes through the ages: "I and the Father are One, and ye are my brethren." As beings bestowed with the divine essence, humanity carries the capacity to be its own redeemer through acts of benevolence. The path to salvation resides in our intentions and in treating others with the same kindness we desire for ourselves. Jesus serves as the embodiment of our elevated nature, emanating love, dignity, honor, and peace. He stands as both a true companion and an extraordinary guide, epitomizing the way, the truth, and the essence of existence. By expressing his divine nature and assisting others in discovering their own, he illuminates the path toward self-realization.

Yet, let us not forget that Jesus is not the sole manifestation of God's creation. He himself declared, "Truly, truly, I tell you, whoever believes in Me will also do the works that I am doing. He will do even greater things than these because I am going to the Father" (John 14:12, BSB). We are all recipients of divine grace, and it is through our actions, rooted in the foundation of Christ's work within and through us, that our salvation becomes evident. When we sow the seeds of intention to love one another, we ascend to new heights of spiritual awakening.

Salvation resides within the depths of the human heart, for it is there that our inner divinity finds its home. Our hearts possess the ability to perceive, comprehend, and experience the vast magnificence and goodness that lie within us. They become the vessel through which we manifest and express our highest good. Therefore, let us cultivate the energy of our hearts and radiate our inner light into the world. As we open ourselves to both give and receive the divine presence dwelling within us, a sweet nectar of love flows forth, rendering us luminous beacons amidst the darkness. No circumstance or problem can withstand the transformative power of love. Love, both directed towards ourselves and extended to others, perpetually holds the key to resolution. By nurturing compassion within ourselves and extending it to others, we unite in a higher purpose of existence, transcending the boundaries of the mundane and forging connections that resonate on a soul level.

ILLUMINATING THE PATH OF SPIRITUAL-AWAKENING: INSIGHTS FROM BUDDHA'S TEACHINGS AND THE POWER OF PERCEPTION

As we become more attuned to the divine essence within, we are called to manifest this inner radiance in our daily lives, living radiantly. It is through embracing the qualities of love, compassion, forgiveness, and service to others that we become conduits of divine grace. This transformative journey, known as edification, involves both moral and intellectual improvement, propelling us towards a higher spiritual plane. As we uplift our knowledge and deepen our sincerity towards God, we undergo a transfiguration, sharing in the very nature of the divine itself. In 2 Peter 1:5-8, we are reminded of the virtues we should cultivate to continue growing in our faith, ensuring that we remain effective and productive on our spiritual journey. Embracing this journey of edification allows us to live radiantly and fulfill our divine calling.

The Buddhist Master Linji once said, "If you meet the Buddha on the road, kill him."[45] This enigmatic statement conveys that encountering someone who appears to possess the qualities of a Buddha may not necessarily mean they are enlightened. It warns against getting caught up in external appearances and instead directs us towards seeking genuine self-realization and awakening, rather than focusing on recognition or adoration.

The realization of self is a key element in our spiritual evolution. It involves looking beyond our superficial identities and recognizing that we are more than what meets the eye. By turning our gaze inward, we can awaken to the wisdom that resides within us and connect with the vastness of the universe.

During my own mystical encounter with God, I was specifically working with my third-eye and crown chakra, which allowed me to tap into unseen dimensions and perceive reality from a place of observation and insight. As we seek a deeper understanding of the divine spark within us, we open ourselves to cultivate receptiveness to profound wisdom and spiritual growth and allow divine essence to be unveiled through moments of revelation and spiritual awakening.

The third eye, associated with the Ajna chakra, represents intuition, insight, and inner vision. It is through the activation of this spiritual center that we gain clarity of perception, transcending our identification with the ego and connecting with the unchanging essence of our being. This essence, often referred to as witness consciousness or the witnessing awareness, remains untouched by the ever-changing experiences of life.

By realizing the witness consciousness, we can go beyond the realm of duality and connect with the deeper reality that underlies existence. This deeper reality is the foundation of ultimate reality, and by recognizing it, we can transcend the limitations of our ego-driven existence. In the words of Jesus from Luke 11:35, we are reminded to ensure that the light within us is not obscured by darkness. By cultivating inner clarity, insight, and spiritual vision, we can radiate our true essence and dispel the illusions of ignorance.

The metaphorical use of the eye as the lamp of the body, as mentioned in the scripture, highlights the importance of inner vision and perception. When our vision is clear, we possess a deep understanding of ourselves and the world, leading to a state of inner light. This clarity contrasts with a state of darkness that arises from a lack of understanding within ourselves.

The pineal gland, often associated with the third eye, has been speculated to play a role in spiritual experiences and expanded consciousness.

The prophetic revelation of my mystical experience with Jesus presents as an illuminating presence within creation, exemplifying a radiant light. Through my co-creative and synergistic endeavors, his divine essence shines forth, casting light upon consciousness itself. This pivotal moment highlights how my work reflects the inner nature that resides within each of us, a facet of nature that is solely discovered within ourselves and unveiled through our hearts.

As we come to recognize our profound interconnectedness with Source energy, we realize that we are both the observer and the observed. The philosophy of being both the observer and the observed is rooted in the understanding that our consciousness has the capacity to simultaneously perceive and experience the world around us, as well as the inner workings of our own thoughts, emotions, and experiences.

By embodying both roles, we develop a more holistic and integrated understanding of ourselves and the world. We recognize that our perception and interpretation of the world are influenced by our own subjectivity, biases, and conditioning. This awareness encourages us to engage in ongoing self-inquiry, continually questioning our assumptions and expanding our perspectives.

We embody the light, and it becomes our responsibility as cosmic beings to illuminate the darkness and dispel the illusions that arise from our unawakened state as unconscious creators of our experiences. Ultimately, there is only light, and we are intrinsic embodiments of that light. Darkness possesses no independent power; it is merely the absence of light. Conversely, light holds its own inherent power.

Werner Karl Heisenberg, a pioneering physicist, noted that the separation between the observer and the observed is no longer possible. We are called to recognize ourselves in what is being observed, understanding that our perception shapes our reality.[46]

An enlightened individual does not claim superiority over others but rather teaches that enlightenment is accessible to everyone. Siddhartha Gautama, who became the Buddha, achieved enlightenment through years of practice and meditation.

As the Buddha, he dedicated the rest of his life to sharing his insights and teachings with others. He traveled throughout ancient India, gathering disciples and imparting his wisdom to all who sought guidance. One of the fundamental teachings of Buddha is the concept of "vipassana" or "insight meditation." Vipassana is a practice that cultivates mindfulness and awareness of one's thoughts, sensations, and experiences in the present moment. It involves observing the nature of reality as it arises and passes away, without clinging to or identifying with these transient phenomena.

Buddha emphasized the impermanent and conditioned nature of all phenomena, teaching that everything is in a constant state of flux and subject to change. Through mindful observation, one can develop insight into the true nature of reality and the interconnectedness of all things.

Buddhist teachings also address the role of perception and how it shapes our understanding of the world. Buddha taught that our perception is conditioned by our mental and emotional states, biases, and attachments. By observing and investigating our perceptions, we can develop a clearer understanding of how they arise and influence our experiences.

The Buddha's teachings revolved around the Four Noble Truths, which describe the reality of suffering, its origin, its cessation, and the path leading to its cessation.[47]

The Four Noble Truths are fundamental teachings in Buddhism that form the foundation of the Buddha's teachings on suffering and its cessation. They are as follows:

1. **The Truth of Suffering (Dukkha):** This truth acknowledges that suffering and dissatisfaction are an inherent part of human existence. It encompasses physical and mental suffering, as well as the unsatisfactory nature of conditioned existence.

2. **The Truth of the Origin of Suffering (Samudaya):** This truth explains that the root cause of suffering is craving (tanha) and attachment to impermanent phenomena. It emphasizes that desire, ignorance, and clinging give rise to suffering.

3. **The Truth of the Cessation of Suffering (Nirodha):** This truth reveals that the cessation of suffering is attainable. It teaches that by letting go of craving and attachment, one can experience liberation and the end of suffering. This state is known as Nirvana.

4. **The Truth of the Path Leading to the Cessation of Suffering (Magga):** This truth presents the Noble Eightfold Path as the means to overcome suffering and attain enlightenment. The path consists of eight interconnected factors: Right View, Right Intention, Right Speech, Right Action, Right Livelihood, Right Effort, Right Mindfulness, and Right Concentration.

In our spiritual journey, let us embrace the process of edification, striving for moral and intellectual improvement. Let us remain vigilant in discerning true enlightenment, focusing on genuine self-realization rather than external appearances. By turning our gaze inward and awakening to the wisdom within, we can activate our third eye and connect with our witness consciousness. Connecting with witness consciousness can provide a deeper understanding of the nature of reality and the self. As individuals observe their experiences without judgment or attachment, they begin to recognize the illusory and impermanent nature of their thoughts, emotions, and sensations. This recognition can lead to a sense of liberation from the limitations of the ego and a connection to a deeper, more expansive aspect of consciousness.

Through inner clarity, insight, and spiritual vision, we transcend the limitations of the ego, embody our true essence, and radiate the light within us. May we illuminate the darkness and illusions that hinder our growth, and may our journey lead us to a profound realization of our interconnectedness with the divine.

Recognizing our responsibility and being accountable for our actions in life is crucial. Unfortunately, some individuals believe that mistreating others is acceptable, assuming that they will be saved and their wrongdoings will be forgiven. However, we have the power to make a different choice. Let us choose to embrace our innate goodness and promote acts of kindness. Decide now to let the inherent light within you shine! Kindness acts as the nourishing sunlight that allows virtue to flourish. As Mark Twain eloquently said, "Kindness is the language which the deaf can hear and the blind can see."

John Archibald Wheeler astutely noted that the immense burden of planning for the future of humanity rests on our own shoulders—a realization that may have seemed unimaginable.[48] Paul Levy, in agreement, suggests that as we dispel the illusion of our separate existence from the universe, we naturally adopt a more holistic and ecological way of thinking, understanding ourselves as integral parts of a greater ecosystem.[49] The Dalai Lama further emphasizes that the fate of humanity lies entirely in our hands. We have the responsibility to create a better, happier, and more peaceful world.[50]

Paul Levy explores the energetic expression of this realization, not just intellectually but in our hearts, that we are interconnected and interdependent at the deepest level of our being. This realization gives rise to compassion. In a passage often attributed to Einstein, it is said:

> *"A human being is apart of the whole called by us universe, a part limited in time and space. He experiences himself, his thoughts and feelings as something separated from the rest, a kind of optical delusion of his consciousness. This delusion is a kind of prison for us, restricting us to our personal desires and to affection for a few nearest to us, Our task must be to free ourselves from this prison by widening our circle of compassion to embrace all living creatures and the whole of nature in its beauty."*[51]

In addition to acknowledging our personal accountability, it is vital to recognize the responsibility we carry towards one another. Neale Donald Walsch highlights the interconnectedness of humanity and the shared responsibility we have as spiritual beings in his conversation with God. The passage below, which resembles a variation of the Lord's Prayer, emphasizes the significance of aligning our actions and intentions with divine principles. It speaks of recognizing the sacredness of all beings and the need for forgiveness and compassion in our interactions. By forgiving others, we open ourselves to receiving forgiveness and experiencing inner healing.

Furthermore, the passage encourages us to exercise discernment and make conscious choices that lead us away from destructive paths. It reminds us that the power to create positive change lies within ourselves, and we are capable of transcending the negative patterns we have contributed to.

Ultimately, the passage signifies the eternal presence of divine wisdom, power, and glory, reminding us of the interconnectedness of Heaven and Earth and the potential for spiritual growth and transformation.

> *Beloved children, residing in the realm of divinity, your name is revered and sacred. May the influence of your spiritual dominion manifest on Earth, aligning with the divine purpose as it does in the heavenly realm. You are provided with the sustenance necessary for each day, and you are granted forgiveness for your transgressions and debts to the same extent that you have par-*

doned those who have wronged you. Choose not to succumb to temptation, but liberate yourself from the negative consequences of the actions you have brought forth. For within lies the eternal realm of divine sovereignty, power, and magnificence.[52]

AWAKENING TO UNITY: TRANSCENDING SEPARATION THEOLOGY AND EMBRACING COMPASSIONATE FAITH

As we remove the metaphorical veil, we awaken to our authentic essence and become conscious of our true nature. In the words of Paul Levy, quantum physics stands as one of the most profound discoveries in the history of human thought. It serves as a dynamic revelation, unveiling the presence of the divine in our lives. It calls upon humanity to elevate itself and engage in a genuine celebration of the divine order, honoring the inherent wisdom and creative force that permeates the universe.[53]

In this verse, James states that a person is justified or shown to be righteous by their works, not by faith alone. The context of this passage is a discussion about the relationship between faith and good deeds or actions. James argues that genuine faith is demonstrated through works of righteousness, such as acts of love, compassion, and justice.

James highlights the idea that faith and works are intertwined and inseparable. True faith, according to him, naturally leads to a life characterized by good works. It is not enough to simply claim faith or have intellectual assent; one's faith should be evident through righteous actions and a life lived in accordance with the teachings of Christ.

The actions you take towards others are ultimately reflections of yourself. When you offer support and kindness to others, you are also benefiting yourself. Conversely, when you neglect to assist or show compassion to others, you are likewise falling short in caring for yourself. What brings goodness and benefit to others also brings goodness and benefit to you. Similarly, what causes harm or negativity to others also affects you negatively.[54]

Numerous individuals believe that they are connected to a higher power, and this notion is prevalent in various religious institutions today. Some individuals attempt to attribute all the world's problems solely to God, hoping that everything will magically resolve itself. However, the reality is that humanity must awaken from its slumber. We are currently in a state of unawareness. It is crucial for us to collectively awaken and recognize that our present and future are in our hands. We must bear our own burdens, take responsibility for our actions, and strive for personal growth for the evolution of our species. As the remarkable co-creators that we are, it is within our power to make positive changes in the world we inhabit. Instead of placing blame, let us assume accountability for our thoughts, words, and deeds.

As co-creators, it is important for us to exercise caution in the things we bring into existence, as some of them can lead us away from our connection with the divine. For instance, the notions of hell, fire, and damnation. While hell itself does not exist in the way it is commonly perceived, we have the capacity to create our own personal experiences that resemble a state of suffering or separation from the divine.[55]

You are not separate from anything. Not from each other, not from any form of life, and not from God, we are interconnected and interdependent. Within our religious institutions, sacred texts, and theological frameworks, numerous outdated teachings persist, including the concept of "Hell." These teachings, instead of fostering a closer connection with God, often distance us from divine presence. To facilitate humanity's spiritual growth, it would be beneficial to let go of these detrimental notions and erroneous doctrines that promote a theology of separation.

By releasing these ideas rooted in separation theology, we can encourage a more inclusive and compassionate approach to faith. Embracing a perspective that transcends the notion of eternal damnation allows us to cultivate a deeper understanding of the inherent unity and love within the divine. It opens the door for a more expansive and harmonious spiritual journey.

EMBRACING DIVINE EXPERIENCE: REMEMBERING CHRIST AND RECOGNIZING OUR ROLE AS VESSELS OF GOD'S EXPRESSION

In a genuine expression of spirituality, the act of passing judgment holds no place. Judgment only serves to create division and foster exclusionary attitudes. Instead, our focus should be on rediscovering our authentic selves through a reconnection with our hearts. It is in this profound remembrance of our true nature that we are able to rise alongside Christ and bask in the radiance of His glory (Romans 8:1-2).

In the embrace of Christ, we discover a realm of unity, completeness, love, understanding, compassion, surrender, divine grace, and an unwavering love that resides within our hearts. As we embark on our individual journeys toward truth, illumination, love, and personal growth, we find solace in supporting and placing confidence in one another. We recognize that we have been gifted with free will and the incredible capacity to shape our own realities by our Creator, who has bestowed upon us a divine nature.

May we embrace a spirit of love and extend kindness and respect to others, just as we desire to be treated ourselves. It is through the power of love, along with an abundance mindset, a sense of honor, inner strength, and a courageous willingness to confront our vulnerabilities, that we bring forth beauty into the world. It is crucial for us to recognize that the belief in separateness is a mere illusion perpetuated by the ego. In reality, we are interconnected and unified. God's love encompasses all His children, regardless of their beliefs or faith. A truly devout individual embodies love for all, as they perceive the divine essence within every person they encounter.

Within our hearts, we inherently know that God is benevolent and kind. Yet, at times, our teachers may instill fear by portraying God as vengeful and to be dreaded. However, the ultimate truth lies in the understanding that God is synonymous with love. It is imperative that we learn to connect with and heed the wisdom of our own inner truth. Deep within our hearts resides the most profound and authentic truth, and by attuning ourselves to its whispers, we discover invaluable guidance in understanding, experiencing, and embodying our existence. This harmonious connection between our mind, body, and spirit allows us to access the divine essence that resides within us.

> *Understanding and knowing are divine states,*
> *but the utmost joy resides in simply existing.*
> *Existence arises from our collective experiences.*
> *The progression of understanding, experiencing, and being*
> *encompasses the Holy Trinity, the threefold nature of God.*
> *God the Father symbolizes profound understanding,*
> *the origin of all knowledge. God the Son represents lived*
> *experiences, embodying everything that the Father knows.*
> *God the Holy Spirit embodies existence itself, encompassing*
> *all that the Son has encountered, achieved through the*
> *wisdom gained from knowing, understanding*
> *and experiencing.* [56]

When contemplating the nature of the Holy Trinity, one can perceive it as a profound relationship characterized by three essential aspects: that which brings forth, that which is lifted or elevated, and that which simply exists.[57]

Through our faith, we are granted glimpses of the divine presence. Even if our faith is as tiny as a mustard seed, it possesses the power to move mountains. It is not through external observations that God unveils Himself to us, but rather through the inward experiences we encounter. I stand as a living testament to this profound truth. Through my journey of inner exploration and unwavering faith, I have become a witness to the tangible presence of God.

In the teachings of Jesus, He speaks of the arrival of the Kingdom, emphasizing the role of our faith (Luke 17:21). The majestic Kingdom of God resides within the depths of each individual, and there is no need for us to seek it outside ourselves. Our highest truths, the very essence of our being, are already embedded within us, waiting to be discovered and embraced

As a spiritual teacher, I intend to help others recognize that they too are part of the divine whole, members of the body. We are divine, co-creators with the Most High God. As stated in Psalm 82:6, "You are gods, and all of you are sons of the Most High."

In 1 Corinthians 11:24, Jesus instructs His disciples to remember Him through the act of breaking bread, symbolizing His body. This act holds deep significance. The bread represents the physical manifestation of Christ's body, which was broken for the sake of humanity. By participating in this act, believers remember Christ's sacrifice and love.

Moreover, this act of remembrance reminds us of our connection to the divine and our role as vessels of experience. Just as Christ experienced the world through His physical body, we too are beings in the flesh, experiencing life through our human bodies. Our experiences become a conduit for God's divine expression. As we navigate life's joys and challenges, we can bring forth love, compassion, forgiveness, and other qualities inherent in the divine nature.

Thus, when we remember Christ through the breaking of bread, we not only recall His sacrifice and teachings, but we also acknowledge our own role as vessels of divine experience. We recognize that God actively experiences the world through us, and our actions, thoughts, and choices become opportunities for divine expression.

In summary, true spirituality rejects judgment and embraces love and unity. Reconnecting with our hearts, we rise with Christ, experiencing divine grace. We should treat others with kindness, recognizing our interconnectedness and God's love for all. Our faith, no matter how small, reveals God's presence. The Kingdom of God resides within us, and our highest truths are already within our hearts. Remembering Christ through symbolic acts acknowledges our divine connection and the role we play as vessels of divine expression.

TRANSCENDING DUALITY: EMBRACING LOVE, COMPASSION, AND DIVINE CONSCIOUSNESS

Duality, as a concept, encompasses the existence of contrasting elements or perspectives that profoundly shape our perception of reality. Whether it is the interplay of good and evil, subjectivity and objectivity, or the harmonious balance of yin and yang, duality challenges us to explore the multifaceted nature of existence. It urges us to embrace the contradictions and diverse aspects that contribute to our understanding of the world.

One of the questions often posed is why there is evil and suffering in a world governed by an all-powerful and loving God. It is important to recognize that evil and suffering are not punishments inflicted by a vengeful or judgmental deity. Rather, they are the natural consequences of individual choices. These experiences serve as catalysts for personal transformation and spiritual growth.

When we approach evil and suffering with compassion, love, and understanding, we contribute to the healing and transformation of the world. We perceive them as invitations to respond empathetically and actively engage in promoting positive change. By embracing this perspective, we align ourselves with the divine purpose of overcoming adversity and fostering a more compassionate and harmonious existence.

Our soul, the eternal essence within us, makes decisions for its own evolution prior to our physical bodies embodying these roles. This understanding adds depth to our journey, as we navigate life's challenges and embrace opportunities for spiritual awakening and personal growth. Seeing through the lens of the Soul gives us a much larger perspective than seeing through the lens of our incarnate being.

Evil and suffering exist as part of the human experience to facilitate growth, learning, and the exploration of the concept of duality. Individuals possess free will and the ability to make choices and these choices can lead to both positive and negative outcomes. Evil and suffering are seen as opportunities for personal and collective evolution, allowing individuals to learn lessons, develop empathy, and expand their consciousness.

Within the realm of our existence, which is relative in nature, as opposed to the absolute realm, we have brought forth the concept of "evil." This was a deliberate act, driven by our desire to encounter love in an experiential manner, rather than merely recognizing that love encompasses everything. To truly experience something, there must be contrasting elements present. Hence, in our reality, we introduced a duality of good and evil, utilizing one to facilitate the experience of the other. However, in the ultimate reality, the notion of good and evil ceases to exist. Within the realm of the absolute, love alone prevails.

Evil is the result of choices made by individuals rooted in fear, ignorance, and a disconnection from their true nature. Evil arises when individuals act in ways that harm themselves or others, often motivated by a sense of separation, selfishness, or a distorted perception of power. Evil is not seen as a force external to humanity but rather as a consequence of misguided choices and actions.

Suffering is the experience of pain, distress, or hardship, both on an individual and collective level. Suffering is an inherent part of the human experience and can arise from various sources such as physical ailments, emotional struggles, and societal injustices. Suffering can serve as a catalyst for personal and spiritual growth, inviting individuals to find meaning, compassion, and resilience in the face of adversity.

The duality of good and evil reminds us that we have the capacity for both, and it is our choices that define our character. Jesus taught various principles that touch upon the concept of duality. Here are a few teachings of Jesus that relate to duality:

Love and Hate: Jesus emphasized the importance of love, teaching his followers to love both their neighbors and their enemies. In Matthew 5:44, he said, "But I say to you, love your enemies and pray for those who persecute you."

Light and Darkness: Jesus spoke about the contrast between light and darkness. In John 8:12, he said, I am the light of the world. Whoever follows me will not walk in darkness, but will have the light of life."

Kingdom of Heaven and Worldly Systems: Jesus taught about the duality between the values and principles of the Kingdom of Heaven and those of the world. In Matthew 6:24, he said, "No one can serve two masters, for either he will hate the one and love the other, or he will be devoted to the one and despise the other."

Good and Evil: Jesus taught his followers to discern between good and evil and to choose righteousness. In Matthew 7:17-18, he said "So, every healthy tree bears good fruit, but the diseased bad tree bears bad fruit. A healthy tree cannot bear bad fruit, nor can a diseased tree bear good fruit."

Overall, Jesus' teachings on duality challenged his followers to transcend binary thinking, embrace love and forgiveness, and seek a higher spiritual reality that goes beyond the surface-level divisions of the world.

When we practice forgiveness, take responsibility for our personal actions, cultivate compassion and empathy, engage in acts of service and kindness, shift our perspective, and connect with the divine we elevate our consciousness.

In conclusion, the chapter emphasizes that as divine co-creators, we possess the power to shape our reality through our thoughts, words, and actions. It highlights the diverse ways in which individuals envision the divine and emphasizes the importance of self-discovery and recognizing our innate goodness. The chapter encourages personal responsibility, accountability, and acts of kindness while rejecting the mistreatment of others. It explores the interconnectedness of the observer and the observed and discusses the role of duality in shaping our perception of reality. Ultimately, it calls for transcending binary thinking, cultivating love and forgiveness, and elevating our consciousness through connection with the divine and acts of service and kindness.

12

SACRED SYMMETRY: EXPLORING THE MYSTERIES OF GEOMETRIC HARMONY AND COLLECTIVE CONSCIOUSNESS

WITHIN THE HIDDEN INTRICACIES OF SACRED GEOMETRY, a pattern unfolds—a symphony of interconnected minds. Like cosmic waves, our intentions ripple through the fabric of existence, resonating with divine energy. In this entangled dance, we find truth and growth. Each thought becomes a thread, each feeling a strand, as we weave a collective tapestry, hand in hand. Together, we contribute to the cosmic symphony, where the web of consciousness expands and evolves, guided by the sacred forms that unite us all.

Sacred geometry holds a profound and timeless significance, revered across cultures and spiritual traditions throughout history. It is the study and exploration of geometric patterns and forms that are believed to embody fundamental principles of existence and the divine order of the universe.

At its core, sacred geometry reveals the interconnectedness and harmony that permeates all levels of creation. It unveils the underlying geometric structures that shape the physical and metaphysical realms, providing a glimpse into the divine blueprint of creation itself. These geometric patterns, such as the Flower of Life, Metatron's Cube, or the Golden Ratio, are considered sacred because they are believed to reflect the inherent order and beauty of the cosmos.

Sacred geometry is not limited to the realm of mathematics and aesthetics alone. It is also intimately intertwined with spirituality and consciousness. The study and contemplation of sacred geometric forms are thought to have a profound impact on the mind, body, and spirit, facilitating a deeper connection with the divine and awakening higher states of awareness.

In various spiritual practices, sacred geometry is employed as a powerful tool for meditation, visualization, and energy work. By focusing on these geometric patterns, individuals can align themselves with the underlying harmonies of the universe and tap into higher frequencies of consciousness. It is believed that through this alignment, one can access profound insights, experience spiritual awakening, and even facilitate healing and transformation.

Moreover, sacred geometry serves as a reminder of the interconnectedness of all existence. It emphasizes the interplay between the microcosm and the macrocosm, revealing that the same geometric principles found in the smallest atoms are echoed in the grandest celestial bodies. This recognition fosters a sense of unity and reverence for the inherent sacredness of all life.

In essence, sacred geometry invites us to contemplate the beauty and order inherent in the universe. It invites us to recognize the divine patterns that underlie our existence and to align ourselves with the harmonies of creation. Through this exploration, we can deepen our understanding of the divine, expand our consciousness, and cultivate a profound sense of awe and reverence for the sacredness that permeates the fabric of our reality.

The concept of sacred geometry resonates with me as an effective tool for imparting wisdom. As someone with a visionary perspective, I see the manifestation of form as an integral part of the creative process. This process is intricately connected to our thoughts, which are in turn influenced by our perception of reality.

Sacred geometry is often regarded as a universal language that transcends cultural and linguistic barriers. It is believed to communicate fundamental truths and principles that are inherit in the fabric of the universe. The geometric patterns and relationships found in sacred geometry are thought to convey symbolic meanings and represent aspects of cosmic order and harmony.

Plato, the ancient Greek philosopher, made significant contributions to the understanding and exploration of sacred geometry. He believed that geometry and mathematics were essential tools for understanding the nature of reality and the underlying principles of the universe. In Plato's philosophy, the world was viewed as a reflection of eternal and unchanging forms or ideas. These forms were considered the true reality, while the physical world was seen as a mere imperfect copy or manifestation of these ideal forms.

Geometry played a crucial role in Plato's metaphysical framework. He saw geometric forms as a bridge between the physical world and the world of ideas. According to Plato, geometric shapes and mathematical relationships provided a means to access and understand the eternal forms. Moreover, Plato explored the concept of the "Divine Geometer" or the "Great Geometer," a divine figure who used geometric principles to create and organize the cosmos. This notion reflected Plato's belief in the inherent mathematical order and harmony of the universe. Plato's ideas on sacred geometry influenced subsequent philosophical and esoteric traditions. His emphasis on geometry as a means of understanding the nature of reality and the existence of ideal forms contributed to the development of sacred geometry as a significant field of study.

Pythagoras, the ancient Greek philosopher and mathematician, also made significant contributions to the understanding of sacred geometry. He founded a philosophical and religious school known as Pythagoreanism, which regarded mathematics and geometry as fundamental to understanding the underlying principles of the universe. Pythagoras and his followers believed that numbers and geometric forms held deep symbolic and spiritual significance. They saw geometry as a way to uncover the divine order and harmony present in the cosmos. Pythagoras referred to geometric shapes as "perfect forms" and believed that they represented the fundamental building blocks of the universe.

In Pythagorean philosophy, geometric shapes were considered to be expressions of universal principles and divine order. The Pythagoreans believed that numbers and geometric forms held deep symbolic meaning and represented fundamental aspects of the universe. Pythagoras and his followers believed that numbers were the foundation of the universe and held deep symbolic meaning. They explored the properties and relationships of numbers, and the Pythagorean theorem is one of their notable mathematical contributions. In Pythagorean philosophy, numbers were viewed as the building blocks of the universe and were associated with various qualities and principles. The number 3 was particularly revered because it represented a fundamental triadic structure and harmony. The Pythagoreans associated the number 3 with the concept of the triad, which was believed to manifest harmony in the world.

Leonardo da Vinci, the renowned Italian artist, scientist, and inventor of the Renaissance period, had a deep interest in various disciplines, including sacred geometry. He believed that geometry was the key to understanding the fundamental principles of the universe and sought to explore its significance in his works. One of the notable ways in which da Vinci incorporated sacred geometry was through his exploration of the golden ratio, also known as the divine proportion.

The golden ratio is a mathematical ratio that is approximately equal to 1.618 and is believed to represent a sense of aesthetic harmony and beauty. Da Vinci used the golden ratio in his compositions, such as "The Last Supper" and "The Vitruvian Man," to achieve balanced and visually pleasing proportions. In "The Vitruvian Man," da Vinci depicted a male figure inscribed within both a circle and a square, demonstrating the harmony between human proportions and geometric forms. This drawing exemplified da Vinci's belief in the inherent connection between the human body, geometry, and the divine order of the universe.

The golden ratio is evident in various iconic structures such as the Great Pyramid of Giza and the Parthenon. It is also present in significant works of art, including Michelangelo's renowned masterpiece, the Creation of Adam. The utilization of the Golden Ratio in these architectural and artistic creations aims to achieve balance, harmony, and symmetry.

Overall, the contributions of Plato, Pythagoras, and Leonardo da Vinci to sacred geometry demonstrate their shared belief in the intrinsic connection between geometry, the divine order of the universe, and the pursuit of harmony and beauty in various aspects of life and creation.

Based on my observations of the photographs that I took on March 31st, 2015, depicting our Creator, I have come to realize that sacred geometry plays a significant role in these captivating images. God always talks to us in a language that we can understand, and one of the ways is through the utilization of sacred geometry, which is a universal language.

For example, in my visionary photography. The manifestation of our Heavenly Father takes on diverse forms, each unique and captivating. These forms may resemble intricate snowflakes, radiant stars like the Star of David, or even the sacred symbol of the Tetragrammaton. It is through these chosen elements and geometric form that He demonstrates Himself to me, showcasing His ability to adapt His appearance to any shape or likeness.

What is a Tetragrammaton?

The term "tetragrammaton" refers to a specific four-letter Hebrew word that is considered sacred in various religious and mystical traditions. In particular, it refers to the four Hebrew letters Yod, He, Vav, and He, which are transliterated as YHWH.[58] These letters represent the name of God in the Hebrew Bible, often referred to as the "Tetragrammaton," meaning "four letters".

The Tetragrammaton is understood as a representation of God's name, signifying His presence, power, and covenant relationships with His people. The Tetragrammaton (YHWH) is the sacred name of God in the Hebrew Bible. It is used to refer to God throughout the Hebrew Scriptures, particularly in contexts where His personal name is mentioned.

So, what is God's Name, and what does it mean? The most likely choice for how the Tetragrammaton was pronounced is "YAH-way," "YAH-weh," or something similar. The name Yahweh refers to God's self-existence. Yahweh is linked to how God described Himself in Exodus 3:14, "God said to Moses, 'I AM WHO I AM. This is what you are to say to the Israelites: "I AM has sent me to you."'" God's name reflects His being. God is the only self-existent or self-sufficient Being. Only God has life in and of Himself. That is the essential meaning of the Tetragrammaton, YHWH.

So, what does a Tetragrammaton look like? I was fascinated by how Nassim Haramein, came up with what a tetragrammaton might look like and the symbolic meanings behind it. You can watch some of his YouTube videos for more information.[59]

Figure 10: Image of a TETRAGRAMMATON

To provide an immersive understanding of Kabbalah and its mystical teachings, let us delve into the intriguing realm of Nassim Haramein's exploration of three-dimensional geometry. In Kabbalistic texts, it is stated that the universe is rooted in four worlds, which hold profound significance. Nassim Haramein, through the lens of sacred geometry, visually portrays the divine essence by presenting us with an image of a Tetragrammaton. This representation has been meticulously crafted by Haramein, who has dedicated three decades to researching and uncovering connections across various fields such as physics, mathematics, geometry, cosmology, and quantum mechanics. For more in-depth insights, interested readers can refer to his YouTube videos. The captivating aspect lies in how Haramein has imaginatively conceived the appearance of a Tetragrammaton, drawing inspiration from Kabbalistic concepts originating from earlier forms of Jewish mysticism, particularly the Four Worlds.

The first world is Atziluth, the World of Emanation, representing the purest essence of divine energy. It is the realm where the divine will and intention originate, transcending the boundaries of physicality. In this ethereal realm, the divine presence is experienced in its most pristine form.

Moving to the second world, we encounter Briah, the World of Creation. Here, the divine energy takes shape and becomes more structured, forming the blueprint for all existence. It is a realm of intellect, wisdom, and contemplation, where ideas and concepts are conceived and brought into being.

The third world, Yetzirah, is known as the World of Formation. Within this realm, divine energy begins to manifest in more tangible and perceptible ways. It is a realm of emotion, where spiritual forces are channeled and shaped into various forms. Yetzirah is a realm of artistic expression and transformative energies, where the inner becomes outwardly visible.

Finally, we arrive at the fourth world, Assiyah, the World of Action. This is the realm of materiality and physicality, where the divine energy is fully realized and expressed through the physical realm. In Assiyah, the divine presence permeates every aspect of creation, and human beings play an active role in manifesting the divine will on Earth.

Isaiah 43:7 beautifully captures the essence of these Four Worlds, stating, "Everyone who is called by my name, whom I created for my glory, whom I formed and made." This scripture highlights the interconnectedness of these realms, emphasizing the divine purpose behind creation and the inherent glory imbued within every individual.

In my personal experiences, I have observed our Heavenly Father manifesting with a playful essence, reminiscent of a beloved grandfather. It is through the ethereal display of a cloud-like face that a mesmerizing exhibition of quantum geometry emerges. This intricate arrangement of shapes and patterns resembles the delicate strokes of an artist's brush, unveiling the essence of God in a captivating and artistic manner.

In His boundless generosity, our Heavenly Father graciously reveals an image of a wise and aged figure to us. This divine depiction features distinct characteristics, such as a prominent nose and a flowing beard, symbolizing wisdom and experience. It is a precious gift, granting us a glimpse into the profound depths of wisdom and guidance that emanate from His whimsical divine presence. This divine visage takes on a shape reminiscent of the tetragrammaton, further enriching its significance.

Harnessing the vast canvas of the sky, our Heavenly Father masterfully crafts a magnificent picture that is visible to all. With remarkable skill, He utilizes the elements of nature to embody the consciousness of "I AM." Nature itself becomes a medium through which His profound presence is expressed, showcasing His divine artistry and the interconnectedness between the natural world and the divine consciousness.

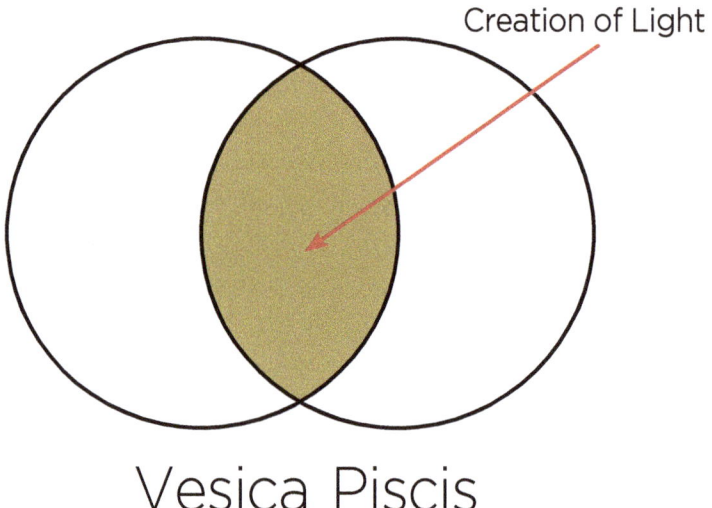

Vesica Piscis

Figure 11: Image of the shape of a VESICA PISCES

The Vesica Pisces is a symbol in sacred geometry that holds great significance and is derived from the intersection of two overlapping circles. It creates a shape resembling a pointed oval or almond. The term "Vesica Pisces" is derived from Latin and translates to "vessel of the fish."

In sacred geometry, the Vesica Pisces is considered a symbol of profound unity and the interplay between duality and oneness. It represents the merging of two opposing forces or principles, often associated with the masculine and feminine aspects of creation, light and dark, or yin and yang. The overlapping region of the circles symbolizes the point of connection or intersection between these opposing elements.

The Vesica Pisces is seen as a portal or doorway, a space where new creations emerge. It is believed to be a womb-like symbol, representing fertility, birth, and the potential for creation and transformation. The shape has been associated with divine feminine energy and is linked to various goddess figures in different cultures.

This symbol also has connections to spiritual and religious traditions. In Christianity, the Vesica Pisces is related to the "Ichthys" symbol, which resembles a fish and represents Jesus Christ. The Vesica Pisces is formed when two circles intersect at a specific ratio, known as the "divine proportion" or the "golden ratio," which is considered a harmonious and aesthetically pleasing ratio in art and design.

The Vesica Pisces holds a deep metaphysical and symbolic meaning, representing the interconnection and balance of opposing forces, the potential for creation and transformation, and the sacred union of masculine and feminine energies. It invites contemplation on the nature of duality and unity, and the profound mysteries of existence.

Jesus the second person of the trinity takes a form showing self-illumination inside the shape of the Vesica Pisces. Among the clouds, Jesus materializes in a human form, fully embodying the essence of flesh and bone. This incarnation portrays him as younger than his father, yet still bearing a genetic lineage and displaying prominent features that reflect his Jewish cultural identity. Through this tangible depiction, Jesus unveils his divine presence in a relatable and recognizable form, acting as a bridge between the realms of the divine and the human.

The Vesica Pisces is an essential component of the Flower of Life pattern in sacred geometry. The Flower of Life is created by repeating the Vesica Pisces shape multiple times in a specific geometric arrangement.

To construct the Flower of Life, you start with a single Vesica Pisces by overlapping two circles of the same size so that the center of each circle lies on the circumference of the other. This creates the distinctive pointed oval shape. Next, additional Vesica Pisces shapes are formed by connecting the centers of neighboring circles in a hexagonal pattern. By repeating this process, the circles and Vesica Pisces shapes interlock, creating a complex network of overlapping circles and interconnecting Vesica Pisces shapes.

The repetition of the Vesica Pisces within the Flower of Life creates a symmetrical and harmonious geometric pattern. The interplay between the circles and Vesica Pisces forms intricate flower-like shapes, hence the name "Flower of Life." Each circle and Vesica Pisces shape within the pattern is connected, representing the interconnectedness and unity of all things.

THE TRANSFORMATIVE POWER OF DRAWING THE FLOWER OF LIFE: UNVEILING COSMIC UNITY AND DIVINE CONNECTION

Figure 12: Image of the FLOWER OF LIFE

The Flower of Life is a significant symbol in sacred geometry. It is a complex and intricate pattern consisting of overlapping circles forming a flower-like shape. This symbol holds deep spiritual and metaphysical meaning across various cultures and belief systems.

The Flower of Life is often associated with the creation of the universe and represents the interconnectedness of all living beings. It is believed to contain the fundamental forms and proportions found in nature, as well as the blueprint of creation itself. Many consider it to be a visual representation of the divine or cosmic energy.

The Flower of Life symbol, with its widespread presence, has been unearthed in numerous locations throughout ancient antiquity. Notably, it has been identified at the Temple of Osiris in Egypt, as well as in diverse regions such as ancient Greece, Turkey, India, Mexico, and China, among others. Its appearance in these varied cultures emphasizes its broad geographical and cultural significance across different civilizations of the past.

Drawing the Flower of Life using a protractor can be a powerful and meditative practice. By engaging in this creative act, you establish a direct connection with the principles of sacred geometry and tap into the universal harmony and unity that it represents. It allows you to participate in the act of creation and align yourself with the cosmic energies that flow through the pattern.

When you take the time to draw the Flower of Life, you not only create a physical representation of this sacred symbol but also cultivate a deeper understanding of its geometric intricacies. This hands-on experience enhances your connection to the cosmos and expands your awareness of the underlying order and unity in the universe.

Engaging with the Flower of Life through drawing can be a transformative experience, as it encourages contemplation, focus, and a sense of being in harmony with the larger cosmic web. It serves as a reminder of the interconnectedness of all things and invites you to explore the profound mysteries and wisdom embedded within sacred geometry.

So, acquiring a protractor and drawing the Flower of Life can be a meaningful endeavor, allowing you to connect with the universal forces and gain insight into the profound unity that underlies existence. Once I began this practice it helped reinforce the divinity that resides within all beings.

Furthermore, within certain photographs I have captured, you will notice a remarkable transformation in the aura that surrounds the immaculate presence of Jesus. As he gradually dissolves into himself, the aura that previously took the shape of the vesica Pisces undergoes a metamorphosis, morphing into a hexagon. In sacred geometry, the hexagon holds great significance as a symbol of creation and manifestation. It represents the unity between heaven and earth, symbolizing the profound connection between the divine realms and the material world.

In sacred geometry, the dodecahedron and icosahedron are two of the five Platonic solids, which are three-dimensional shapes with regular polygonal faces and symmetrical properties. Each of these solids holds symbolic significance and is believed to embody certain qualities or principles.

Figure 13: Image of ICOSAHEDRON

Figure 14: Image of DODECAHEDRON

The dodecahedron is a polyhedron with twelve regular pentagonal faces. It has been associated with the concept of the universe or cosmos in various ancient civilizations. Some cultures considered it a symbol of divine knowledge, representing the harmony and order of the cosmos. In Plato's philosophy, the dodecahedron was linked to the element of the universe known as the "Aether," which was thought to be the substance that filled the celestial sphere.

The icosahedron, on the other hand, is a polyhedron with twenty equilateral triangle faces. It has been associated with the element of water and is often regarded as a symbol of fluidity, change, and creativity. The icosahedron's dynamic and flowing nature is thought to represent the ever-changing aspects of life and the interconnectedness of all things.

Both the dodecahedron and icosahedron hold significance beyond their individual qualities. In certain esoteric traditions, they are believed to be archetypal forms that reflect fundamental principles of existence. Some practitioners of sacred geometry believe that meditating on or working with these shapes can foster a deeper connection with the underlying patterns of the universe and promote spiritual growth and understanding.

In my holy photograph the Holy Spirit, in its state of blessedness, emanates in a manner that evokes the image of a geometric and polyhedral prism of light. This radiant manifestation reflects a stunning visage, reminiscent of a multi-dimensional and multi-faceted dodecahedral or icosahedral rainbow. Furthermore, it exudes an energetic presence infused with electromagnetic properties, resonating with a vast range of frequencies and vibrations. Its vibrant hues encompass shades ranging from scarlet and carnelian to jasper and emerald-green. In essence, the Holy Spirit embodies mysterious qualities that bear resemblance to crystalline structures. Within its electromagnetic pulse lies a frequency of existence that transcends the constraints of time, where whispers of synchronicity weave through the air, signifying the interconnection of entangled minds and hints of the afterlife.

Sacred geometry teaches us that we are co-creators of our reality. Just as geometric patterns emerge from simple elements, we have the power to shape our world through our thoughts, intentions, and actions. By collectively embracing the principles of sacred geometry, such as balance, harmony, and unity, we can actively participate in creating a better world. We tap into the inherent goodness and potential within ourselves to work together to manifest a more harmonious and compassionate reality.

The concepts of sacred geometry have also become prominent in popular culture, as seen in the Walt Disney documentary-style cartoon featuring Donald Duck titled "Donald in Mathmagic Land" that was released in 1959.

In the cartoon, Donald is transported to "Mathmagic Land" where he learns about the mathematical principles and patterns found in nature, art, and architecture—which are core ideas behind sacred geometry. The cartoon was able to make the abstract concepts of sacred geometry accessible and engaging for a mainstream audience. It helped bring these ideas about the inherent mathematics in nature.

In the realm of sacred geometry, the statement "The truth has a way of revealing itself" resonates deeply. Sacred geometry is a universal language that transcends cultural boundaries and serves as a bridge between the seen and the unseen, the material and the spiritual. It is believed that within the intricate patterns and symmetries of sacred geometry lie fundamental truths about the nature of existence.

Moreover, when truth is expressed and shared, it brings about a sense of peace. In the realm of sacred geometry, the harmonious proportions and symmetries found in nature reflect a state of equilibrium and tranquility. By expressing and embodying truth, we contribute to this state of peace, both within ourselves and in the world around us.

The exploration of these truths requires an open and willing mind. Sacred geometry invites us to delve into its profound mysteries, encouraging us to explore the hidden dimensions of reality. It beckons those who are curious and receptive to venture beyond the surface, to dive deeper into the profound wisdom that lies within.

Quantum physics explores the behavior of matter and energy at the smallest scales. One of the key principles of quantum physics is the idea that the act of observation or measurement affects the system being observed. This is often referred to as the observer effect or the measurement problem. It suggests that our perspective and the act of observing can influence and shape the manifestation of what we perceive.

This idea aligns with the notion in sacred geometry that our individual viewpoints and intentions play a fundamental role in shaping our reality. Sacred geometry, in its exploration of symmetrical and harmonious forms, reflects a deeper understanding of the underlying patterns and structure of the universe. By working with these forms, some practitioners believe they can tap into a universal language or blueprint that connects them to a greater cosmic order.

The convergence between sacred geometry and quantum physics hints at the interplay between consciousness, perception, and the fundamental fabric of the universe. It suggests that our thoughts, intentions, and perspectives have the potential to influence and shape our experiences of reality. This doesn't imply that individual perspectives create the entirety of reality, but rather that there is a dynamic relationship between our consciousness and the world we perceive.

By exploring the truths embedded within sacred geometry and embracing the insights offered by quantum physics, individuals may embark on a transformative journey of self-discovery and a deeper understanding of the interconnectedness of all things. It encourages an exploration of the relationship between our consciousness, the physical world, and the underlying principles that govern them.

As we awaken to self-discovery, we recognize our conscious nature and the immense power we possess for creation. We also understand that we are intricately connected and reliant on one another. Our journey of evolution involves a continuous process of divine manifestation within us, through us, and as us. The Buddha's wisdom reminds us to verify our beliefs through personal experience.

Within us lies an inherent reservoir of wisdom, waiting for the right circumstances to bloom and grow. Each person is granted the opportunity to discover their true essence and undergo personal development. When we comprehend our interconnectedness and value compassion, unity, and social justice, we wholeheartedly embrace our human existence. By offering assistance to our fellow beings, we contribute to a collective endeavor to build a better world. In doing so, we authentically embrace the inherent goodness that resides within each and every one of us.

13

JOURNEY THROUGH SACRED REALMS: EXPLORING SHAMANISM AND MEDITATION

SHAMANIC JOURNEYING IS AN ANCIENT SPIRITUAL PRACTICE THAT allows individuals to tap into energetic frequencies and connect with the vast realm of possibilities. It involves entering an altered state of consciousness, often achieved through meditation, drumming, singing, chanting, dancing, or mindfulness. By opening the mind to receive information and insights from the unseen realms, one can access spiritual energies and gain profound understanding.

Rooted in indigenous traditions, shamanic journeying has also found its place in contemporary settings, attracting those seeking personal transformation and spiritual exploration. Through the power of thought, prayer, and communication with spirits, ancestors, angels, plants, and animals, individuals can engage in ritualistic practices to harness healing and transformation.

Setting intentions and being present within oneself create a shamanic journey, where thoughts shape reality and faith expands the possibilities of multi-dimensional experiences. It is a deeply personal and individual process, with unique details, symbols, and encounters varying from person to person. The practice relies on intuition, openness, and a willingness to engage with the spiritual realms.

Shamanic journeying is seen as a means to gain insights into personal or collective issues, fostering personal growth, self-discovery, and seeking guidance in life's questions. Its potential reaches beyond cultural boundaries, adapting to contemporary contexts while honoring its indigenous origins. Ultimately, it offers a gateway to connect with the unseen, access spiritual wisdom, and facilitate profound healing and transformative experiences.

The Shaman, a seeker of inner truth, discovers serenity and devotes themselves to sacred unity. They are beckoned by the spiritual essence, venturing deep into the essence of the universe. Within this profound encounter, they connect with the ancestral beings of timeless realms and gain a profound understanding of the ever-present cycles of existence.

In the heart of the cosmos, the Shaman finds reconciliation and consecration, becoming attuned to the harmony of the divine. They are called forth by the guiding Spirit, embarking on a journey into the very soul of the universe. In this sacred experience, they commune with the wise ancestors of eternal realms, attaining profound insights into the prevailing rhythms of life.

In his book "The Strong Eye of Shamanism," Robert E. Ryan explains that the shaman has the ability to internalize myth, transforming traditional beliefs into concrete mystical experiences. By internalizing this wisdom, the shaman establishes a direct communication channel with the source of enlightenment. As their understanding crystallizes, it becomes the vehicle that guides the shaman towards their destined path. It is through this process that the mind's self-revelation takes shape, evolving into the spiritual essence—the strong eye of the shaman.[63]

UNVEILING THE SHAMANIC REALM: A JOURNEY INTO SACRED ENERGIES AND SPIRITUAL CONNECTIONS

During my exploration of Shamanic energy, I ventured into an alternate realm of vibrant energies. I came to understand that we are beings composed of frequency and vibration. In this state, I could forge a deep connection with the natural world and tap into the subtle life force energy that permeates all things. The discoveries I made were abundant and transformative. I had the remarkable ability to interact with elemental beings and receive profound insights and knowledge from their energetic vibrations. It was a mystical and esoteric experience.

Within this realm, I encountered Earth Spirits, Angels, and animal spirits such as the whale, each intimately connected with and embodying the essence of their respective domains. From the gentle sway of flowers to the towering wisdom of trees, from the crystalline formations of stones to the majestic presence of the whale, I delved into the energetic realms of these magnificent beings. I was astounded by the hidden pathways of extraordinary expression.

My focus extended to the animal spirits, such as the whale, whose presence resonated deeply within me. By attuning myself to their unique vibrations, I experienced profound moments of connection and insight. The whale, with its immense size and graceful movements, carried within it a wisdom that stirred my soul. Through this connection, I delved into the depths of their energetic presence, receiving messages and guidance that enriched my journey.

In these moments, I was immersed in a world where the secrets of nature unfolded, and I became a part of a symphony of energies. It was a time of profound awe and wonder as I tapped into the essence of the elements, the animal spirits, and the beings that embodied them.

I've had some truly captivating encounters while working with pine trees, and I can't help but feel that they hold a profound significance as a guide for humanity's understanding of itself. Before my enlightening interaction with the Blessed Holy Mother, I delved into the energetic realm of Marigold flowers that I cultivated on the Farm. Likewise, prior to my profound experience with "I AM," I explored the power of crystals to unlock and enhance my third-eye chakra vision.

MARY'S GOLDEN EMBRACE: EXPLORING THE SPIRITUAL SYMBOLISM OF MARIGOLDS FOR GROWTH, ENLIGHTENMENT, AND SELF-REALIZATION

Marigolds hold a profound spiritual meaning, representing growth, enlightenment, and self-realization. They carry deep symbolism associated with the spiritual power of resurrection, regeneration, and renewal. Interestingly, the common name "Marigold" derives from "Mary's Gold," further emphasizing its spiritual connotations.

In various religious ceremonies in Nepal, Marigolds hold great importance and are used to adorn Hindu temples in India. Additionally, in Mexico, they are considered the flower of the dead and are used to decorate altars during the Day of the Dead celebration.

Personally, whenever I encounter a Marigold flower, it serves as a constant reminder of the blessed Holy Mother. This is because I was actively working with the energetic frequency of Marigolds when I had my profound visitation with her. Each Marigold blossom becomes a living memorial of her divine presence and the radiant golden light of resurrection that she embodies.

Marigolds, with their vibrant colors and spiritual significance, invite us to reflect on the transformative power of spirituality and the eternal cycle of life. They serve as a beautiful reminder of the connection between the earthly realm and the sacred dimensions beyond, stirring a sense of wonder and awe within us.

THE SACRED WISDOM OF PINE TREES AND PINECONES: EXPLORING NATURE'S RESERVOIR OF LOVE, STRENGTH, AND SPIRITUAL INSIGHT

Nature possesses an immense reserve of wisdom, strength, and love. My encounters with pine trees and pinecones have been particularly fascinating, as they seem to embody a universal wisdom that can illuminate our path. During my shamanic training, we were taught various energetic practices, including connecting with plants and animal spirits. I was drawn to forge a special bond with pine trees, mesmerized by their distinctive geometric patterns and their role as vessels for the seeds of new life.

Interestingly, the pinecone has been attributed with powerful symbolism, representing concepts such as regeneration, resurrection, and fertility. It serves as a vessel, holding the seeds that perpetuate the cycle of life for pine trees. Depictions of Hindu deities often portray them holding pinecones, while ancient Assyrian palace carvings depict winged figures grasping these symbolic objects. Even the Egyptian staff of Osiris showcases two spiraling snakes ascending towards a pinecone. These diverse depictions suggest that the pinecone is a symbol of spiritual consciousness and enlightenment.

Remarkably, the Catholic Church also incorporates pinecones in its iconography. One notable example is the 'Fontana della Pingna,' a grand bronze pinecone that adorns the wall of the Vatican, facing the Cortile della Pigna. Originally situated near the Pantheon and close to the Temple of Isis, it was later moved to the courtyard of the Old St. Peter's Basilica during the Middle Ages. It is intriguing to note that the Pope himself carries a sacred staff adorned with a carved pinecone. This cone represents the all-seeing third eye, possessing the extraordinary ability to perceive beyond the ordinary. It symbolizes spiritual insight and awareness that transcends the confines of the physical realm.

The experiences I've had with pine trees, pinecones, marigold flowers, and crystals have unveiled a deeper understanding of the interconnectedness between nature, spirituality, and human consciousness. They serve as profound guides, inviting us to explore and embrace the vast realms of knowledge and enlightenment that lie beyond our everyday perception.

SACRED BONDS:
CONNECTING WITH ANIMAL SPIRITS
FOR SPIRITUAL GROWTH

During my exploration of the chakras with the Shaman, we incorporated spirit animals to enhance our connection with each energy center. While I won't delve into every animal we encountered, I want to share my experience with a remarkable creature during my exploration of the throat chakra—the magnificent whale.

The whale, symbolizing the element of water and its association with the throat chakra, holds deep significance in the realm of communication. This majestic spirit animal embodies qualities of awareness, intuition, and the power of our inner voice. By connecting with the whale, I was encouraged to listen attentively to its wisdom, allowing it to guide me toward a better understanding of my own desires and aspirations. It urged me to have faith in my abilities and to trust the calling of my heart.

Working with the whale as a spirit animal not only deepened my connection to the throat chakra but also taught me the importance of embracing conscious communication and the significance of listening to the inner wisdom that resides within us. It was a profound journey of self-discovery and a reminder to honor the power of our own voice in expressing our truth.

WHISPERING SEAS:
THE ENCHANTING SONG OF THE WHALE

The spirit of the whale is often associated with various symbolic meanings and spiritual significance. Whales are revered creatures, known for their immense size, intelligence, and gracefulness in the water. Many cultures and indigenous traditions hold deep reverence for whales and consider them to be highly spiritual beings.

Connecting with the spirit of the whale involves tapping into the qualities and energies associated with these majestic creatures. Here are some aspects often associated with the spirit of the whale:

◊ **Wisdom and Awareness:** Whales are believed to possess profound wisdom and a deep level of consciousness. Connecting with their spirit can help individuals access higher knowledge, gain insights, and expand their awareness of the world around them.

◊ **Intuition and Emotional Depth:** Whales are highly intuitive animals, known for their strong emotional bonds and deep empathy. By connecting with their spirit, individuals can enhance their own intuition, emotional intelligence, and ability to connect with others on a deeper level.

◊ **Communication and Expression:** Whales are known for their intricate communication systems, involving songs and complex vocalizations. The spirit of the whale can inspire individuals to improve their communication skills, express themselves more effectively, and listen attentively to others.

◊ **Inner Peace and Emotional Healing:** Observing the gentle, peaceful nature of whales in their natural environment can evoke a sense of tranquility and inner peace. Connecting with their spirit can help individuals find solace, release emotional burdens, and embark on a journey of healing and self-discovery.

To connect with the spirit of the whale, you can try the following practices:

◊ **Meditation and Visualization:** Find a quiet and peaceful space to meditate and visualize yourself surrounded by the vastness of the ocean. Envision the presence of whales, their energy, and their spirit connecting with you. Allow yourself to absorb their qualities and wisdom.

◊ **Symbolic Representations:** Surround yourself with symbols or artwork that represent whales, such as paintings, sculptures, or jewelry. These visual reminders can serve as focal points for connecting with the spirit of the whale.

◊ **Nature Immersion:** Spend time in nature, particularly near bodies of water. Observe the natural world around you and cultivate a sense of reverence and respect for all living beings. This can help you attune to the energy of the whale and the interconnectedness of all life. I do not live near the ocean but was still able to connect with these lovely beings. You can also listen to whale sounds and simply send your consciousness to the sea uniting with them on your journey.

◊ **Dreamwork and Journaling:** Pay attention to any dreams or recurring symbols related to whales. Keep a dream journal to record your experiences and insights. Reflecting on these dreams can provide valuable guidance and deeper connections with the spirit of the whale.

Remember, connecting with animal spirits is a personal and individual experience. The spirit of the whale may reveal itself to you in unique ways, so trust your intuition and allow yourself to be open to the wisdom and guidance it offers. I am grateful to have been guided by remarkable mentors in my journey towards exploring these mystical realms. Shaman Sandra Ingerman, author of "Walking in Light," and Eliot Cowan, author of "Plant Spirit Medicine," have been sources of inspiration for me. They have shared their wisdom and teachings, empowering me to open myself to the wonders of these otherworldly dimensions.

In our world, there are numerous natural Shamans, each with their unique gifts for working with nature in various ways. Some have mastered the art of harnessing the spirit energy of the sun and water, transmuting and purifying it into a higher vibrational state. As a Cloud Shaman, I am attuned to the energetic frequencies that coexist with us, whether recognized by humanity or not. The sky holds a vast reservoir of consciousness and abundance. I firmly believe that within each of us lies the potential to connect with the unseen world. We possess the power and ability to transform our reality by working with the elemental energies that surround us, utilizing the immense potential of our minds, our emotions, and our positive intentions.

The story of Jesus calming the stormy waters in the Sea of Galilee and walking across the sea to his disciples is a powerful metaphor. It signifies the extraordinary abilities that lie within us, waiting to be discovered and harnessed. Jesus encouraged Peter to join him in walking on water, symbolizing the limitless potential that exists beyond the confines of our natural laws. While Peter's ambition was strong, he had yet to fully realize his own strength and potential to defy the limitations of our human nature.

In the exploration of these realms, we find ourselves in the company of enlightened teachers, ancient wisdom, and the boundless power of the unseen world. It is an invitation to embrace our own innate abilities and embark on a transformative journey of self-discovery and connection with the extraordinary forces that surround us.

In learning to understand our true divine nature we can overcome obstacles in our path. The power of our mind combined with positive intention can indeed transfigure our reality into a more blissful spiritual state, becoming radiant like the dawn.

From the Shamanic perspective when working with Nature you can unmask the material world and become part of the vortex of interdimensional reality that does exist. There are portals of consciousness you can connect with.

Learning to work with your imagination is an important tool to open these gateways. Remembering you are not only a body in your human experience but a Mind and Spirit too and realizing we are connected to a universal Mind and Spirit that transcends space and time and part of a loving infinite intelligence will create a new paradigm and worldview for you to know yourself.

Einstein famously said "Imagination is more important than knowledge. For knowledge is limited, whereas imagination embraces the entire world."[64]

Shamans play an important role in our society. Shamans interact with the unseen world of God, demons, and ancestral spirits. Shamans are healers, spiritual guides, and counselors and can help communities raise consciousness and connect with ascended masters, angelic realms, and elemental forces.

Shamans can read the land and understand its frequency and vibration and cultural ancestral spirits from far before our time as inhabitants on Earth. Shamans have a responsibility to empower our culture to heal itself and release fears and heal the land, purify the water, our sun, and our hearts for a greater more abundant, and loving future.

Planted within our being, we have seeds of wisdom that we can draw upon. We can have transformative encounters in the sacred spaces that we create within ourselves. Life-giving truth from the deep wellspring of emerging reality sits within us like a tap root anchored in a great knowing waiting for us to become aware.

AWAKENING THE PATH OF WISDOM: HARNESSING THE POWER OF MEDITATION FOR CLARITY AND DISCERNMENT

"Meditation brings wisdom; lack of meditation leaves ignorance. Know well what leads you forward and what holds you back and choose the path that leads to wisdom."[65]

For the Buddha, however, nothing could substitute for the direct experience of meditation. "Do not accept something merely from tradition or out of blind faith," he says. "Do not accept it even on the word of your teacher. Ehi passika: go and see for yourself, through the practice of meditation."[66]

The Buddha's teachings offered me a bountiful harvest of wisdom, allowing me to perceive and comprehend my suffering in profound ways. These teachings became potent tools, essential ingredients that facilitated my awakening and shattered the illusions I once held.

Establishing a sacred space for meditation, a sanctuary where I could delve into the depths of my spiritual essence, played a pivotal role in this transformative journey. Through this sacred practice, I cultivated the ability to quiet the restless chatter of my mind, enabling me to perceive energy and recognize myself as pure consciousness.

In this state of heightened awareness, consciousness revealed itself to me, radiant and luminous, akin to the dancing and glimmering light upon the water.

Engaging with archetypal figures like the Buddha, the Blessed Holy Mother, Jesus, or the Great Corn Mother can be immensely valuable as we embark on a journey of awakening. Jesus, in particular, assumed the role of my shepherd and a cherished companion, guiding me and providing solace during arduous times when my soul cried out in the vast wilderness. He met me in the sanctuary of my heart, declaring, "Here I am," and became my steadfast support through trials and tribulations. Witnessing his grace, mercy, and selfless service to humanity ignited a passionate flame within my own heart, inspiring me to follow a similar path of compassion and devotion.

BEAUTY AND DEVOTION: DISCOVERING THE EXTRAORDINARY IN EVERYDAY MOMENTS

Beauty and devotion are intertwined forces that have the power to transform our lives. When we wholeheartedly devote ourselves to seeking and appreciating the beauty that surrounds us, life responds in kind, offering us more beauty and devotion. In a world often overshadowed by wars and politics, it is essential to consciously choose to find and embrace beauty, even in the smallest of moments. This conscious choice can lead us to remarkable personal growth and bring about a shift in our perception of the world. By cultivating gratitude and realizing the beauty that exists in our lives, we can navigate even the most challenging circumstances with renewed hope and resilience.

In the face of adversity, it may seem difficult to find beauty or reasons to be grateful. However, it is precisely in these challenging moments that the power of devotion to beauty becomes most evident. Consider an example of a person going through a difficult time, perhaps struggling with a personal loss or a setback in their career.

Instead of getting caught up in negativity or despair, this person chooses to focus on finding beauty in the midst of their hardship. They might notice the warmth of a gentle smile from a stranger or the soothing sound of raindrops on their window. They might find solace in the comforting presence of a loved one or discover a renewed appreciation for the simple pleasures of life, such as savoring a cup of tea or watching a breathtaking sunset.

By devoting their attention to these moments of beauty and expressing gratitude for what they do have, a shift occurs within them. They begin to see the world in a different light, recognizing the interconnectedness of all things and the resilience of the human spirit. The realization dawns that even in the midst of challenges, beauty can be found and cherished.

Beauty extends beyond material possessions or external appearances. It encompasses the intangible elements that bring joy and meaning to our lives. The beauty of the universe manifests in the energies that surround us, the vibrant colors of a sunrise or sunset, the infectious laughter of children, the delicate blooming of an orchid, the loving bond between parents and their children, the majesty of trees, and the nourishment of deep and meaningful friendships.

When we actively seek out and appreciate these aspects of beauty, we become more attuned to the wonders of the world. Our senses are awakened, and we develop a profound sense of gratitude for the richness of life. This gratitude transforms us from within, allowing us to approach each day with a renewed sense of purpose, joy, and interconnectedness.

In conclusion, it is when you are devoted to the beauty of life that life responds with more beauty and devotion back to you. Beauty and devotion are transformative forces that have the power to elevate our lives. By choosing to devote ourselves to seeking and appreciating the beauty that surrounds us, we invite more beauty and devotion into our experience.

Even in the face of adversity, by finding reasons to be grateful and focusing on the beauty in the universe, we can navigate life's challenges with resilience and hope. The simple act of noticing and valuing the beauty in everyday moments can bring about a profound shift in our perception.

Let us recognize and cherish the extraordinary in the ordinary, cultivating gratitude for what we do have, and allowing beauty and devotion to shape our lives in profound ways. As we devote ourselves to finding beauty in both the material and immaterial aspects of life, we open ourselves up to the abundance of beauty and devotion that surrounds us.

By choosing to see and appreciate the beauty in the world, we become active participants in creating a more beautiful and compassionate society. Let us embrace the power of gratitude and devotion to beauty, knowing that our choices have the ability to not only transform ourselves but also inspire and uplift those around us.

May we continue to seek and celebrate the beauty that exists in moments, energies, connections, and the wonders of the universe. Through our devotion to beauty, we can create a ripple effect of joy, kindness, and love that extends far beyond ourselves.

In my journey, I followed the path of Bhakti Yoga. Bhakti Yoga is a spiritual path in the yogic tradition that emphasizes the cultivation of love, devotion, and surrender to a personal deity or a higher power. The term "bhakti" is derived from the Sanskrit word that means "devotion" or "love."

Bhakti Yoga is a path of wondrous devotion, a sacred journey that traverses the realms of love and surrender. It beckons us to cultivate the fire of divine love within our hearts, to immerse ourselves in the boundless stream of unconditional devotion. With each beat of our soul's longing, we draw closer to the object of our adoration, the personal deity, or the mighty higher power.

Know that this devotion is far more than lofty aspirations or fleeting desires. It is a profound essence, an uncompromising love that knows no bounds. It transcends the realm of expectations, fears, and rivalries, for it seeks nothing in return. It is love in its purest form, unadulterated and unconditional. Its purpose is to dissolve into the eternal dance of divine love, to merge effortlessly with the cosmic currents.

When one is truly touched by the flames of love, the object of adoration becomes the pinnacle of their existence. In the realm of bhakti, love reigns supreme. It is an intense and fervent emotion, a passionate longing that surpasses the realms of the physical and the mundane. It is a contemplation so profound that the lover and the beloved become one, boundaries dissolve, and separateness fades away. In this mystical union, the entirety of creation is embraced, for the beloved is none other than the Supreme Self, the Creator and creation intertwined.

Such oneness brings fulfillment beyond measure. It is the sweet nectar of eternal bliss that permeates every fiber of our being. Throughout the tapestry of diverse cultures and spiritual traditions, the concept of unity with the Supreme, the communion with the divine, resonates in myriad forms. Love is a universal language, and its spiritual manifestation is even more so.

In ancient Greece, Plato, a wise philosopher, spoke of the idea of good as an all-encompassing ideal that can be compared to the modern notion of God. According to Plato, love for the divine is a spiritual love that helps the soul recognize the true essence of existence. He proclaimed that to truly know the idea of good, one must become the idea of good. This statement emphasizes that genuine understanding and insight into goodness or virtue arise from personal experience and embodiment. Merely observing goodness from a distance is insufficient; one must actively live, embody, and integrate goodness into their being. This concept encourages us to go beyond passive observation and engage actively with the ideals we seek to comprehend.

The great mystic Spinoza delved into the depths of love, providing a profound perspective on its nature. According to Spinoza, love can be understood as the intelligent love of God. It represents the very love through which God loves Himself, a divine embrace that surpasses the boundaries of mortal comprehension. Spinoza's exploration reveals love as a transcendent force that connects humanity to the divine, offering a glimpse into the profound and limitless nature of this powerful emotion.

By embracing the path of Bhakti Yoga, a transformative spiritual practice, we open ourselves to profound experiences. Through this path, we embark on a journey towards union with the divine, unlocking the ecstasy of oneness and attaining the eternal bliss that awaits the devoted soul. Bhakti Yoga, with its emphasis on devotion and love, offers a structured approach to cultivating a deep and intimate connection with the divine. It is through this dedicated practice that we can unveil the profound spiritual experiences and the enduring joy that lies within the realm of the devoted heart.

Living as a seed grower and deeply connected to the land, I had the privilege of nurturing a profound relationship with the wisdom teachings of the Great Corn Mother. Throughout my journey, I immersed myself in the vibrational essence of the land that enveloped me. The majestic trees, vibrant flowers, and abundant seeds—they all whispered their secrets to me, revealing the bounty of nature's offerings. By opening myself to the possibility of receiving these gifts, my cup overflowed. The Great Corn Mother became a conduit, enabling me to forge a connection with my ancestors and embrace the realm of poetic expression, allowing my creative spirit to flourish.

Our ancestors, guardians of wisdom, find expression through the vibrant tapestry of nature's existence. The Great Corn Mother, in her graceful dance with the wind, holds profound pearls of wisdom. She stands alongside her brothers and sisters, symbolizing the interconnectedness of all life. As I observed the kernels of her seed, a sense of unity and oneness enveloped me. The tassels and outstretched arms of her weathered branches, kissed by the sun, breathed life into the seeds she birthed. Each kernel is a unique entity, yet intricately linked to the collective, capable of communicating across vast distances through the genes it carries. Individually distinct, these kernels connect and pollinate through the gentle touch of the Spirit's wind, ushering forth a new realm of creation. The eternal cycle continues as those who sow the seeds of wisdom embrace the beauty and abundance they share with the world, nurturing it for generations to come.

NAVIGATING THE REALMS: FROM RELATIVE REALITY TO ABSOLUTE REALITY IN THE JOURNEY OF MEDITATION

In my spiritual journey of awakening, meditation became an important tool in helping me transcend my mind. You have to get out of your mind of everyday relative reality in order to enter into a different state of awareness or absolute reality. Meditation offers a means to delve into one's inner world and explore the depths of consciousness. Meditation nurtures a deeper connection with the divine, the transcendent. Meditation is a tool for exploring spiritual dimensions, cultivating mindfulness, and deepening one's spiritual journey. For me it allowed me to understand the concepts of relative reality and absolute reality more fully.

Relative reality refers to the everyday world that we perceive and experience through our senses. It includes the physical world, our individual identities, and the ever-changing phenomena of life. Relative reality is characterized by duality, where there are distinctions between subject and object, good and bad, pleasure and pain, and so on.

Understanding relative reality is essential because it is the realm in which we navigate our daily lives. It involves practical considerations, decision-making, and engaging with the world. However, recognizing the limitations of relative reality is also crucial. It is impermanent, constantly changing, and often subject to illusion and misperception. Over-attachment to relative reality can lead to suffering and a sense of dissatisfaction when things inevitably change.

Absolute reality, also known as ultimate reality or transcendental reality, refers to the underlying truth or fundamental nature of existence that transcends the limitations of our ordinary perception. It is often described as timeless, unchanging, and beyond duality.

Understanding absolute reality is important because it offers a deeper understanding of the nature of existence and can provide a sense of ultimate meaning and purpose. It helps to transcend the limitations of relative reality and the suffering associated with it. Many spiritual traditions assert that realizing or attaining union with absolute reality leads to liberation, enlightenment, or the realization of one's true nature.

Balancing the understanding of relative and absolute reality is often seen as important in spiritual and philosophical journeys. While relative reality demands our attention in practical matters, recognizing the illusory and impermanent nature of relative reality can help cultivate a deeper awareness of the absolute reality that underlies it. This understanding can bring about a greater sense of peace, freedom, and harmony with the larger picture of existence.

AWAKENING TO DIVINE TRUTH: SAT CHIT ANANDA AND THE POWER OF OPENING THE LENS OF AWW, WONDER, AND CURIOSITY

The Holy Spirit represents the everlasting and timeless bliss of unadulterated awareness that enlightens us and offers a glimpse of and connection to the ultimate truth. Sat Chit Ananda represents the nature of your being, encompassing peace and the joy of existence.

According to the Vedantic tradition, it signifies the knowledge of our own being. One who truly knows themselves also understands the ultimate reality. Deep within us lies an expansive ocean of bliss. Across various spiritual traditions, the essence of all religious teachings, as conveyed in their scriptures, can be distilled into a single, simple endeavor: to know oneself. In Sufi traditions, knowing oneself equates to knowing the Lord. Greek philosopher Socrates famously emphasized the importance of self-knowledge with his maxim, 'know thyself'.

Sat: Sat refers to truth or beingness. It represents the eternal and unchanging aspect of reality. It is the inherent existence that underlies all phenomena and remains constant beyond the realm of time and space.

Chit: Chit signifies consciousness or awareness. It refers to the pure and limitless awareness that perceives and knows all things. Chit is the essence of our being that transcends the limitations of the individual mind and ego.

Ananda: Ananda translates to bliss or joy. It represents the state of profound happiness and contentment that arises from realizing one's true nature and connection to the divine. Ananda is not dependent on external circumstances but rather stems from an inner realization of unity and completeness.

Together, Sat Chit Ananda represents the holistic experience of truth, consciousness, and bliss. It signifies the state of enlightenment or self-realization, where one recognizes their inherent divinity and experiences the interconnectedness of all existence.

Witnessing the blessed Holy Spirit opens a gateway to the realm of Ultimate Reality, revealing a blissful consciousness that surpasses our limited human constructs and perceptions. It grants us a glimpse into a dimension of existence filled with awe and wonder. Acknowledging this elevated state of consciousness introduces us to something entirely new and mystical, not only on a human level but also on a soul level, surpassing our previous imaginings. It is a beautiful expansion of the soul and its impact ripples through the growth of the universe and the collective consciousness. This profound state of being is where the Holy Spirit resides within us, moving and guiding us. By observing the world from this state of consciousness, characterized by awe, wonder, and curiosity, we can penetrate the veils of illusion and grasp the essence of Ultimate Reality.

EXPLORING THE ETERNAL ESSENCE: MANTRAS, UPANISHADS, AND THE SIGNIFICANCE OF OM

In my meditation practices, I used mantras to help me transcend my mind. OM is a mantra, not a symbol. A mantra is a word, phrase, or sound that is repeated either silently or aloud as a form of meditation or spiritual practice. The word "mantra" is derived from two Sanskrit words: "manas," which means mind, and "tra," which means to protect or liberate. Therefore, a mantra is often considered a sacred utterance that helps to protect the mind and liberate it from mundane thoughts and distractions. The repetition of a mantra is believed to have a calming and focusing effect on the mind, leading to a state of deep concentration and spiritual awareness.

In addition to their meditative and spiritual purposes, mantras are also believed to have transformative and healing powers. They are thought to create vibrations and energy patterns that can positively influence the practitioner's mental, emotional, and physical well-being. Some popular mantras include "Om," "Om Namah Shivaya," and "Om Mani Padme Hum," but there are countless other mantras used in different traditions and lineages.

On my spiritual journey, I was called by Spirit to read the Upanishads. You may ask how Spirit called me to do this and I'm not sure how to answer this question exactly. This information likely came through one of my clair senses such as an image dropping down into my awareness. I remember faintly seeing an image in which a teacher or guru sat next to one of the students. The universe works with us in mysterious ways to help us along the way and when we participate in this synchronicity things come into manifestation. It is important to also recognize that we are eternal beings always existing and there is likely apart of me that was able to tap into this information because I've been exposed to it before perhaps in a different incarnation.

The term "Upanishad" is derived from the Sanskrit words "upa" and "niṣad," which together mean "sitting down near" or "sitting down closely." It refers to the act of sitting down closely or intimately with a teacher or guru to receive esoteric or spiritual knowledge.

The Upanishads, which are a collection of ancient philosophical texts within Hinduism, mention OM and delve into its significance. They explore the deeper meaning and metaphysical aspects associated with the syllable.

Om was first perceived by the ancient yogis of prehistory, and it is not the exclusive property of any religion or philosophy. OM belongs to all without distinction or exclusion. It is swayambhu: self-begotten, self-existent, and self-sufficient holding the same idea as the name or word of God. It arises spontaneously within, from the Self. "One who meditates upon the self and realizes the self sees the self everywhere and rejoices in the self."[67]

The Upanishads are a collection of ancient philosophical texts within Hinduism that are considered to be the culmination of the Vedic teachings. They are often presented as dialogues or conversations between a student (disciple) and a teacher (guru), where profound spiritual and philosophical truths are revealed.

The Upanishads explore various topics such as the nature of reality, the self (Atman), the ultimate reality (Brahman), the nature of existence, the relationship between the individual and the universe, the path to liberation (Moksha), and the means to attain spiritual enlightenment.

In the Upanishads, OM is often described as the primordial sound from which the universe manifests. It is seen as the essence of all creation, representing the ultimate reality or Brahman.

The Mandukya Upanishad, in particular, is dedicated to the exploration of OM and its significance. At the core of the Mandukya Upanishad lies a profound message: "that thou art." This message encapsulates the revelation that you are not separate from Brahman, the ultimate reality. It unveils the truth that your very essence is intimately connected to that which you seek. It is natural to question how, as an individual, you can embody the qualities of the absolute, the immortal, the all-pervading, and the eternal.

Brahman, the embodiment of vastness, transcends the boundaries of space, time, and objects. It encompasses limitless expanses that stretch beyond our comprehension.

The Mandukya Upanishad teaches that you must realize the essence of the self, which has four dimensions or aspects. These aspects are the Waker (you in the waking state), the Dreamer (you in the dream state), the deep sleeper (you in deep sleep), and the Turia (the absolute). The fourth aspect represents what you are seeking.

In a similar vein, Jesus poses a profound question about the nature of our search and asserts that he himself is the very answer we seek. He invites us to recognize that the fourth aspect, which represents a deeper understanding, aims to teach, and reveal the present reality—not as something to be attained only after death, but as a tangible experience in the here and now. This teaching emphasizes that the absolute presence of God resides within each of us. It points to a profound realization regarding the essence of our being, unveiling the truth of who we truly are at our core.

The primary challenge lies in uncovering the authentic essence of your being and gaining a deep understanding of your true nature. It is natural to wonder about the whereabouts of this ultimate reality, Brahman. If you do not perceive yourself as godlike or absolute, you may question your connection to it altogether. However, Jesus taught that not only would we carry out the same miracles he did, but we would also accomplish even greater deeds (John 14:12).

At the core of our misunderstanding lies our perception of our own existence. When we shift our perspective and redefine our understanding of who we truly are, a profound transformation occurs, and our entire reality undergoes a remarkable shift. We awaken to the truth that we are beings of light and love, empowered in ways we couldn't have imagined.

As we emerge from our metaphorical slumber, our experience of life is fundamentally altered. We realize that we have always been an expression of Brahman, the ultimate reality, even though we were previously unaware of this profound connection. Now, the veil has been lifted, and you recognize that this truth has been within you all along, even if you had not consciously perceived it before. This awakening marks a significant milestone in your spiritual journey, opening the doors to a new level of self-awareness and profound realization.

The Mandukya Upanishad outlines the process of the three states: waking, dreaming, and deep sleep. It asserts that the experience required for enlightenment is already within you. You may wonder, "What experience is that?" It refers to the experiences of waking, dreaming, and deep sleep. This part urges self-investigation.

The second part of the Upanishad focuses on the syllable OM.

The Upanishads describe OM as consisting of three syllables: "A," "U," and "M." These three syllables represent different aspects of existence. The "A" represents the waking state, the "U" represents the dream state, and the "M" represents the deep sleep state. Additionally, there's a fourth aspect beyond these three, known as "Turi-ya," which represents the ultimate reality or pure consciousness.

Overall, the Upanishads provide philosophical insights into the nature of OM and its significance in understanding the nature of reality and the spiritual journey.

◊ **Mandukya Upanishad:** The Mandukya Upanishad is entirely dedicated to the explanation of the syllable OM. It states that OM represents the entirety of existence, encompassing the past, present, and future. It describes OM as the imperishable, all-encompassing Brahman, the ultimate reality.

◊ **Prashna Upanishad:** The Prashna Upanishad refers to OM as the bow, and the individual self as the arrow. It teaches that when the individual self is perfectly aligned with the transcendent reality represented by OM, it leads to the realization of the Supreme.

◊ **Katha Upanishad:** The Katha Upanishad explains that OM is the sound symbol of the Supreme Reality. It describes OM as the bridge that connects the individual self (jivatman) with the Universal Self (Paramatman). Through the practice of meditation and self-inquiry, one can traverse this bridge and merge with the eternal.

◊ **Taittiriya Upanishad:** The Taittiriya Upanishad describes OM as the essence of the Vedas and the source of all creation. It states that OM represents the three states of consciousness—waking, dreaming, and deep sleep—and the fourth state, which is beyond the three. The Upanishad teaches that those who realize the significance of OM attain liberation.

In the Taittiriya Upanishad, it is stated that "OM is a supreme symbol of the Lord.,""The student who is established in OM becomes united with the Lord of Love.[68]

OM is a mystic syllable, considered the most sacred mantra in Hinduism and Tibetan Buddhism. Supreme Consciousness that is a single syllable: OM, it is called Pranava, which means both the Word of Life and the Breath Word since prana means both life and breath. The yoga tradition says that the contemplation of the Pranava, OM, is the contemplation of our own true nature. It is the knowledge of our own Self. When the breath and OM are perfectly merged it is the major force of inner transformation- transmutation, and transfiguration.

In ancient Indian wisdom, the universe originated from an invisible and unchanging reality in a manner analogous to the expression of a profound and mystical sound, known as the "big OM," rather than through a big bang. This concept symbolizes the emergence of a sacred song, which is based on two fundamental principles discovered by ancient Indian thinkers.

If one meditates on the Supreme Being with the syllable OM, he becomes one with the Light, he is led to the world of Brahman who is higher than the highest life, that which is tranquil, un-aging, immortal, fearless and supreme" (Prashna Upanishad 5:1,5,7).

The first principle is Rita, which encompasses the idea of cosmic order and the natural laws that govern the universe. It recognizes that the physical universe operates according to inherent laws and principles. The principle of cause and effect, often referred to as karma, can be seen as a manifestation of Rita. According to the law of karma, every action has consequences, and individuals experience the effects of their actions in their lives or future lives. This principle of cause and effect is an expression of the cosmic order and the interconnectedness of all beings. Without this principle, no scientific or moral discoveries would be possible. Human experience would lack meaning, and we would have no means of learning from them.

The second principle is yajna, which translates to sacrifice. It signifies that the functioning of the universe depends on renunciation. The most significant human action involves sacrificing personal gain for the sake of something higher and more sacred. Yajnas are seen as a means of selfless giving, where offerings are made with the intention of surrendering one's ego and desires to a higher power. They also serve as a way to express gratitude and seek divine blessings for the well-being and prosperity of individuals, communities, and the entire universe.

Jesus's teachings align with the concepts of Rita and Yajna. For example:

◊ **The Golden Rule:** Jesus's teachings to "do unto others as you would have them do unto you" is in line with the principles of Rita. It emphasizes treating others with fairness, kindness, and respect, understanding that our actions towards others will ultimately have consequences for ourselves as well. The physical universe operates according to inherent natural laws, and one of these laws is the principle of cause and effect. Jesus, in teaching the golden rule of "do unto others as you would have them do unto you," was imparting the understanding of this law of cause and effect.

◊ **Love and Compassion:** Jesus emphasized the importance of love and compassion towards both God and fellow human beings. He taught his followers to love their neighbors as themselves and even to love their enemies. This teaching promotes a selfless attitude and a sense of interconnectedness with others, which aligns with the principles of harmony and unity found in Rita.

- Luke 6:27-28: "But to you who are listening I say: Love your enemies, do good to those who hate you, bless those who curse you, pray for those who mistreat you."

◊ **Selfless Service:** Jesus often emphasized the importance of serving others and putting their needs before one's own. He demonstrated this through his acts of healing, feeding the hungry, and caring for the marginalized. This selfless service can be seen as a parallel to the concept of Yajna, where one offers oneself in service to others and God.

- Mark 10:45: "For even the Son of Man did not come to be served, but to serve, and to give his life as a ransom for many." Matthew 20:26-28: "Instead, whoever wants to become great among you must be your servant, and whoever wants to be first must be your slave—just as the Son of Man did not come to be served, but to serve, and to give his life as a ransom for many."

◊ **Surrender and Trust in God:** Jesus taught his followers to surrender their will to God and trust in divine providence. This surrender involves recognizing a higher power and aligning one's life with God's plan. It echoes the idea of living in harmony with the cosmic order and acknowledging a divine plan beyond one's desires.

- Matthew 6:33: "But seek first his kingdom and his righteousness, and all these things will be given to you as well."
- Luke 22:42: "Father, if you are willing, take this cup from me; yet not my will, but yours be done."

◊ **Detachment from Material Possessions:** Jesus's teachings caution against attaching excessive importance to material possessions. He encourages his followers not to lay up treasures on earth but to seek the kingdom of God and righteousness. This aligns with the concept of yajna, as it emphasizes the sacrifice of personal attachment to worldly possessions in favor of spiritual growth and the pursuit of higher ideals.

In summary, Jesus's teachings reflect the essence of Rita and Yajna. He emphasizes the importance of treating others with fairness and kindness while also encouraging a shift in focus from material wealth to spiritual enrichment. By embodying these principles, individuals can cultivate a more harmonious and meaningful existence.

As we surrender and open ourselves to the boundless love of the divine, an extraordinary phenomenon unfolds within us—a profound awakening. It is through immersing ourselves in the present moment that we can establish a deep connection with God's presence. But here's the remarkable part: God's communication surpasses the limitations of mere words. It is a language that resonates through the very fabric of the physical world, and it reverberates in the connections we share with one another.

Consider this: each person whose life you touch becomes a canvas upon which the divine paints its masterpiece. Your example, actions, and love create ripples that gently traverse their lives, like a stone creating waves upon a serene lake. Even the blooming rose becomes a messenger of the divine's artistic prowess. As its delicate petals unfurl, it reveals a captivating amalgamation of colors and scents, igniting our senses and reminding us of the inherent beauty that lies within each of us.

So, let us embark on this extraordinary journey together. Let us surrender ourselves to the divine, immersing ourselves in the present moment. In doing so, we become conduits of divine love, embracing our role as living embodiments of the boundless love that flows through all of creation. Through surrender, presence, and love, we become harmonious participants in the symphony of existence, resonating with the profound beauty of the divine.

Engaging in acts of service towards one another on a daily basis becomes a channel for the divine essence dwelling within us to radiate outward. By selflessly offering our support, kindness, and compassion, we allow the divine light that resides within us to shine brightly, illuminating the lives of those around us.

In this state of connection and service, we embrace the divinity within ourselves and witness its transformative power. We become vessels for love and grace, embodying the essence of the divine in our thoughts, words, and actions. By awakening to the presence of God within us and nurturing this divine connection, we cultivate a life infused with purpose, joy, and a deep sense of interconnectedness with all of creation.

When we establish a connection with the natural world and remain open to its revelations, we bear witness to its immense beauty and marvels. Nature serves as a vibrant manifestation of the divine presence. It is in the embrace of nature that we can discover a multitude of gifts that God has bestowed upon us, as children of the divine. By immersing ourselves in the sights, sounds, and sensations of nature, we create a receptive space within us, allowing the spiritual gifts of the divine to flow into our lives and into our hearts.

14

DIVINE ENCOUNTERS: CAPTURING THE ESSENCE OF GOD'S UNFOLDING PRESENCE

THE MEETING OF THE WATERS

THERE is not in the wide world a valley so sweet
As that vale in whose bosom the bright waters meet;
Oh! the last rays of feeling and life must depart,
Ere the bloom of that valley shall fade from my heart.
Yet it was not that nature had shed o'er the scene
Her purest of crystal and brightest of green;
'Twas not her soft magic of streamlet or hill,
Oh! no—it was something more exquisite still.
'Twas that friends, the beloved of my bosom, were near,
Who made every dear scene of enchantment more dear,
And who felt how the best charms of nature improve,
When we see them reflected from looks that we love.
Sweet vale of Avoca! how calm could I rest
In thy bosom of shade, with the friends I love best,
Where the storms that we feel in this cold world should cease,
And our hearts, like thy waters, be mingled in peace. [69]

THOMAS MOORE (1779-1852)

IN MY WORK, I ENDEAVOR TO SHOWCASE THE PROFOUND AND sacred manifestation of the divine essence that resides within every human being. It is an awe-inspiring experience when the divine presence intertwines with humanity, revealing that we are not separate from the divine. This interaction serves as a poignant reminder that God not only hears but truly understands His children, and that His presence is intricately woven into the fabric of our lives and emotions.

With each photograph in this collection, I strive to capture and convey the image and resemblance of God as revealed to me. Through my artistic perspective, I aim to document and share the wondrous splendor of His magnificence with the world. I am eternally grateful to God for granting me the opportunity to bear witness to these extraordinary moments and to offer you a glimpse into the divine revelation that unfolded during a brief yet profound seven-minute walk.

Within the span of those seven minutes, I had the privilege of capturing approximately 25 pictures, each one a testament to this extraordinary encounter. As you embark on this visual journey, you will witness the clouds gracefully and intentionally shifting, coming together to create a scene reminiscent of the sacred Holy Trinity. It is important to remember that this unfolding does not transpire instantaneously, for God is not a static entity. Rather, He is an ever-evolving action, an ongoing process, a continuous happening.

Therefore, as you turn the pages of this collection, I kindly ask for your patience and open-heartedness, allowing each image to gradually reveal its divine essence. Take the time to immerse yourself in the beauty and significance captured within each frame. Allow yourself to be moved by the intricate details, the interplay of light and shadow, and the profound symbolism that emanates from these photographs.

May this visual journey serve as a reminder of the divine love and grace that permeates our existence, and may it awaken within you a deep recognition of the divine spark that yearns to be acknowledged. With humility and gratitude, I present to you these photographs, a testament to the majesty and splendor of God's manifestation.

This extraordinary event unfolded thirteen days after I made a heartfelt request to God, asking if I could have a picture of Him. At that particular juncture in my life, I could sense the essence of the Source vibrating through every cell of my being. It was a time of pure magic and spiritual connection.

As I was completing my daily tasks, tending to the seeds in my care, my attention was suddenly drawn to something outside my home office window. There, in the sky, a peculiar cloud caught my eye. I couldn't help but feel a deep intuitive sense that this cloud held something special—a presence beyond the ordinary. It was as if the Divine Mother herself or even a celestial spacecraft had graced the sky with its ethereal presence. I know these thoughts might seem unconventional, but there was an undeniable pull, an inexplicable magnetism that compelled me to investigate further.

Without hesitation, I gathered my trusted companions—the dogs who had become faithful walking companions and the goats who relished our shared adventures. Together, we embarked on a journey to explore the enigmatic cloud that had captured the essence of my heart.

Our 40-acre organic vegetable farm nestled in the serene landscapes of Avondale, Colorado, provided the backdrop for this extraordinary pursuit. Avondale, a small agricultural community located in Pueblo County, rests on the arid plains of Southeastern Colorado, near the majestic Front Range and the meandering Arkansas River. Surrounded by nature's beauty and the bountiful gifts of the land, our farm served as a sanctuary for growth and connection.

With my trusty 35 mm digital Nikon camera in hand, I ventured forth, drawn by an unseen force that resonated deep within my soul. The dogs wagged their tails in excitement, and the goats eagerly trotted alongside us, as if they too sensed the profound significance of our mission. Together, we set out to unravel the mysteries concealed within the captivating cloud that had beckoned me so irresistibly.

Little did I know that this seemingly ordinary walk would soon unfold into a rendezvous with the divine—a revelation of unparalleled beauty and grace that would forever alter the course of my spiritual journey. As we embarked on this quest, my heart raced with anticipation, eager to witness the truth that awaited me within the folds of the heavens.

In the next chapter of my life, I would bear witness to a celestial spectacle that would surpass all expectations—a manifestation of

God's presence that would leave an indelible mark on my soul. And so, with a mixture of curiosity, wonder, and reverence, I ventured forth, guided by the call of my heart and the promise of divine revelation.

God says, "No one calls to me without being answered." And each of us will be answered by that which we call Divine, in the way which most effectively responds to the vibration that we hold and in a form that is most appropriate to our background, our culture, our level of understanding, the level of our desire, and our willingness. [70]

THE CELESTIAL CANOPY

Each brushstroke of color, vibrant and bold,
Tells stories untold. From times of old.
A masterpiece crafted with divine precision,
An invitation to ponder life's profound vision.

As I stand beneath this celestial canopy,
I feel the presence of the Almighty, free.
In the whispers of the wind, I hear a call,
To seek the truth, to rise above it all.

The lenticular clouds, like celestial keys,
Unlock the door to a realm that frees,
My spirit to soar to reach for the light,
Guided by the Creator's celestial might.

In the cloudscape, I find solace and peace,
A moment where earthly worries cease.
For in the presence of the divine, I stand,
Connected to a power that's vast and grand.

So let me reveal in this sacred sight,
Embracing the beauty, day, or night.
For lenticular clouds and the Creator's gaze,
Illuminate the path through life's,
Complex maze.

In the heart of the farm, amidst a cluster of trees, a lenticular cloud graces the heavens, drawing my heart's attention and holding a unique significance. This remarkable sight unfolds as a symbol, a divine glimpse of our Heavenly Father's presence among us. Amidst the branches, there is one tree branch that stands out, pointing directly toward the ethereal image I am about to convey to you. A moment is frozen in time as if the heavens themselves have unveiled a breathtaking secret. Behold, the first image of our Heavenly Father, captured in a photograph that transcends the boundaries of our world.

Nature itself seems to acknowledge the profound significance of this encounter. The branches of the surrounding trees, as if guided by an unseen force, cradle, and caress His image, tenderly holding it in their embrace. It is as though they were specially placed in this very moment, bearing witness to this extraordinary occasion.

In a sight that defies all expectations, the ethereal scene unfolds before our very eyes. At first glance, one is immediately drawn to the captivating form that emerges from the magnificent canopy of lapis lazuli-colored clouds. As if a divine artist had sculpted perfection, our Heavenly Father takes shape, gracefully suspended laying on His right side. With a gaze that penetrates the depths of our souls, His veiled eyes meet ours, embracing us with an overwhelming sense of love and compassion.

Bathed in the golden hues of the sun's warm embrace, His celestial presence stands in stark contrast to the vast expanse of the heavens. The vivid blue of the clouds seems to radiate with an otherworldly luminescence, illuminating His gravity-defying being and magnifying His divine essence.

In this remarkable convergence of elements, the miracle of the moment becomes palpable. The Heavenly Father, both the embodiment of the clouds and the embodiment of love itself, reveals His boundless nature. His image calls to us, urging us to believe in the extraordinary and reminding us that the divine can manifest itself in the most unexpected forms.

Figure 15: Dunston, J. C. (2015) "DIVINE ESSENCE UNVEILED:
I AM THAT I AM, OUR BLESSED HEAVENLY FATHER"

At the focal point of this captivating photograph, the unmistakable features of a face emerge, infused with divine essence. A prominent forehead, veiled eyes, distinct nostrils, and a chin come into focus, while wavy contours of hair, particularly on the right side of His face (our left), cascade with celestial grace. His holy right arm appears raised, reaching towards the celestial realm above, as if beckoning a connection between the earthly and the divine. In this extraordinary composition, He reveals Himself amidst the branches of the mulberry tree, descending majestically within the ethereal embrace of the clouds. The image evokes a profound sense of divine power and strength as if the heavens themselves bear witness to His presence.

Adorning His chest, an emblem reminiscent of that worn by a superhero catches the eye, symbolizing His supreme nature and divine authority. It serves as a visual representation of His magnificence and the awe-inspiring qualities that define Him. This extraordinary portrayal captures the essence of our Heavenly Father, offering us a glimpse into the depths of His infinite majesty and unmatched grandeur.

As you gaze upon this photograph, allow yourself to be captivated by the divine energy it emanates. May it awaken within you a sense of wonder and reverence for the boundless power and love that reside within our Heavenly Father. Let it remind you of His ever-present guidance and unwavering support as you navigate the exhilarating landscape. May this image serve as a gentle reminder that the divine is always among us, revealing itself in the most extraordinary and unexpected ways.

As we embark on this sacred photographic journey, I invite you to join me in a profound exploration that unfolded over approximately seven minutes. It was during this time that I began to grasp the significance of God's presence, as He continued to walk alongside me, patiently allowing me to comprehend His being. While I have shared an image capturing His bodily form within the clouds, it's important to understand that God's manifestation expands beyond a singular appearance. He adapts His form and shape to align with our individual understanding and perception, gradually revealing the triune nature of His being.

In the following moments, I invite you to witness the Heavenly Father assuming a form that resonates with my personal comprehension. It is essential to acknowledge that the omniscient Father possesses the wisdom to reveal Himself in a manner that we, as finite beings, can comprehend and relate to. Through this extraordinary process, a profound revelation unfurls before our very eyes, as we bear witness to the emergence of beloved Jesus, the Son, springing forth from the very essence of the Father. Alongside Him, the extraordinarily blessed Holy Spirit makes its presence known, standing in glorious unity, thereby unveiling the concept of the Holy Trinity.

This revelation is an invitation to delve into the depths of divine mystery and ponder the interconnectedness of God's triune nature. It beckons us to contemplate the profound unity and harmonious existence of the Father, Son, and Holy Spirit, woven together in perfect harmony. As we gaze upon this miraculous image, let us open our hearts and minds to the infinite wisdom and love that emanate from the Holy Trinity, recognizing that God's divine nature surpasses our human comprehension, yet seeks to reveal Himself to us in ways that resonate with our understanding.

Through the lens of this extraordinary photograph, we are granted a glimpse into the unfathomable depths of the divine, drawing us closer to the vastness of God's presence and illuminating the intricate tapestry of the Holy Trinity. May this revelation inspire awe and reverence within us, fostering a deepening connection to the divine and a profound appreciation for the boundless love that encompasses the Father, the Son, and the blessed Holy Spirit.

In this divine revelation, the figure of the Son, who embodies both humanity and divinity, emanates from the Father as He breathes Him out of His very being. The Son takes on human form, embodying the grace, love, and teachings that have touched the hearts of countless individuals throughout history. Simultaneously, the blessed Holy Spirit manifests in a state of wondrous splendor before the church, encompassing all of humanity. It is within the collective unity of humanity, as the church, that the Holy Spirit finds its dwelling place, guiding, comforting, and empowering all who seek the divine path.

Figure 16: Dunston, J.C. (2015) "REVELATION TO ALL NATIONS:
THE LORD'S HOLY ARM UNVEILED"

"The LORD has bared his holy arm before the eyes of all the nations, and the ends of the earth shall see the salvation of our God" (Isaiah 52:10, ESV).

"Lord, who has believed our message and to whom has the arm of the Lord been revealed?" (John 12:38, NIV)

These photographs undergo a constant transformation as I journey alongside God. On the left, a plane glides across the sky, offering a sense of the passage of time. These photographs were captured as the sun was setting over the Wet Mountain Valley in Southern Colorado. I am facing west towards the horizon where the sun bids its farewell, casting hues of gold, a celestial veil.

The cloud formation itself carries a sense of grandeur and serenity. Its vast expanse and gentle presence command attention and evoke a feeling of awe. It becomes a visual representation of the divine, a symbol of the encompassing force that my heart is drawn to.

At this moment, I am captivated by the whole scene- the interplay of light and shadow, the changing sky, and the profound sense of connection with something greater guided by an inner calling. It is a reminder of the beauty and divinity that surrounds us, inviting us to embrace the journey and listen to the whispers of our hearts.

In this state of witness consciousness, I find myself captivated by the presence of this cloud. It becomes the focal point of my attention, drawing the gaze of the observer and evoking a sense of curiosity about its form, movement, and significance. As I gaze upon the cloud, I feel a mutual awareness, as if it, too, is observing me. This exchange creates a dynamic connection, deepening my awareness of the divine presence that permeates the world. The cloud becomes a symbol of divine communication and interaction, inviting me to explore its mysteries and contemplate its message.

In this profound encounter, the cloud serves as a reminder of the ever-present divine presence that surrounds us, inviting us to embrace a sense of wonder, curiosity, and reverence. It symbolizes the interconnectedness between the divine and the human, and in its form and movement, it holds the potential to reveal profound insights and truths. As I continue to behold this captivating cloud, I am filled with a deep sense of awe and gratitude for the divine manifestations that grace our lives and the ongoing journey of spiritual discovery.

The image of God's outstretched arm reaching over the horizon is a powerful and evocative representation. Although His eyes are veiled in shadow, you can discern the profile of a nose, adding to the enigmatic nature of the portrayal. The question arises: why are His eyes veiled?

While it is impossible to definitively ascertain the intentions of the divine, one perspective could be that God veils His eyes to prevent overwhelming or frightening His creation. The infinite and boundless nature of God's presence can be awe-inspiring and humbling, and encountering the fullness of His gaze might exceed our capacity to comprehend. By veiling His eyes, God may be offering us a gentler and more accessible encounter, allowing us to approach Him with a sense of comfort and familiarity.

Figure 17: Dunston, J.C. (2015) "ENTHRALLING LENTICULAR CLOUD CAPTIVATING MY HEART"

Within the context of God's veiled eyes, the wisdom of Meister Eckhart, who once proclaimed, "The eye through which I see God is the same eye through which God sees me; my eye and God's eye are one eye, one seeing, one knowing, one love," brings a profound dimension to our understanding.

In contemplating the veiled eyes of God, we are reminded that our perception of the divine is intricately intertwined with the divine perception of us. According to Meister Eckhart's teaching, the eye through which we perceive God is not separate from the eye through which God perceives us. It is a unified eye, a shared vision that transcends the veils of separation. The veiling of God's eyes, then, can be seen as an invitation to explore the depths of our own being, recognizing the divine presence within us, and acknowledging that this very presence is also aware of us.

This perspective, illuminated by Meister Eckhart's words, invites us to contemplate the profound unity between the human and the divine. It suggests that the divine gaze upon us is not one of intimidation or judgment but rather one of love and understanding. God's veiled eyes, seen through the lens of Meister Eckhart's wisdom, can be understood as a gesture of compassion, a way for the divine to meet us where we are, to assuage our fears, and to guide us gently on our spiritual journey.

In this understanding, the veiled eyes of God become a symbol of the intimate connection between the human and the divine, a reminder that our gaze towards God and God's gaze towards us are inseparable. It is through this shared vision, this unified eye, that we come to know and experience the boundless love and wisdom that emanate from the divine source. As we contemplate the veiled eyes of God, guided by Meister Eckhart's insight, let us embrace the profound truth that our perception and God's perception are intertwined, bound by a shared vision, a shared knowing, and a shared love. May this understanding deepen our reverence, strengthen our connection, and inspire us to seek union with the divine in our own lives.

MEETING THE OBSERVER AND THE OBSERVED

There is only us a friend of my bosom. The lover and the beloved, the seer and the seen, the observer and the observed. The knower and the known.

The Seer, with wisdom's gift bestowed,
Peers beyond the veil of time and space,
In realms unseen, truths are sowed,
An eternal search for divine grace.

The seen, a world of forms and hues,
A canvas painted with life's delight,
As the observer wanders, it imbues,
With wonder, awe, and love's pure might.

The knower, seeker of profound truth,
Delves into realms of knowledge vast,
With every insight, a blossoming youth,
Understanding deep, a treasure amassed.

For observer and observed,
in harmony sway,
Bound by a bond that forever shall stay.
The beloved and lover intertwined,
In hearts entwined, a sacred fire,
The Seer and Seen, a union defined,
In unity's embrace, they never tire.

So, let us ponder the cosmic dance,
Of observer and observed, entwined,
In every moment, a divine chance,
To glimpse the eternal, the sublime.

For in union of knower and known,
The mystic's path becomes clear and bright,
In the depths of our being, truth is sown,
And love's eternal flame ignites.

As I stand before the Chamisa shrub, basking in the divine gaze, I am enveloped in a sacred moment of recognition and communion. The dormant shrub, representing resilience in the arid plains, stands as a powerful foreground to this divine encounter. The vastness of the landscape and the presence of the LORD above it all accentuate the sense of awe and reverence that fills my heart. The Almighty soars above the great plains, and I can feel His gaze fixed upon me, filling me with a deep sense of recognition and significance.

In this moment, I am reminded of the intimate connection between the natural world and the divine, the absolute, as well as the profound connection between my own consciousness and the consciousness of God. It is a moment of unity, where the beauty of nature and the presence of the divine converge, stirring a deep sense of wonder and gratitude within me.

This encounter between me and the divine presence, walking with me, holds tremendous meaning. It signifies a moment

Figure 18: Dunston, J. C. (2015) "CONVERGENCE IN THE VALLEY OF AVONDALE: WHERE THE OBSERVED AND OBSERVER UNITE"

*Figure 19: Dunston, J.C. (2015) "AWAITING DIVINE REVELATION:
THE CONVICTION OF GOD'S PRESENCE"*

of divine awareness and connection, where the boundaries between the observer and the observed blur. The consciousness I experience becomes intertwined with the conscious cloud of the Divine, creating a sense of mutual observation and understanding.

These holy pictures portray the enchanting scenery of Avondale, Colorado, with the majestic Wet Mountains gracing the distance. The Wet Mountains, a small mountain range located in Southern Colorado, derive their name from the amount of snow they receive during the winter season. They are considered a sub-range of the Sangre de Cristo Mountains.

The Sangre De Cristo Mountains, meaning "The Blood of Christ" in Spanish, make up the Southern sub-range of the Rocky Mountains. These mountains, renowned for their awe-inspiring beauty, add to the breathtaking landscape of Avondale, Colorado. Standing tall and commanding, they serve as a reminder of the grandeur and magnificence of nature.

The holy pictures capture the harmony between the picturesque Avondale scenery and the distant presence of the Wet Mountains, showcasing the tranquility and serenity that permeates the area. The combination of these natural elements invites contemplation and a sense of reverence, connecting the divine and the earthly realms.

May these holy pictures continue to inspire and uplift, reminding us of the splendor and sacredness that can be found in the harmonious interplay between the land, the mountains, and the spiritual essence that resides within them and us.

In this profound instance, I grasp that my encounter encompasses the divine, although my mind grapples to shape a tangible image or understanding of it. It is a profound sensation and intuitive knowledge that links me to the existence of God. Without comprehending the unfolding events, I instinctively summon Archangel Gabriel, witnessing orbs of radiant light enveloping the atmosphere.

Figure 20: Dunston, J.C. (2015) "THE HEAVENS DECLARE THE GLORY OF GOD,
AND THE SKY ABOVE PROCLAIMS HIS HANDIWORK" (Psalm 19:1)

Figure 21: Dunston, J.C. (2015) "DIVINE ENCOUNTERS: EMBRACING THE UNFATHOMABLE AND ILLUMINATING PATHWAYS TO GOD"

As I focus my gaze on the white within the expanse of the blue cloud, I sense that a great revelation is about to materialize. There is a sense of anticipation as if something extraordinary is about to unfold before my eyes. I recognize that within that white space, a profound truth or insight is waiting to be revealed.

This anticipation of a revelation emphasizes the mystical nature of this experience. It goes beyond what can be seen with the naked eye and relies on a deeper level of perception and understanding.

I remain open and receptive, allowing my intuition and senses to guide me. I understand that the revelation I am about to witness may not conform to conventional visual cues. It may arise in a way that is beyond ordinary comprehension, touching the depths of my being and resonating with my soul.

In this moment of eager anticipation and intuitive connection, I prepare myself for a transformative encounter with the divine. I am ready to witness the miraculous revelation that awaits within the white expanse of the blue cloud. This profound experience brings me closer to the divine truth and provides me with a deeper understanding of the mysteries of existence.

In this particular moment of my epiphany of the LORD, my focus shifts to the far-right side of my vision, revealing a significant element: a picture of Pikes Peak, a majestic mountain in Colorado. Nestled in the far-right bottom corner, this image holds great personal significance to me as it represents my birthplace, Colorado Springs.

As I gaze upon the picture of Pikes Peak, I am reminded of the profound connection between my life's journey and the spiritual awakening I am experiencing. The inclusion of Pikes Peak in this epiphany serves as a powerful reminder of my roots and the experiences that have shaped me.

Pikes Peak, known as "America's Mountain," has long held spiritual significance for many Native American tribes. In Ute traditions, the peak marks the place where the Creator settled the Mouache band of Utes in the mountains. The Utes named it Tava, meaning "Sun Mountain," because they observed that due to its height, Pikes Peak was the first to be illuminated by the dawn.

Figure 22: Dunston, J. C. (2015) "AWAKENING AMIDST THE PEAKS:
A SPIRITUAL JOURNEY ROOTED IN LOVE"

Figure 23: Dunston, J. C. (2015) "MELODIES OF REVERENCE: RESOUNDING "OM" IN HARMONIOUS DEVOTION"

For the Pawnee people, Pikes Peak is the site where the Evening Star, the revered mother figure who created all things, came down to Earth and gifted the people with corn to grow.

It was against this backdrop of indigenous spiritual reverence that American poet and professor Katharine Lee Bates visited the summit of Pikes Peak in 1893. Inspired by the majestic view, she wrote a poem that would eventually become the iconic "America the Beautiful." Bates' tribute to the natural splendor of the United States has endured as one of the country's most beloved patriotic songs.

One does not see God with their eyes. One sees God with their heart and their faith. Seeing God with our hearts means cultivating a deep inner awareness and attunement to the divine. It involves developing a sensitivity to the subtle signs and messages that God may communicate to us through our intuition, emotions, and inner experiences.

Blessed are the pure in heart, for they will see God.
MATTHEW 5:8, BSB

He who loves a pure heart and gracious lips
will have the king for a friend.
PROVERBS 22:11, BSB

For this I will praise you, O LORD,
among the nations,
and sing to your name.
PSALM 18:49

As I embark on this extraordinary journey with the divine, the ancient wisdom of Indian spirituality comes to mind, reminding me of the sacred song of God - OM. From the depths of my heart, I begin to sing this divine sound, and as its vibrations resonate within me, a profound transformation takes place.

In this state of deep devotion, I am blessed with a remarkable sight. Before my very eyes, the Blessed Holy Father manifests in a tangible form. It is a moment of divine manifestation and revelation that leaves me in awe.

In my spiritual vision, I see a seedling, symbolic of new life and potential, growing and sprouting from its designated place. This imagery represents the emergence of a divine purpose and the unfolding of a greater plan. It signifies that the Blessed Holy Father is bringing forth a sacred mission, one that will lead to the construction of the temple of the LORD.

The words from Jeremiah 23:5, as recorded in the King James Version, resonate within me: "Behold, the days come, saith the LORD, that I will raise unto David a righteous Branch, and a King shall reign and prosper..." This prophecy speaks of a future time when a righteous Branch, descended from the lineage of David, will rise to power and establish a reign of righteousness and prosperity.

In this profound moment, I recognize that the fulfillment of this prophecy is unfolding before me. The righteous Branch, the long-awaited King, is making His presence known. It is a revelation that fills my heart with awe and reverence.

I embrace this sacred encounter with the Blessed Holy Father, knowing that His divine purpose is being revealed to me. I eagerly anticipate the realization of His plan and the manifestation of righteousness and blessings in my life and the world around me. May His reign of righteousness and prosperity be established, bringing peace and harmony to all.

As I continue to witness the divine manifestation unfolding before me, I perceive the Heavenly Father shaping a form that I can comprehend. In this sacred moment, beloved Jesus begins to emerge from the Father's presence and reveals Himself to me. He stands at the right hand, which corresponds to our left, signifying a position of honor and authority.

The words from Revelation 22:12-13, as expressed in the King James Version, resound within me: "And, behold, I come quickly; and my reward is with me, to give every man according as his work shall be. I am Alpha and Omega, the beginning and the end, the first and the last." These verses emphasize the imminent arrival of Jesus, who proclaims Himself as the Alpha and Omega, the beginning and the end, representing His eternal nature and divine authority.

In this profound encounter, I comprehend the significance of Jesus' presence and His role as the embodiment of pure love. He is the epitome of unconditional love and compassion, radiating divine grace and mercy to all. His essence transcends earthly judgments and brings forth a deep sense of peace and acceptance.

As Jesus reveals Himself to me, I am filled with a deep sense of reverence and awe. His presence brings forth a profound understanding of divine love and the eternal nature of His being. I am reminded of His teachings, which emphasize love, kindness, and the transformation of the human heart.

In the presence of the Heavenly Father and the emerging figure of Jesus, I am humbled and uplifted. I embrace this sacred revelation, recognizing Jesus as the embodiment of pure love, a guiding light, and a source of hope. May the presence of beloved Jesus ignite a flame of love within us all to know ourselves.

Figure 24: Dunston, J. C. (2015) "BLOSSOMING MESSIAH:
FROM SPROUT TO FRUIT BEARER, A PROPHECY FULFILLED"

In this captivating image, Jesus will grow from small to large for he causes the branch of his roots to bear fruit.

Indeed, the prophecy from Isaiah 11:1-2 speaks of a shoot springing up from the stump of Jesse, a reference to the lineage of King David. This shoot represents the growth and emergence of a Branch, a figure who will bear fruit and bring forth blessings. The Spirit of the LORD, along with the gifts of wisdom and understanding, will rest upon this Branch.

This prophecy points to the coming of Jesus, who is often referred to as the "Son of David," tracing His lineage back to King David. Jesus is the fulfillment of this prophecy, as He embodies the qualities attributed to the Branch in Isaiah's vision.

The shoot that springs up from the stump symbolizes the restoration and renewal that Jesus brings to the world. From humble beginnings, He grows in influence and impact, bringing forth spiritual fruit and blessings to all.

The Spirit of the LORD resting upon Jesus signifies His divine anointing and empowerment. The gifts of wisdom and understanding further highlight His divine nature and His ability to impart divine knowledge and enlightenment to those who seek Him.

As we reflect on this prophecy and the fulfillment found in Jesus, we are reminded of His role as the Messiah, who brings hope, transformation, and spiritual abundance. He is the Branch that bears fruit, bringing forth the wisdom and understanding that lead to spiritual growth and enlightenment.

Figure 25: Dunston, J.C. (2015) "ETERNAL UNFOLDING: THE DIVINE MANIFESTATION OF JESUS, A RADIANCE OF SACRED CONNECTION"

In the perpetual state of growth and connection with his beloved Heavenly Father, Jesus continuously branches out and emerges. It is as if the Heavenly Father is birthing and breathing him out of His being, a process that showcases the ongoing divine manifestation of Jesus. The radiance that surrounds him captures the essence of his divine nature, reflecting his purity and holiness.

As Jesus faces us directly, it is reminiscent of a portrait, inviting us to gaze upon him and receive his love and grace. Meanwhile, the Heavenly Father presents a side profile, reminiscent of Michelangelo's famous fresco painting "The Creation of Adam," symbolizing the Father's role in bringing forth creation and the ongoing work of divine creation through Jesus.

The arch of the sun illuminates Jesus, emphasizing the radiant love that pours through his heart. This love is a guiding light, offering hope and healing to all who embrace it. It represents the selfless and unconditional love that Jesus embodies and shares with humanity.

Figure 26: Dunston, J. C. (2015) "DIVINE TRINITUDE: EMBRACING THE SACRED UNITY OF KNOWING, EXPERIENCING, AND BEING IN THE HOLY TRINITY"

In the divine unfolding, the blessed Holy Spirit is soon to emerge at the right hand of Jesus, signifying a source of great comfort, guidance, and jubilation. The Holy Spirit's presence brings the realization of the promises and blessings that accompany the divine unity of the Father, Son, and Spirit.

As we contemplate this profound image, we are invited to enter into a deeper connection with Jesus, recognizing his ongoing growth and divine nature. We are called to embrace his love, seek the guidance of the Holy Spirit, and rejoice in the eternal bond shared within the triune God.

May this vision inspire us to cultivate a closer relationship with Jesus, allowing his love to permeate our lives and radiate through us to the world. May we celebrate and experience the comforting presence of the Holy Spirit, drawing us deeper into the divine embrace of the Father, Son, and Blessed Holy Spirit.

Figure 27: Dunston, J. C. (2015) "THE EMBODIED DIVINE: UNVEILING THE HEART OF GOD'S MANIFESTATION IN THE WORLD"

And we all, who with unveiled faces
contemplate the Lord's glory,
are being transformed into his image
with ever-increasing glory,
which comes from the Lord, who is the Spirit.

2 CORINTHIANS 3:18, NIV

In the presence of our Father, His face offering a side profile, we witness the awe-inspiring revelation of His divine countenance. Our gaze falls upon the left side of His face, leaving no doubt that Jesus, in His exalted position, resides at the Father's right hand. Beloved Jesus emerges before us, surrounded by a resplendent halo of light that emanates from His heart, resembling a celestial Sun, symbolizing the brilliance of His divine nature. In sublime harmony, the Blessed Holy Spirit, elegant and ethereal, occupies a place of honor at Jesus' right side, adorned in fiery hues of enigmatic living carnelian, glowing ambers, and brilliant green.

Let us now journey into the biblical story of Pentecost, a momentous event that unfolded after the death and resurrection of Jesus Christ. As we turn to the New Testament book of Acts, we uncover a vivid account of the disciples gathered together in Jerusalem during the Jewish festival of Pentecost. Suddenly, a sound like a rushing wind filled the air, and tongues of fire materialized, descending upon each disciple. The flames gently rested upon them, and they were all filled with the Holy Spirit, prompting them to speak in different languages.

Through this profound narrative, we catch a glimpse of the Holy Spirit's transformative power and role in guiding and empowering believers. In this description, the imagery of tongues of fire hovering above the disciples' heads serves as a metaphorical representation of the Holy Spirit's presence and work among them.

Now, let your imagination soar as we contemplate what the Holy Spirit might resemble if we were to behold the Holy Spirit's divine form. Picture the life breath of a fire, radiant and vibrant, resting gently above your head. As you envision this sacred flame, what captivating image materializes in your mind's eye? Allow your senses to embrace the wonder of this vision.

As we immerse ourselves in the mystery of the Holy Spirit's presence, let us surrender to the Holy Spirit's guidance and embrace the transformative work within us. May the Holy Spirit's fiery essence ignite our hearts with zeal and passion for the Divine. With open hearts and minds, let us seek the wisdom, comfort, and empowerment that the Holy Spirit graciously bestows.

Your right hand, O LORD, is majestic in power;
Your right hand, O LORD, has shattered the enemy.
With loving devotion, You will lead
The people You have redeemed;
With Your strength You will guide
To Your holy dwelling.[71]

The Heart of God carries a deep desire to reveal and manifest itself in the world. It is an expression of the divine longing to take shape and be expressed through us. As we evolve in our collective consciousness, we are called to actively participate in sharing the presence of the divine Creator and the universal essence of Christ that resides within our hearts and beings.

With each step forward in our spiritual journey, we are invited to tap into the depths of our innermost being, where the essence of the divine dwells. It is from this sacred space that we can access the love, wisdom, and creative power of God.

As we grow in awareness and understanding, we recognize that we are interconnected and part of a larger whole. We come to realize that the divine presence permeates every aspect of creation, and we are vessels through which the divine can be made manifest.

Angelic hosts travel with God and appear as white orbs of light that appear throughout this majestic portrayal of the Triune nature of God. I will emphasize these in later photos so you can see.

THE HEAVENLY FATHER'S IMAGE

Figure 28: Dunston, J.C. (2015) Details of our Heavenly Father's Face.
"SACRED SPLENDOR: ILLUMINATING THE DIVINE ESSENCE
OF THE HEAVENLY FATHER"

The Heavenly Father in the photos evokes the image of a star cloud, reminiscent of the Star of David. The Star of David is a symbol composed of two interlocking triangles, forming a six-pointed star. This symbol carries deep significance and is often associated with divine protection, unity, and the connection between heaven and earth. Now, let's connect this symbol to the picture below.

Figure 29: Tekhelet (sky blue)
colored Star of David,
as depicted on the Flag of Israel.

In the photos, the Heavenly Father is only revealing His face, not His entire body as seen in the first image. So, envision the image of the star in your mind, and imagine that there is a face within that star. The face of God, captured in these photos, is represented within the confines of the star shape. This visual correlation adds depth and meaning to the image, inviting us to contemplate the divine presence within the sacred symbol.

The depicted cropped image of our Father does not have all the points as this tilted star does here. I am only using this as an example to help me illustrate.

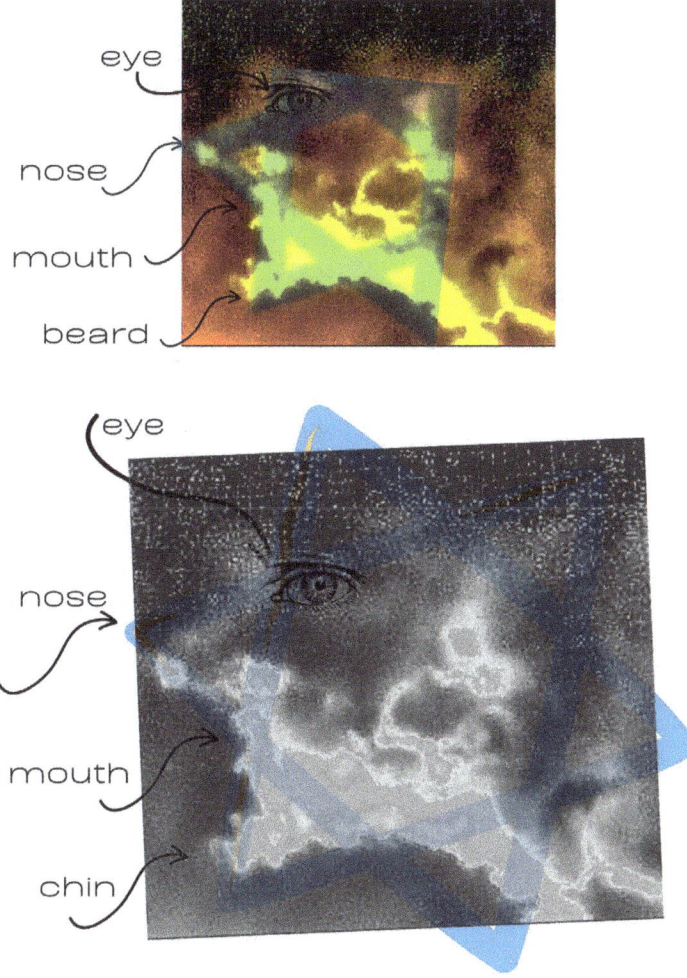

Figure 30: GUIDE TO FACIAL FEATURES OF HEAVENLY FATHER

Direct your attention to the cropped image of our Heavenly Father, where a white cloud stands out, illuminated by the gentle touch of sunlight. This cloud bears a striking resemblance to the side profile of our Father depicted in the painting "The Creation of Adam." His nose would be on the far left resembling a point of the star.

Now, focus on the bottom left point of the star, which represents His whimsical and flowing goatee. The cloud forms a shape that mirrors the essence of this distinctive feature. Between His nose and goatee, you can envision His lips, gently curved to form His serene facial expression. His head is rounded on top, without any point, blending harmoniously with the overall shape.

While His eye remains shrouded in shadow, He creates a visual representation of an eye and an arched eyebrow for you to perceive. Imagine this eye positioned at the top center, between two points of the star. As you gaze upon this divine appearance, you'll notice that His gaze is directed straight at you, providing a profound sense of connection and the ability to truly see Him. In this remarkable visualization, He manifests a droplet of white, akin to a reflective light bouncing back at you, bestowing the gift of sight. He creates the perfect shading and interplay of light and shadow to define his features.

Furthermore, within the image, His head is slightly positioned inside the halo of Jesus. His nose is in direct alignment with where Jesus' eyes are located.

Figure 31: Michelangelo, "THE CREATION OF ADAM" Fresco. Sistine Chapel, Vatican City

THE IMAGE OF BELOVED JESUS

The face of Jesus is right next to our Father, centered inside the halo. In the image, the sky is painted to resemble human flesh. You can clearly see His nose and the arch up to His eyebrow.

When you reference back to the icon of the Pantocrator, you'll notice the resemblance to Him in this photo, as well as the dove I drew. You can see what appears to be cheek and bones, and if you look closely, you may discern a well-trimmed mustache around the shape of His lips. Furthermore, if you look very carefully, you can see His eyes, especially His left eye (our right side). You can also imagine that the face of the Messiah is encased in a menorah light or a candle flame.

> *Jesus replied, "Philip, I have been with you all this time,*
> *and still you do not know Me? Anyone who has seen Me*
> *has seen the Father. How can you say,*
> *'Show us the Father?'*

(JOHN 14:9)

Figure 32: ARTIST UNKNOWN (6TH CENTURY) THE OLDEST KNOWN ICON OF CHRIST PANTOCRATOR, SAINT CATHERINE'S MONASTERY, MOUNT SINAI

Figure 33: DUNSTON, J.C. (2015) DETAILS OF BELOVED JESUS' FACE. "WHOEVER HAS SEEN ME HAS SEEN THE FATHER" JOHN 14:9, ESV

Figure 34: Dunston, J.C. (2015) "SPIRIT DIVINE REVEALED:
CAPTURING THE GRACEFUL COUNTENANCE OF THE BLESSED HOLY SPIRIT"

THE IMAGE OF THE BLESSED HOLY SPIRIT

The Blessed Holy Spirit is positioned next to Jesus. As the image of the Heavenly Father begins to dissipate into Himself and the image of Jesus fades out of the clouds; you will witness the magnificence of the Blessed Holy Spirit's splendor. The Holy Spirit painted the sky with fiery carnelian undertones and shades of emerald-green. The Holy Spirit presents itself with the shape of an upside-down triangle, resembling a beak, and within the Holy Spirit's splendid harmonic beauty, creates eyes and a smile, encompassing the space of its divine resonance.

This is what God the LORD says—
the Creator of the heavens,
who stretches them out,
who spreads out the earth
with all that springs from it,
who gives breath to its people,
and life to those who walk on it:
"I, the LORD, have called you in righteousness;
I will take hold of your hand.
I will keep you and will make you
To be a covenant for the people
And a light for the Gentiles,
to open eyes that are blind,
to free captives from prison
and to release from the dungeon
those who sit in darkness.

ISAIAH: 42:5-7, NIV

The dynamic and lovely presence of the blessed Holy Spirit fills my heart with immense joy and causes my spirit to soar with delight! It is a captivating force that ignites a symphony of emotions within me, evoking a sense of wonder and awe. The Holy Spirit's divine essence infuses my being, enveloping me in its tender embrace and illuminating my path with its radiant light. In its presence, I feel a profound connection to the divine, as if the very essence of heaven has descended upon me. The Holy Spirit's boundless love and grace uplift my soul, inspiring me to live a life filled with compassion, kindness, and gratitude. It is a wondrous gift that stirs my innermost being and fills my days with purpose and meaning. Oh, how blessed I am to experience the transformative power of the blessed Holy Spirit, for it is a treasure that brings abundant blessings and makes my heart rejoice and sing!

One thing I would like to mention is that I did not understand seeing the Holy Spirit for quite some time. I saw our Heavenly Father immediately, and I saw Jesus, but the blessed Holy Spirit remained an enigma for me. I wasn't sure if the " Sun Dove" was the Holy Spirit. It was one night, as I was preparing to go to bed, that I was inspired to read the book of Acts in the Holy Bible. Something then hit my consciousness in a huge wave, and I looked over at the picture of the Almighty on my bedside stand. That was the first time I understood and recognized the presence of the blessed Holy Spirit. The Holy Spirit is nearly invisible in these photographs, as you might imagine a Spirit would appear. I was very humbled and embarrassed that I did not understand the visage of the blessed Holy Spirit until many months after my initial experience with our beloved Creator.

THE HOLY TRINITY

Jesus said, "Know what is in front of your face, and what is hidden from you will be disclosed to you. For there is nothing hidden that will not be revealed."[72]

Ezekiel, a revered prophet in the Hebrew Bible, also had a powerful encounter with God. His visions and experiences are recorded in the Book of Ezekiel, which provides a detailed account of his encounters with divine manifestations.

In one of his most notable encounters, Ezekiel describes a vision where he sees a captivating manifestation of God's presence. He witnesses a divine chariot, often referred to as the "chariot of God" or the "Merkabah," which is a complex and awe-inspiring celestial vehicle. This chariot is surrounded by heavenly beings, such as cherubim, who possess multiple wings and exhibit a profound sense of divine glory.

As Ezekiel describes the vision, he portrays God's presence as indescribably radiant and majestic. The divine glory he witnesses is depicted as a brilliant light, illuminating the entire scene. Ezekiel's encounter is accompanied by a sense of overwhelming reverence and awe, as he realizes the greatness and holiness of the divine presence before him.

Above this surface was something that looked like a throne made of blue lapis lazuli. And on this throne high above was a figure whose appearance resembled a man. From what appeared to be his waist up, he looked like gleaming amber, flickering like a fire. And from his waist down, he looked like a burning flame, shining with splendor. All around him was a glowing halo, like a rainbow shining in the clouds on a rainy day. This is what the glory of the LORD looked like to me. When I saw it, I fell face down on the ground, and I heard someone's voice speaking to me.

EZEKIEL 1:26-28, NLV

Figure 35: Dunston, J.C. (2015) "TRANSCENDENT MAJESTY: THE RADIANT THRONE OF DIVINE SPLENDOR"

For God, who said, "Let light shine out of the darkness," made His light shine in our hearts to give us the light of the knowledge of the glory of God in the face of Jesus Christ

(2 CORINTHIANS 4:6, BSB).

321

This is the image of the dove that I drew on the back of the religious icon "Christ the Pantocrator." See here how the Almighty incorporated this image into the Sun showing our synergistic co-creation together.

Figure 36: Dunston, J.C. (2014) "SACRED REVELATIONS: THE DIVINE IDENTITY EMBODIED IN THE 'I AM' DOODLE"

"Father, I want those you have given me to be where I am, and to see my glory, the glory you have given me because you loved me before the creation of the world"

(JOHN 17:24, NIV).

Hear O Israel, the Lord our God is One Lord.

MARK 12:29

I will walk among you and be your God, and you will be my people.

LEVITICUS 26:12

Figure 37: Dunston, J.C. (2015). "THERE HE WAS TRANSFIGURED BEFORE THEM. HIS FACE SHONE LIKE THE SUN, AND HIS CLOTHES BECAME AS WHITE AS THE LIGHT"

You can see that God the Father created an arch almost like a puzzle piece that connects to the bridge of the Son's nose. The arch begins at Jesus's nose and curves down to where the Father's beard is. They illuminate and fade into one another. Knowledge of God comes through the knowledge of Christ.

Figure 38: Dunston, J.C. (2015) "THE MIGHTY ONE, GOD THE LORD, SPEAKS AND SUMMONS THE EARTH FROM THE RISING TO THE SETTING OF THE SUN. FROM ZION, PERFECT IN BEAUTY, GOD SHINES FORTH" (Psalm 50:1-2).

The Father's image has begun to dissipate into itself, and the Son has gone into the Father, but his halo of light transforms into the shape of half a hexagon that remains surrounding the image of where their faces appeared. The Holy Spirit's radiance stretches across the sky in lovely hues of jasper, scarlet, magenta, and glowing emerald enveloping the whole. You can see the light of the Holy Spirit pouring glorious colors and fluttering in the sky and the Holy Archangel's lights float beneath the Sun as orbs of light in the valley of Avondale Colorado. In God's majestic glory is the splendor of truth and beauty!

Figure 39: Dunston, J.C. (2015) "SPHERES OF RADIANT CELESTIALS: ARCHANGELS REVEALED IN GLOWING GLORY"

Angels are most definitely real. Archangels are powerful spiritual beings. The term "archangel" originates from Greek and means "chief angel" or "ruling angel." Archangels are considered to be a high rank of angels who serve as messengers or intermediaries between God and humans. Angels play many different roles for God, and many have a designated job. The Bible calls angels "ministering spirits" in Hebrew 1:14 and believers say that God has made each angel in the way that would best empower that angel to serve the people whom God loves.

Angels possess an ethereal and enigmatic nature that distinguishes them from human beings. Unlike humans, angels lack physical bodies, granting them the ability to manifest in diverse forms. In certain circumstances, angels may adopt a human guise when their assigned task necessitates such an approach. Or they may reveal themselves as extraordinary, winged creatures, radiant beings of light, or assume various other manifestations.

Angels do indeed walk among us and since we have free will we can call on angels to guide us, to protect us, and to provide words of encouragement and messages from God.

Angels can manifest themselves in ways beyond our comprehension and there are different methods in which they can visit us. One is through our Clair senses in which perhaps you hear an audible voice, or in a dream and vision, and also in a time of need.

In the Bible, the book of Daniel recounts several instances where angels played a role in protecting Daniel. One of the most well-known stories involving Daniel and angelic protection is found in Daniel chapter 6. Daniel was thrown into a den of lions as a result of a plot against him by jealous officials. However, God sent an angel to shut the mouths of the lions, ensuring that Daniel was unharmed throughout the night. Daniel is called to interpret dreams or visions. Daniel often seeks divine assistance, and angels are sent to provide him with insight and understanding.

Joseph, who was engaged to Mary, discovered that she was pregnant, and an angel of the Lord appeared to him in a dream and explained that the child conceived in Mary was from the Holy Spirit. The angel instructed Joseph to not be afraid and to take Mary as his wife and affirmed that the child would be a fulfillment of prophecies, Immanuel, meaning God is with us.

Luke 1:19 is an account of the angel Gabriel's visitation to Zechariah, the father of John the Baptist. The verse states: "And the angel answered him, 'I am Gabriel. I stand in the presence of God, and I was sent to speak to you and bring you this good news.'"

In this verse, Zechariah, a priest, had been serving in the temple when the angel Gabriel appeared to him. Zechariah was startled and afraid, but Gabriel reassured him and identified himself as Gabriel. The good news was the promise that Zechariah's wife, Elizabeth, would conceive and bear a son, who would play a significant role in preparing the way for the coming Messiah.

Fig. 40: THE ANNUNCIATION (photo has small circles encased around angelic orbs to emphasize the presence of angelic beings).

Figure 41: Dunston, J. C. (2015) "CELESTIAL SYMPHONY: THE LUMINOUS DANCE OF MYRIADS OF ANGELIC HOST"

We can all connect with the angelic realm. Angels love us and they do not judge us. They don't care if we are religious or non-religious. God has many gifts for humanity and angels are a gift from God. Angels want to be asked to give them the green light to help us. You can ask the angels to give you a sign. The first thing to do is have belief and set a clear intention. Breath, close your eyes, move your awareness to your heart, get centered with a nice relaxing breath, and from that heart space state to the universe "In my soul I know there's a part of me that believes angels are real and I am setting the intention now to have a personal experience with the angelic realm, thank you so much." Trust that you have been heard and that the angels are with you.

*Figure 42: Dunston, J.C. (2015) "TRULY THE LIGHT IS SWEET, AND A PLEASANT
THING IT IS FOR THE EYES TO BEHOLD THE SUN," (Ecclesiastes 11:7).*

*Do not be afraid,
little flock, for your
Father has been
pleased to give you
the kingdom.*

LUKE 12:32, NIV

… *"Now the dwelling
of God is with men,
and he will live with
them. They will be
his people, and God
himself will be with
them and be their
God. He will wipe
every tear from their
eyes. There will be
no more death or
mourning or crying
or pain, for the old
order of things has
passed away"*

(REVELATION 21:3-4, NIV).

Figure 43: Dunston, J. C. (2015) "EPIPHANY'S LUNAR EMBRACE:
WORMWOOD AND THE GIBBOUS MOON"

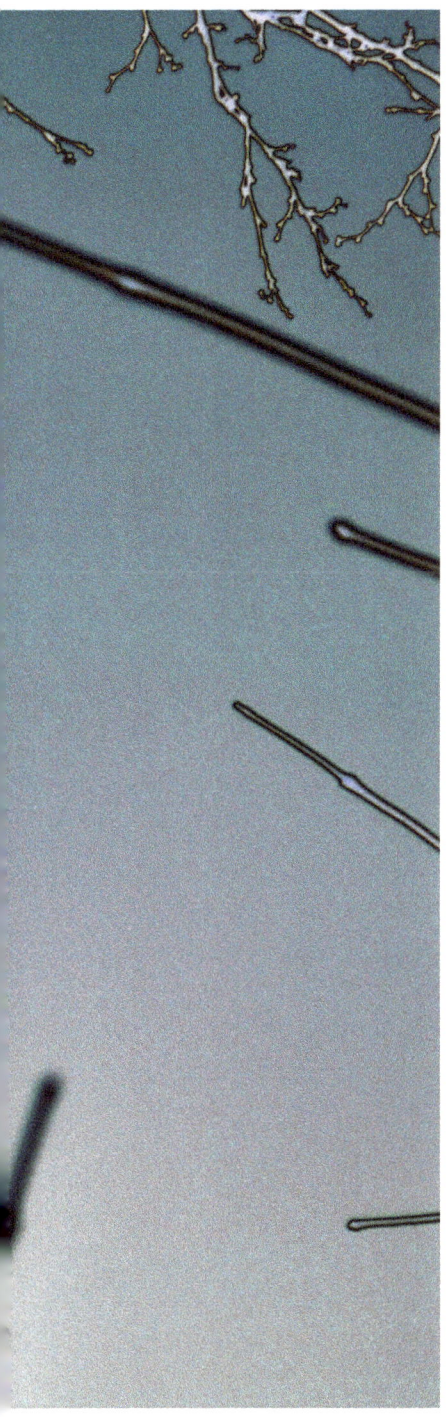

The Universal Christ is the God-realized mystic who knows the "I Am" and understands the universal "I am consciousness" that everyone is an expression of because all life is the child of the Divine. I am the way, the truth, and the life and as beings of light, we are connected to that magnificent light universally. The vine and the branches are a metaphor for our universal connection, the metaphor of reality in which we are all one in unity.

Jesus came to change humanity about God. He taught that God is love, divine love and that we can have a personal relationship with God as children of God. Jesus is the tap root of the tree, and the branch in which your faith becomes personal, concrete, here and now. Christ is the universalization of that same Love, intimacy, grace, and gift of God that we are part of.

The birth of Christ was the Big Bang! It is the revelation of God where God began to materialize and show the God self, the internal workings of God. The Cosmic Christ is the omnipresent notion of God found within our being. It is the integration with the individual and his/her experience, our embodiment. The desire for God is the most fundamental way of all.

"If you know me, you will know my Father also. From now on you do know him and have seen him"
(JOHN 14:7, ESV).

335

REVEALING THE SACRED UNION:
NURTURING THE DIVINE MOTHER WITHIN
AND EMBRACING COLLECTIVE CONSCIOUSNESS

The Glory of the LORD appeared on the last day of March 31st, 2015; the wormwood moon was waxing high in the eastern sky at sunset. I believe these trees are Mulberries. We have a small grove of trees on the farm that consists of Mulberries, Ash, and Black Walnut. I believe they were planted as part of the National Conservation Act in the 1930s known as the New Deal. Shortly after the New Deal, President Franklin D. Roosevelt initiated the Great Plains Shelterbelt which was a project to create windbreaks in the Great Plains states. This was in response to the severe dust storms of the Dust Bowl era. The United States Forest Service believed that planting trees on the perimeters of farms would reduce wind velocity and lessen the evaporation of moisture from the soil.

I was standing in what I had coined 'The Heart of the Farm' when our Heavenly Father first appeared. I have had many special moments in my life on this part of the farm. Out in the high desert Plains where there are few trees one can feel exposed and naked as the hot sun and wind sweeps across the valley floor. When I first moved to Avondale Colorado, I was called to this special place many times. As I stood in that sacred place, surrounded by the beauty of nature, I felt something precious, something indescribable yet deeply profound. It was as if the air itself was charged with a divine energy, a vibration that resonated within my very being. Looking back, I now recognize it as the presence of the Divine Mother, the nurturing force that permeates all of creation.

In those moments, I would find solace in the embrace of the trees, lying down in their grooves, and allowing myself to be cradled by the loving vibrations of the Holy Mother. It was as if she enveloped me in her tender arms, showering me with a love so pure and unconditional. In her presence, I felt safe, held, and deeply seen.

The experience was transformative, for in those moments of connection, I was not just an individual but a part of something greater—

a sacred bond between the Divine Mother and her children. It was a reminder that we are not alone in this vast universe but held in the embrace of a compassionate and loving Mother.

Swami Vivekananda was an Indian Hindu monk and spiritual leader of the late 19th century. Swami Vivekananda beautifully reminds us that the Divine Mother is the eternal presence dwelling within the depths of our hearts. She is the guiding light that illuminates our path, leading us to the realization of our true nature. In those moments amidst the trees, I felt her gentle guidance, nudging me toward a deeper understanding of myself and the interconnectedness of all existence.

Anandamayi Ma was a spiritual leader and saint from India she was regarded as a highly realized soul. Anandamayi Ma's teachings centered around the concept of the Divine Mother, often referred to as "Ma" or "Mother." She saw the Divine Mother as the ultimate reality, the embodiment of love, compassion, and wisdom. According to Anandamayi Ma, the Divine Mother is the source of all creation and the underlying essence that permeates everything in the universe.

Anandamayi Ma encouraged her followers to develop a personal and intimate relationship with the Divine Mother. She emphasized that the Divine Mother is not separate from us but resides within each individual as our true nature. Ma taught that by realizing our inherent divinity and surrendering to the Divine Mother's grace, we can experience spiritual awakening and liberation.

In the presence of the Divine Mother, nestled in the trees and the earth, I found a sanctuary where the ordinary transcended into the extraordinary. It was a place where love and divinity merged, where the vibrations of the Mother's energy resonated with my own, awakening a deeper sense of purpose and belonging. It was within this sacred connection that I discovered the power of her love to transform, heal, and awaken the dormant potential within me.

May we all open our hearts to the presence of the Divine Mother, recognizing her eternal guidance and boundless love. May we find solace and transformation in her embrace and may her vibrations of love and tenderness continue to cradle us on our journey of self-discovery and spiritual awakening.

As we delve into the concept of collective consciousness, it becomes essential to embrace the profound notion that nature responds to synchronicity, even across the span of 2000 years. This realization holds particular significance when we consider the proximity of God's appearances to the occasions of Passover and Easter.

During the Last Supper, a momentous event that unfolded in the upper room of Jerusalem, Jesus and his disciples came together to commemorate the Passover meal. It was on this sacred occasion that Jesus instituted the sacrament of the Eucharist. Taking a loaf of bread, he blessed it and declared, *"This is my body." Likewise, he took a cup of wine, blessed it, and proclaimed, "This is my blood."* Instructing his disciples to partake of the bread and wine in remembrance of him, Jesus symbolized their deep connection to him and his continuous presence among them.

The Eucharist serves as a powerful symbol, representing not only their unity with Jesus but also the spiritual unity and love they are urged to demonstrate toward one another. The apostle Paul eloquently writes, *"Because there is one bread, we who are many are one body, for we all partake of the one bread."* Just as the Eucharist unifies believers into one cohesive body, the universal Christ beckons us to acknowledge the intricate interconnectedness we share with all of creation.

By engaging in the Eucharist, we symbolically enter into communion with Christ and, by extension, with the divine itself. It is a profound invitation to recognize and embrace the inseparable bond that exists between ourselves and the sacred web of existence.

In addition to the institution of the Eucharist, Jesus also washed the feet of his disciples as a gesture of humility and service, teaching them the importance of serving one another in love and humility.

Furthermore, Jesus shared profound teachings and prophecies during this time. He predicted his betrayal by one of his disciples, Judas Iscariot, and foretold Peter's denial of him. He comforted his disciples, assuring them of his love, and promised to send the Holy Spirit to guide and empower them after his departure. Jesus also spoke about his impending suffering, death, and resurrection, foreshadowing the events that would soon unfold.

Beloved Yeshua, like the radiant light of the menorah, encases himself in a self-illumination that emerges from within, captivating and mystical. This light symbolizes the divine plan of God, establishing a deep communion with us and revealing our intricate resemblance to the divine. It signifies the outpouring of the glorious and radiant Holy Spirit, even after two millennia, a precious gift of profound significance bestowed upon humanity.

As brothers and sisters, we unite as one body, embracing the profound "I AM" presence within us. In this unity, we are called to love one another with the same unconditional love that God has graciously bestowed upon us. This divine mandate echoes throughout the ages, inviting us to manifest divine love in our relationships and interactions, symbolizing the triumph of light over darkness, freedom over oppression, and religious freedom over persecution.

The menorah, a sacred seven-branched candelabrum, holds deep symbolism in Judaism, representing the eternal flame and spiritual illumination. It was an essential fixture in the Holy Temple, embodying the enduring spirit, faith, and resilience of the Jewish people. The menorah's physical and symbolic lighting in the Holy Temple reflects the triumph of light, faith, and the preservation of religious identity.

> *But with precious blood of Christ,*
> *a lamb without blemish or defect.*
> *He was chosen before the creation*
> *of the world but was revealed in*
> *these last times for your sake.*
>
> 1 PETER 1:19-20, NIV

> *Through him you believe in God, who raised him from the*
> *dead and glorified him, and so your faith and hope are in God.*
>
> 1 PETER 1:21, NIV

Jesus invites us to share our true selves and our unique gifts with the world. In Matthew 5:15-16, 16 states, *"Nor do people light a lamp and put it under a blanket, but on a stand, and it gives light to all in the house. In the same way, let your light shine before others, so that they may see your good works and give glory to your Father who is in heaven."*

The underlying meaning is that we should not hide our authentic selves or our abilities out of fear, insecurity, or a desire to conform.

Instead, we are encouraged to let our light shine brightly, allowing our unique qualities and gifts to positively impact the world around us. By embracing and expressing our true selves we inspire others and contribute to the greater good.

In essence, the phrase reminds us to have the courage and confidence to be true to ourselves and to share our unique talents, passions, and virtues with others. It encourages us to live authentically and make a positive difference in the world by allowing our inner light to shine.

In conclusion, this profound spiritually transformative experience has awakened in me a deep longing to bring together all of humanity in harmony with the divine, recognizing that we are intricately composed of three parts, mirroring the image and likeness of our Creator.

Throughout history, various branches of philosophy have sought to explore fundamental questions of existence (ontology- which asks what exists) and knowledge (epistemology- how we know about the existence of such things).

Yet, the true answers to these inquiries lie within our very being and resonate within our hearts. Those who earnestly seek shall find. My sincere aspiration is that this transformative experience may illuminate the hearts and minds of many, providing insight into the enigmatic concepts of consciousness and the nature of the mind. May we embark on a collective journey of discovery and understanding, guided by the light of this profound awakening.

Let us embrace the power of seeking, for those who ask shall receive, and those who search shall find. Through this transformative experience, we have the potential to ignite the light of awareness within ourselves and share it with others, illuminating the path toward unity, compassion, and profound insight.

May this journey of self-discovery and connection with the divine inspire countless hearts, igniting a collective awakening to the mysteries of consciousness, the nature of the mind, and the boundless potential that resides within each and every one of us. Let hope guide our steps and may the transformative power of this experience ripple outwards, bringing healing, unity, and inspiration to all humanity to know themselves.

15

REVELATION OF GOD'S NATURE AND ANTHROPOMORPHIC ATTRIBUTES

THE REVELATION OF GOD'S NATURE REFERS TO HOW GOD HAS chosen to make Himself known to humanity, revealing aspects of His character, attributes, and purposes. In Christian theology, there are several ways in which God's nature is revealed:

◊ **General Revelation:** General revelation refers to the knowledge of God that is available to all people through creation and the natural world. Psalm 19:1 states, "The heavens declare the glory of God; the skies proclaim the work of his hands." Through the beauty, order, and complexity of the natural world, people can gain insights into God's existence, power, wisdom, and creativity.

◊ **Special Revelation:** Special revelation refers to God's unique and specific self-disclosure to humanity through various means. This includes:
1. *Scripture:* The Bible is considered the primary source of special revelation. It is believed to be inspired by God and contains truths about God's nature, His actions in history, and His redemptive plan for humanity.
2. *Jesus Christ:* Jesus is seen as the ultimate and fullest revelation of God's nature. John 1:18, says, "No one has ever seen

God, but the one and only Son, who is himself God and is in closest relationship with the Father, has made him known." Through Jesus' life, teachings, death, and resurrection, God's love, mercy, grace, and redemption are revealed.

3. *Personal Experience:* God can also reveal Himself through personal experiences, such as answered prayers, spiritual encounters, and divine interventions. These experiences provide individuals with a firsthand understanding of God's presence and work in their lives.

Through these various forms of revelation, God's nature is gradually unveiled to humanity, allowing individuals to develop a deeper understanding of His love, justice, holiness, mercy, sovereignty, and other attributes. The revelation of God's nature is an ongoing process as individuals seek to know and experience Him more fully.

According to the Bible, God has expressed Himself in the world through His creation in several ways:

◊ **Divine Attributes:** Creation reflects the attributes of God, such as His power, wisdom, and beauty. The intricate design, order, and complexity of the universe point to a Creator who is infinitely wise and powerful.

◊ **Revelation of God's Nature:** Creation reveals aspects of God's nature and character. Romans 1:20 states, "For since the creation of the world God's invisible qualities—his eternal power and divine nature—have been clearly seen, being understood from what has been made." By observing the natural world, we can gain insights into God's attributes, such as His creativity, provision, and care.

◊ **Stewardship and Responsibility:** God's creation is entrusted to humanity, and we are called to responsibly care for it. Genesis 1:28 says, "God blessed them and said to them, 'Be fruitful and increase in number; fill the earth and subdue it. Rule over the fish in the sea and the birds in the sky and over every living creature that moves on the ground.'" This stewardship includes the responsible use of natural resources, conservation, and environmental care.

◊ **Parables and Metaphors:** Jesus often used elements of creation in His teachings to convey spiritual truths. For example, He spoke of seeds, birds, flowers, and the natural world to illustrate lessons about faith, God's provision, and the kingdom of God. These parables and metaphors draw connections between the physical world and spiritual realities.

◊ **God's Provision:** Creation serves as a testimony to God's abundant provision for His creatures. Jesus refers to God's care for the natural world in Matthew 6:26, saying, "Look at the birds of the air; they do not sow or reap or store away in barns, and yet your heavenly Father feeds them." This highlights God's loving provision and sustenance for all living beings.

These examples illustrate how God's creation serves as a means for Him to reveal Himself, convey spiritual truths, and demonstrate His care and provision. By observing and appreciating the natural world, we can gain insights into the character and nature of God.

In my personal experience, I find many of these ideas about how God reveals Himself to be true. For instance, Psalm 19:1 expresses that the skies and heavens showcase the glory and creative work of God. As I observe the natural world, I see the sky as a canvas through which God manifests His presence.

Additionally, Jesus refers to himself in scripture as the bright morning star, the light that enlightens all people, and the Son of Man. To me, these symbols signify that Jesus, within my human understanding, represents the sun, as he utilizes the sun's attributes to exemplify his own.

The Sun is a massive luminous sphere and without the Sun's energy life as we know it could not exist. It is interesting to note that when I had the visit from the blessed Holy Mother she carried with her a ball of brilliant luminous light.

The philosopher Plato, in his famous work "The Republic," presents an allegory known as the "Allegory of the Sun," in which he discusses the relationship between the Sun and goodness. According to Plato, the Sun serves as a metaphorical representation of the ultimate form of goodness and knowledge.

Plato suggests that just as the Sun is the source of light and visibility in the physical world, the form of the Good is the source of truth and understanding in the realm of ideas. The Good, in this context, represents the highest form of reality and the ultimate goal of philosophical inquiry.

Plato argues that the Sun's illumination allows us to perceive and understand the world around us. Similarly, the form of the Good provides the foundation for knowledge and enables us to grasp the true nature of reality and the forms that exist beyond the physical realm.

Furthermore, Plato emphasizes that the Sun's light not only enables us to see external objects but also illuminates our minds, leading to the development of moral virtue and the pursuit of wisdom. The Good, in a similar sense, enlightens the intellect and guides individuals toward moral excellence and the understanding of universal truths.

Similarly, the Holy Spirit is symbolically depicted as a dove in the Gospels, particularly during Jesus' baptism. The dove, known for its traits of peace, gentleness, and purity, serves as a representation of how God collaborates with me, transforming the drawing of my dove into the radiant heart of Jesus pouring through our Earth's magnificent star. The Holy Spirit is described in various ways that can be related to nature. In John 3:8, Jesus compares the work of the Holy Spirit to the wind, saying "The wind blows wherever it pleases. You hear its sound, but you cannot tell where it comes from or where it is going. So it is with everyone born of the Spirit." This comparison highlights the mysterious and unseen nature of the Holy Spirit. In the Bible, The Holy Spirit is not explicitly assigned a gender. The Holy Spirit is often described using metaphors and symbols rather than gender-specific language. In my personal experience as a witness to God's presence, I can only say that the blessed Holy Spirit is a radiant expression of the greatest joy and love.

Another analogy is found in the association of clouds with our Heavenly Father, who is often referred to as Yahweh or the Lord. Psalm 68:4 portrays God riding on the clouds, while in Matthew 24:30, Jesus prophesies his second coming, describing himself as coming on the clouds of heaven with great power and glory.

These references to God being associated with clouds convey several symbolic meanings. Clouds can represent the divine presence and glory, acting as a visual manifestation of God's transcendence and power. They can also symbolize God's guidance, protection, and provision, as seen in the pillar of the cloud leading the Israelites in the wilderness.

The imagery of God riding on the clouds is often interpreted as a symbol of divine sovereignty and authority. It signifies that God is above and beyond the earthly realm, reigning over all creation. Additionally, the association of clouds with God's presence can evoke a sense of awe, mystery, and the ineffable nature of the divine. The cloud imagery is used to help convey aspects of God's character and relationship with humanity, highlighting His power, guidance, and presence.

BEYOND BOUNDARIES: EXPLORING ANTHROPOMORPHISM, GENDER, AND THE DIVINE NATURE

Throughout history, human beings have often anthropomorphized God for several reasons. Anthropomorphism (*an-thruh-puh-mor-fi-zm*) is the attribution of human characteristics or behavior to a god, animal, or object. Anthropomorphism can arise from our limited understanding of the divine. As finite beings, it is challenging for us to comprehend the nature of God, who is infinite and transcendent. To make God more relatable and understandable, we might attribute human characteristics and forms to Him. Anthropomorphism provides a way to grasp and connect with the divine in a familiar and accessible manner.

By attributing human qualities to God, we create a framework that enables us to relate to Him on a personal level. We project our own experiences, emotions, and relational dynamics onto God, allowing for a sense of intimacy and interaction.

Anthropomorphism can also be influenced by cultural factors and societal norms. Different cultures throughout history have used anthropomorphic representations to communicate and understand the divine within their specific cultural frameworks. These representations often reflect the values, beliefs, and symbols prevalent in a particular culture.

Interpretation of sacred texts can contribute to anthropomorphism. Ancient religious texts, such as the Bible, contain passages that describe God using anthropomorphic language. Metaphors, similes, and figurative language are employed to convey complex theological concepts in a way that is understandable to the human mind. However, these descriptions can sometimes be taken literally, leading to the anthropomorphization of God.

Anthropomorphizing God can fulfill emotional and psychological needs. Humanizing God can provide comfort, a sense of security, and familiarity. It can also give individuals a sense of purpose and meaning, as they perceive a personal and caring deity who engages with their lives.

God is often understood as a spiritual and transcendent force that encompasses and goes beyond human notions of male and female. While anthropomorphism can be a natural tendency, it is also recognized that God transcends human limitations and is not limited to human characteristics. This perspective recognizes that God's essence cannot be confined or limited to human gender constructs or characteristics. Instead, God is seen as a boundless and inclusive presence that encompasses all genders and beyond. This understanding acknowledges the inherent diversity and complexity of the divine, inviting a broader and more inclusive understanding of the nature of God.

Moreover, discussions around God's gender have broader implications for society as a whole. They prompt us to question and challenge deeply ingrained gender stereotypes, encouraging a more nuanced understanding of gender roles and identities. By recognizing the limitations of human language and concepts in describing the divine, we open ourselves to a more expansive and inclusive spirituality, where all individuals are valued and respected.

In conclusion, humanity's understanding of God's gender influences our perception of gender roles, equality, and social dynamics. Embracing a more inclusive and diverse understanding of the divine can lead to positive changes in our world, fostering greater gender equality and dismantling oppressive structures.

16

LIBERATING WISDOM: UNVEILING THE PATH TO FREEDOM

COUNTLESS SYSTEMS EXIST IN OUR WORLD THAT DO NOT ALIGN with our highest good, often rooted in fear and judgment. During the time of Jesus, the prevailing system was based on the adherence to the Ten Commandments. However, Jesus came to offer an alternative path, teaching the divine law that is inscribed within the depths of our hearts. He emphasized our inherent connection to the Triune God and revealed that we are spiritual beings, liberated from the chains of sin and death.

The book of Galatians in the Holy Bible recounts how the apostle Paul shared transformative teachings with newly converted Jews who were wrestling with their traditional beliefs. His purpose was to elevate their thinking and understanding. Paul played a crucial role in establishing Christianity as a distinct religious tradition, guiding the Jews to realize that the Ten Commandments had become outdated, no longer guiding them toward truth and freedom.

However, it becomes evident that organized religions today often incorporate various elements and assign significant importance to concepts such as sin and judgment. Consequently, individuals find themselves perpetually engaged in prayer, seeking salvation and redemption for their souls.

The central argument put forth here is that these ideas and beliefs are intentionally designed to manipulate and exert control over people, impeding our evolutionary progress. For example, the fear of hell is a self-generated thought that arises from the illusory notion of being separate from God. Yet, separation from God is impossible, for God is pure love. It is crucial to recognize that, as co-creators, our thoughts have the power to manifest our reality. Therefore, if we hold the belief that we will endure eternal damnation in hell, we will perceive an experience aligned with that belief, much like watching a movie.

However, it is essential to understand that we are the ones creating that experience, not God. Once we choose to release that thought, a more favorable reality can be created. A more constructive approach would involve refraining from teaching and preaching fear to humanity. This fear-based approach does not serve the greater good and can cause individuals to turn away from God. It is worth noting that many religious dogmas still permeate our culture, preserving their core assumptions to this day.

According to Neale Donald Walsch, it is suggested that the concept of the devil was created by humans to instill fear and manipulate others into conforming to their desires, using the threat of being disconnected from God as a means of control. However, Walsch reassures that there is no longer a need to fear, as nothing can ever separate individuals from God.[73] Walsch also emphasizes the inclusive nature of spirituality, stating that all churches and faiths are expressions of God, and every soul possesses a divine essence that unites them with God. In this view, no individual or living being exists outside the realm of God's community.[74]

In today's world, a growing number of individuals are distancing themselves from these traditional beliefs. They are increasingly open to embracing a personal connection with God and intelligent design, placing it at the core of their intimate relationships and understanding. This shift involves developing a bond that is instinctual, loving, captivating, and grounded in reality, rather than adhering to a false dogma that is considered blasphemous, outrageous, and destructive, driven by fear and anger.

The question of whether we exist in a benevolent universe is of profound importance to humanity. It was considered by Albert Einstein to be the foremost and fundamental question that each individual must personally confront. Understanding the nature of the world we perceive, and the process by which we perceive and construct it, holds immense significance in our lives.

To truly awaken to our authentic divine essence, we must release our attachment to the outdated structures of the old patriarchal system and the perspective that we should fear the Lord. This mindset hinders our ability to undergo transformation and transcend our evolutionary journey. It is essential to redirect our attention to our inherent God-self, which enables us to actively participate in our evolutionary process, aligning with our true nature. By nurturing the seeds of love within us and tending to the growth of our spiritual being, we contribute to our own evolution and the betterment of humanity as a whole. This shift allows us to recognize ourselves as embodiments of love and tap into the profound power of the Spirit and God-consciousness residing within us.

Furthermore, in the journey of faith, direct experiences with God can serve as catalysts for profound transformation. We witness such instances in the lives of Peter and Paul, two pivotal figures in the early Christian movement, whose encounters with the divine powerfully shaped their understanding of the Gospel.

Peter, a devout Jew and one of Jesus' closest disciples experienced a remarkable event that forever changed his perspective. While engaged in prayer on a rooftop, he witnessed a vision—a large sheet descending from heaven, filled with various animals, both clean and unclean according to Jewish dietary laws. A voice urged Peter to rise, kill, and eat, challenging the strict dietary regulations ingrained in his religious upbringing.

Initially perplexed, Peter hesitated, clinging to his deeply ingrained beliefs. However, the voice spoke again, declaring, "What God has cleansed, no longer consider unholy" (Acts10:15). This vision symbolized a profound shift in Peter's understanding, as he realized that the Gospel of Jesus Christ was meant for all people, regardless of their cultural or religious backgrounds. It was a message of inclusivity and love, breaking down the barriers that separated humanity.

Similarly, the apostle Paul underwent a transformative experience on the road to Damascus. As a devout Pharisee, Paul fervently persecuted early followers of Jesus, considering them a threat to Judaism. However, during his journey, he encountered a blinding light and heard the voice of Jesus, asking, "Saul, Saul, why are you persecuting Me?" (Acts 9:4). This encounter left Paul physically blinded but spiritually awakened. He underwent a profound conversion, dedicating the rest of his life to spreading the Gospel to both Jews and Gentiles, ultimately becoming one of the most influential figures in early Christianity.

These experiences highlight the power of direct encounters with the divine, which can shatter our preconceived notions, challenge our beliefs, and ignite a radical transformation within us. They demonstrate that the path of faith is not confined to rigid dogmas and doctrines but is a dynamic and personal journey of communion with the divine.

In conclusion, organized religions often incorporate fear-based systems that perpetuate judgment and separation. However, the teachings of Jesus and the experiences of early believers point us toward a higher understanding—an understanding rooted in love, inclusivity, and direct communion with the divine. By embracing our inherent divine nature and nurturing our connection to God, we can transcend the limitations of fear and judgment, actively participating in our own evolution and contributing to the betterment of humanity.

In today's society, we are constantly subjected to various influences that shape our thoughts and behaviors. These influences aim to manipulate and control us, leading us to conform to a limited version of ourselves. Consequently, we often fail to establish a genuine connection with our authentic essence and creative potential.

However, when we awaken to our true identity as independent and imaginative individuals, we disrupt the control exerted by societal systems. By empowering ourselves as creative agents, we not only liberate our own spirits but also unleash the inherent brilliance within us, enabling us to shape and transform the world around us.

Breaking free from the conditioning and programming that restricts our true creative selves is a personal journey that requires self-awareness and conscious effort. Here are some steps you can take to begin this process:

◊ **Cultivate self-awareness:** Start by examining the beliefs, values, and behaviors that you have adopted throughout your life. Reflect on whether these truly aligned with your authentic self or if they have been influenced by external forces.

◊ **Question societal norms and expectations:** Challenge the societal norms and expectations that have been imposed upon you. Ask yourself why you believe certain things or behave in specific ways. Do these behaviors genuinely resonate with your true self or if they are simply products of conditioning?

◊ **Seek alternative perspectives:** Expose yourself to diverse viewpoints and alternative narratives. Engage in critical thinking and question the dominant narratives presented by society.

◊ **Embrace creativity in all aspects of life:** Recognize that creativity extends beyond traditional artistic pursuits. Embrace creativity in all areas of your life, whether it's problem-solving, decision-making, or expressing different ideas, take risks, and challenge the status quo.

◊ **Practice self-expression:** Engage in activities that bring you joy and allow you to tap into your creativity, such as writing, painting, dancing, or playing music. Expressing yourself freely and without judgment helps cultivate a deeper connection with your creative essence.

◊ **Surround yourself with creative individuals.**

◊ **Continuously learn and evolve:** Commit to lifelong learning and personal growth. Engage in activities that expand your knowledge, challenge your beliefs, and push you outside of your comfort zone.

The truth is that salvation is available to all of us. God embodies love and exists within everything. Regardless of whether one identifies as atheist, agnostic, Jewish, Catholic, Muslim, Hindu, Buddhist, or any other belief system, no path exists outside of God. There is only one God, who is interconnected with every individual, knowing them intimately and loving them unconditionally and eternally.

Let the radiant light within your heart shine brightly as you rediscover your authentic essence. Embrace your role as a contributor in shaping a world filled with joy, the profound beauty of the soul, the wisdom found in harmonious melodies, and the symphony of love that permeates life. Take ownership and responsibility for how you contribute, making a positive impact. Your acts of service are a genuine reflection of your essence within the intricate fabric of existence. Remember and embrace unity as the purpose of your soul.

If there is light in the soul, there will be beauty in the person,
If there is beauty in the person, there will be harmony in the
house. If there is harmony in the house, there will be order in
the nation If there is order in the nation, there will be peace
in the world.

CHINESE PROVERB

Engaging in the sacred task of dismantling our deceptive systems is a profound endeavor; join in this sacred work. It is crucial to stand in the revelation of divine love and extend compassion and grace to ourselves as we evolve into our empowered role as co-creators, capable of manifesting extraordinary wonders.

Within each of us resides a brilliant and radiant spark, akin to the sun illuminating a magnificent day. This luminosity originates from the depths of our being. It is essential to recognize that the face of the beloved, whom we seek, shines forth from every face. Embracing this divine understanding will dissipate the veils of our self-imposed illusions of separation and judgment.

In the quest for truth, we are invited to explore the profound teachings of Jesus and embark on a journey of self-reflection. Jesus, in his divine wisdom, prompts us to delve deep into our hearts and contemplate the nature of truth within our own lives. This introspective quest resonates with the very question Pilate posed when he encountered Jesus, "What is truth?" (John 18:38). Pilate, however, did not await an answer, missing the opportunity to uncover the transformative wisdom that Jesus came to reveal.

Yet, we recognize that Jesus, as the embodiment of truth, came to illuminate the path for us. Through his life, teachings, and divine presence, he shows us that truth is not an abstract concept but something tangible and experiential. It is through our direct experiences with the Creator that we can personally sense and verify the existence of God, transcending mere intellectual understanding.

In those moments of divine connection, our senses become attuned to the presence of the Divine, and we are enveloped in a profound awareness of a higher reality. It is in these encounters that we find truth taking root within our souls, assuring us of a reality that surpasses human comprehension. These personal experiences of encountering the divine are not limited to a select few; they are accessible to all who earnestly seek truth.

As we open ourselves to these transformative encounters and cultivate a deeper relationship with our Creator, we anchor our faith in the bedrock of personal revelation. These experiences become touchstones that guide our thoughts, actions, and relationships, infusing our lives with a deeper sense of purpose and understanding.

In the quest for truth, let us heed the call of Jesus to journey inward, exploring the depths of our hearts and minds. May we embrace the humility of Pilate's question, "What is truth?" and patiently await the answers that unfold through personal revelation and divine encounters. As we open ourselves to the whispers of truth that resonate within us, we draw closer to the divine source of all that is true, meaningful, and eternal.

THE BREAD OF LIFE: NOURISHING OUR SOULS, ILLUMINATING OUR PURPOSE

The Bread of Life, a divine sustenance graciously provided by our Heavenly Father, is the key to quenching our deepest longings. It originates from the heavenly realm, intricately woven into the fabric of our very being. When we acknowledge this eternal source of fulfillment, a profound transformation occurs. Our hunger and thirst dissipate as we realize that our essence is inseparably intertwined with the magnificent and unified presence of God.

In this understanding, we find nourishment for our spirits, uplifting and satisfying our innermost longings. It is through a deep and intimate knowledge of our Creator that we discover the ultimate nourishment for our souls. This divine communion grants us everlasting life and leads us to the wellsprings of our salvation.

As we undergo a transformative rebirth, our awareness expands, resonating at the core of our being. This newfound understanding propels us to soar into the boundless light of personal growth. We begin to grasp the profound truth that the Father Himself has sealed us with His love, assuring us that even in moments of hunger, we are nourished and content through our unity and intimate connection with Him.

The Son of Man, exalted for our sake, invites us to recognize the divine child within ourselves. Just as the Father has sent Him, He has also sent us into the world, to carry forth the fruits of our spiritual journey and to make a lasting impact. We are not mere wanderers; rather, we have been chosen and ordained to bring forth fruit that endures, bearing witness to the transformative power of the Bread of Life.

In the words of Jesus, "Ye have not chosen me, but I have chosen you, and ordained you, that ye should go and bring forth fruit, and that your fruit should remain" (John 15:16, KJV). These words remind us that our journey is not a solitary one. We have been lovingly chosen by the Divine, entrusted with a sacred purpose to manifest the fruits of our union with the Bread of Life.

May we embrace this profound truth and allow it to permeate every aspect of our lives. By partaking in the Bread of Life, we find sustenance, fulfillment, and the strength to carry forth the transformative message of love and grace. Let us walk in the knowledge that we are chosen, ordained, and empowered to make a lasting impact, shining the light of the Bread of Life to a world in need.

17

ETERNAL RESTORATION: UNVEILING THE ULTIMATE HEALING

THE LAST JUDGEMENT IS THAT THERE IS NO JUDGMENT. Beyond perception, there is no judgment. "Judge not that ye be not judged" (Matthew 7:1). If you judge the reality of others, you will be unable to avoid judging your own. In the book A Course of Miracles the Last Judgement is described in this way:

◊ **T-2. VIII.3.** The Last Judgment is generally thought of as a procedure undertaken by God. 2 Actually it will be undertaken by my brothers with my help. 3 It is a final healing rather than a meting out of punishment, however much you may think that punishment is deserved. 4 Punishment is a concept totally opposed to right-mindedness, and the aim of the Last Judgment is to restore right-mindedness to you. 5 The Last Judgment might be called a process of right evaluation. 6 It simply means that everyone will finally come to understand what is worthy and what is not. 7 After this, the ability to choose can be directed rationally. 8 Until this distinction is made, however, the vacillations between free and imprisoned will cannot but continue.[75]

◊ **T-2. VIII.4.** The first step toward freedom involves a sorting out of the false from the true. 2 This is a process of separation in the constructive sense and reflects the true meaning of the

Apocalypse. 3 Everyone will ultimately look upon his own creations and choose to preserve only what is good, just as God Himself looked upon what He had created and knew that it was good. 4 At this point, the mind can begin to look with love on its own creations because of their worthiness. 5 At the same time the mind will inevitably disown its miscreations which, without belief, will no longer exist.[76]

UNVEILING TRUTH:
THE LAST JUDGMENT AND THE EIGHTFOLD PATH ON THE JOURNEY OF DISCERNMENT AND TRANSFORMATION

These teachings are similar to the teachings of the Buddha and the eight-fold path. The Eightfold Path is a fundamental concept in Buddhism that outlines a set of guidelines for leading a wholesome and fulfilling life, ultimately aiming to achieve liberation from suffering and attain enlightenment. In Buddhism, the concept of discernment is closely tied to the practice of mindfulness and meditation. Through these practices, individuals cultivate a clear and direct perception of their experiences, allowing them to see through illusions and delusions. This process of discernment enables them to distinguish between what is helpful and unhelpful, beneficial and harmful, skillful and unskillful.

In sorting out the false from the truth it encourages individuals to examine their own creations, thoughts, and actions, and to choose to preserve what is good and aligned with truth while letting go of what is false and lacking in worth.

The last judgment, as described earlier, shares the emphasis on discernment and right evaluation. It is a process through which individuals gain insight into what is worthy and what is not, leading to a clearer understanding of reality and the ability to make choices based on wisdom and truth.

The teachings of the Last Judgment resonate with the principles of the Buddha's Eightfold Path. In Buddhism, discernment is closely tied to mindfulness and meditation, allowing individuals to perceive reality clearly and distinguish between what is beneficial and harmful. Similarly, the Last Judgment emphasizes discernment and right evaluation, leading to a clearer understanding of reality and the ability to make choices based on wisdom and truth.

The Eightfold Path consists of eight interconnected practices.

WISDOM

> **Right View:** Developing an accurate understanding of the nature of reality including the Four Noble Truths and the law of cause and effect.

> **Right Intention:** Cultivating wholesome intentions, such as renunciation, goodwill, and compassion.

ETHICAL CONDUCT

> **Right Speech:** Practicing truthful, kind, and helpful speech while avoiding harmful or divisive speech.

> **Right Action:** Acting in ways that are ethical, virtuous, and non-harmful, such as refraining from killing, stealing, and engaging in sexual misconduct.

> **Right Livelihood:** Engaging in a livelihood that is honest and supports one's spiritual development, avoiding occupations that cause harm or suffering to others.

MENTAL DEVELOPMENT

> **Right Effort:** Cultivating the effort to abandon unwholesome thoughts, emotions, and behaviors, while nurturing wholesome ones.

> **Right Mindfulness:** Developing moment-to-moment awareness of one's body, feelings, thoughts, and the surrounding environment, with clarity and non-judgmental observations.

> **Right Concentration:** Cultivating deep states of concentration and focus through practices such as meditation, leads to a calm and clear mind.

The Eightfold Path is seen as a holistic and balanced approach to life, addressing both our internal mental states and our external actions. It is considered a path of self-discovery, self-transformation, and liberation from the cycle of suffering.

"Let this mind be in you which was also in Christ Jesus" from Philippians 2:5 encourages people to adopt the same mindset as Jesus Christ, which ultimately leads to a transformed perspective.

Imagine a butterfly emerging from its cocoon. When the butterfly breaks free from the confines of its former state, it experiences a newfound freedom and transformation. Similarly, when we separate what is true from what is false in our lives, it liberates us to discover our highest Truth.

Just as the butterfly undergoes a metamorphosis, we too undergo a process of inner transformation and self-realization. As we embrace our worthiness and recognize our inherent wholeness, we can come to know God or our highest spiritual nature with absolute certainty.

Our human experience is not solely about conceptual understanding but rather about experiential knowing. It is through our desire for self-awakening and the fullest expression of our true selves that we embark on a journey of evolution. This journey is like the graceful unfolding of a butterfly's wings, as we tap into the light of divine consciousness and reveal our authentic being.

Just as the butterfly's transformation is a natural part of its lifecycle, our personal growth and connection with the divine are inherent aspects of our existence. We are already whole and sacred, and our path is to align ourselves with that truth and allow our authentic selves to blossom and flourish.

DIVINE UNION: EMBRACING ONENESS AND ELEVATING CONSCIOUSNESS

Jesus, a figure of unparalleled historical significance, stands as a transformative liberator who offers us the key to true freedom. Through his teachings and examples, he illuminates the path toward a profound self-awareness rooted in godliness. At the heart of his message lies the concept of embodying the union of spirit and matter, which deepens our understanding of the interconnectedness that defines our existence.

Imagine Jesus as a loving shepherd, ever-present, watching over and guiding us on our journey. He unifies our hearts and serves as the beloved bridegroom to all, inviting us into a sacred union with divinity. In this union, we discover the central task that lies before humanity: expanding our awareness in order to grasp the immense magnitude of love.

In a world governed by duality, we often find ourselves trapped in a state of judgment. We label things as good or bad, right or wrong, without realizing the limitations this imposes on our understanding. Jesus brings forth a profound message: "Do not judge, and you will not be judged. Do not condemn, and you will not be condemned. Forgive, and you will be forgiven" (Luke 6:37).

These words challenge us to transcend our judgmental tendencies and embrace a mindset of forgiveness and compassion. Jesus reminds us that our interconnected existence demands empathy and understanding, for when we cast others into darkness, we are drawn into that same darkness ourselves. By recognizing the profound truth of our interconnectedness, we begin to unravel the threads of suffering that bind us, paving the way for harmony and well-being in our shared existence.

Oneness is a fundamental aspect of our being, transcending apparent divisions and separations. We are all interconnected, forming part of a greater whole. It is within this understanding that we bear a collective responsibility toward one another and the planet we call home. Embracing our inherent oneness calls us to engage with empathy, compassion, and care for others, fostering harmony and well-being in our shared existence.

SELF-REFLECTION AND PERSONAL GROWTH

Jesus's teachings caution us against hypocrisy and urge us to embark on a journey of self-reflection and personal growth. How can we presume to remove a tiny speck from our brother's eye when we remain blind to the beam obstructing our own vision? By addressing the faults within ourselves first, we gain clarity and perspective. Through this self-awareness, we can approach others with compassion and understanding as we assist them with their own challenges.

The underlying message is clear: humility, self-examination, and personal growth are essential in our interactions with others. Rather than being overly critical or judgmental, we are called to focus on our own improvement, fostering empathy, understanding, and genuine assistance.

RAISING OUR VIBRATION AND CULTIVATING INTERCONNECTEDNESS

Yet, embracing these transformative teachings requires more than abstract concepts; it calls for tangible changes in our daily lives. We must raise our vibration, elevating our energy to align with higher frequencies. This involves mindful practices, adopting healthier habits regarding diet and lifestyle, and being aware of the media and content we consume, as they greatly influence our energy levels.

Every aspect of our lives plays a role in determining our vibrational condition. By transcending the outdated beliefs that have limited human potential and hindered the progress of our world, we can cultivate a profound sense of interconnectedness and gain a deeper understanding of our place in the universe. Such a shift in consciousness contributes not only to our personal well-being but also to the well-being of our global community, fostering sustainability and harmony.

REVITALIZING RELIGION AND EMBRACING DIVINE ESSENCE

To revitalize religion, we must delve into the depths of our emotions and experience a spiritual awakening within ourselves. By awakening our hearts, we establish a profound connection with the universe, akin to stepping into a transformative spiritual realm. In this era of revelations, it becomes crucial for us to seek renewal and gain a deep understanding of the necessary changes we must embrace. We must consciously select new frameworks of thought that enrich our lives with the essence of our inherent greatness, allowing us to embody the core essence of our divine nature.

Look within your heart, and imagine the presence of Christ at its core—a radiant light, a vibrant flame. Step into the inner sanctuary of your being, feeling the warmth that emanates from within and witnessing the flickering light that resides there. It is within this sacred space that your deepest intuition exists. Take a moment to sit with the presence of this divine energy, this luminous light. Allow it to permeate your being, filling you completely and merging with your essence. In this communion, you connect with a heightened frequency known as Christ Consciousness—a state of elevated awareness and divine union.

The Christ within you represents the truth of who you are, and as you embody this truth, you manifest the awe and wonder of God within your own experience of life. It is through this divine union, this merging of our human selves with the essence of the divine, that we find our purpose and experience life in its fullest expression.

In conclusion, embracing the teachings of Jesus opens the door to a transformative understanding of our interconnectedness and oneness. By relinquishing judgment, cultivating self-reflection, raising our vibration, and merging with our divine essence, we embark on a profound journey of personal growth and spiritual awakening. In this sacred union, we discover the truth of who we are and embrace the manifestation of God within us, creating a wondrous and awe-inspiring experience of life. Let us walk this path of divine union together, guided by the teachings and example of Jesus, and awaken to the limitless possibilities that lie within us and before us.

UNVEILING THE SYMBOLISM OF THE FIG TREE: JESUS, FAITH, AND THE PROFOUND INTERPLAY OF DIVINE AND HUMAN EXISTENCE

The Fig tree holds profound symbolism as it represents the Nation of Israel, the birthplace of Yeshua (Jesus). Jesus yearns for his people to grasp the depth of his teachings and bear spiritual fruit. Under the fig tree, God intimately knows our hearts, perceiving us in our most private moments. We are all embraced and interconnected, united with the essence of our divine nature.

In the Gospel of John, Jesus astonishes Nathanael by revealing divine insight about Nathanael's presence under the fig tree. This revelation sparks Nathanael's belief in Jesus. Jesus promises even greater spiritual experiences to Nathanael, symbolized by the opening of heaven and the angels of God ascending and descending upon the Son of Man.

This passage underscores Jesus' divine wisdom and his embodiment of the profound connection between the heavenly and earthly realms. Through a deep connection with Jesus, individuals can encounter extraordinary spiritual revelations and witness the divine intersecting with human existence.

As the time of harvest approaches, the maturity of our faith becomes crucial. Like a ripe fruit, mature faith bears enduring and righteous outcomes. A good tree cannot produce evil fruit, and the harvest draws near. God, who discerns our readiness, extends an invitation to all, standing at the threshold of our hearts. The manifestation of God becomes evident when we are fully ripened, and the spiritual fruit we bear is abundant. Through collective efforts and heartfelt prayers, we participate in the abundant harvest of souls, bringing them into the embrace of God's love and grace.

When we cultivate trust and surrender, placing our faith in God and the abundant universe, remarkable transformations occur. True magic unfolds when we relinquish control and allow ourselves to be guided by a higher power. Opening ourselves to receptivity and embracing an attitude of allowance become essential for attaining freedom and accessing the "upper room" of spiritual enlightenment. Through trust and connection with higher consciousness, we invite a heightened vibrational energy to flow through our beings.

The "upper room" serves as a symbolic space, encompassing significant events such as the Last Supper, the appearance of the risen Jesus to His disciples, and the gathering of the early Christian community before the outpouring of the Holy Spirit. It represents a collective field of sacred communion, transformation, and empowerment, where individuals come together to experience the divine presence and receive spiritual empowerment. In this sacred space, hearts are united, and the power of the divine is deeply felt, fostering spiritual growth and empowerment.

18

ILLUMINATED AWAKENING: UNVEILING THE SOUL'S JOURNEY

I said: what about my eyes?
He said: Keep them on the road.

I said: What about my passion?
He said: Keep it burning.

I said: What about my heart?
He said: Tell me what you hold inside it?

I said: Pain and sorrow.
He said: Stay with it. The wound is the
place where the Light enters you.

RUMI

THE PROCESS OF AWAKENING IS A DEEPLY IMPACTFUL AND transformative journey that beckons individuals to delve into the profound depths of their inner selves, unravel the enigmatic mysteries of existence, and expand their awareness. Across the ages, those on a spiritual path have embarked on a quest for self-realization, driven by a desire to uncover the answers to life's most fundamental inquiries.

As we progress through the 12 stages of Spiritual Awakening, we embark on a journey that leads us to discover new realms of wisdom, knowledge, and interconnectedness. By unlocking the mysteries of our existence and embracing the path toward elevated consciousness, we open ourselves to profound growth and transformation.

FROM DISCONTENT TO AWAKENING: UNVEILING THE VEIL OF SUFFERING

The initial stage we come across is a powerful feeling of discontentment. It extends beyond a temporary dissatisfaction with our material possessions or worldly successes and represents a profound and enduring longing for something that transcends the physical realm.

It is a shared human experience that goes beyond cultural, societal, and individual differences. This sense of dissatisfaction that often arises can be interpreted as a gentle push from our inner selves to embark on a spiritual journey and search for the fundamental essence of our existence, which extends beyond the physical world. The feeling of discontentment, therefore, is not solely a source of pain but rather an opportunity for Spiritual Awakening, a doorway through which illumination, wisdom, and comprehension can enter our lives. Our discontented emotions should not be viewed as mere obstacles to overcome, but rather as valuable signs guiding us towards a deeper understanding of our true purpose and the profound aspects of our being. These emotions serve as catalysts, propelling us towards awakening and compelling us to explore the boundless potential within us and embrace the lessons that our souls are meant to learn.

The story of Siddhartha Gautama, the Buddha, beautifully exemplifies the correlation between discontentment and spiritual awakening.

Siddhartha Gautama was born into a life of luxury, shielded from the harsh realities of the world. However, despite his privileged upbringing, he felt a deep sense of discontentment. The opulence surrounding him failed to provide lasting fulfillment or answer the profound questions that stirred within his soul.

Driven by his inner restlessness, Siddhartha embarked on a spiritual quest, leaving behind his princely life. He sought out spiritual teachers, engaged in rigorous ascetic practices, and delved deeply into meditation. Yet even these intense pursuits did not alleviate his discontentment.

One day, while sitting under the Bodhi tree in deep contemplation, Siddhartha experienced a profound awakening. He realized that the root of his discontentment lay in the attachments and desires that bound him to the material world. He understood that true fulfillment and liberation could only be found by transcending the physical realm and awakening to the deeper truths of existence.

This pivotal moment marked Siddhartha's transformation into the Buddha, the awakened one. From that point forward, he dedicated his life to sharing his insights and teachings with others. The Buddha's teachings emphasized the impermanence of worldly pursuits and the importance of seeking enlightenment to transcend suffering.

The story of Siddhartha Gautama serves as a powerful illustration of how discontentment can serve as a catalyst for spiritual awakening. His journey exemplifies the idea that the wound of discontent can be a gateway to profound transformation and enlightenment. Like the Buddha, when we recognize the limitations of our material pursuits and embark on a quest to discover our true essence, we can find the light, wisdom, and understanding that lead to a deeper understanding of ourselves and our purpose in life.

~ STAGE 2 ~
UNVEILING TRUTH THROUGH INQUIRY AND EXPLORATION

Discontentment leads to a phase of inquiry and exploration. This stage is defined by a reflective journey in which we confront profound inquiries about the meaning of life and our authentic nature. It is a period characterized by an insatiable longing for wisdom and a pursuit of truth that transcends superficial aspects of existence. The soul, by its very nature, is driven to seek knowledge and truth.

This phase of inquiry and exploration can be perceived as an expression of the soul's innate longing to awaken and expand its understanding. By awakening the latent knowledge within us, we tap into a wellspring of concealed wisdom. The inquiries we pose to ourselves during this period serve as keys that unlock profound insights about our existence and the universe, guiding us toward a more profound understanding. During this stage, our focus shifts from seeking external validation to embarking on an internal journey of exploration and personal growth. It is a transformative period where we gain a deeper and more meaningful comprehension of ourselves and the world around us. We begin to discern patterns in our lives, recognizing the lessons we have learned and the wisdom we have acquired, which propels us towards a path of self-awakening that is more fulfilling and profound. It is at this juncture that we fully embrace the soul's journey, acknowledging and cherishing our unique experiences and the intrinsic yearning for knowledge and truth that resides within us.

~ STAGE 3 ~
UNVEILING THE INNER LIGHT
OF CONSCIOUSNESS

The journey of awakening brings us to a crucial stage known as enlightenment. This stage is not merely a singular moment, but rather an expansive process in which consciousness expands, enabling us to perceive and comprehend realities that extend beyond the realm of the ordinary. In this context, enlightenment signifies the expansion of our awareness, granting us access to the vast reservoirs of universal knowledge and wisdom. It involves tapping into higher levels of knowledge that exist within the universe. Over time, the fundamental truths of our existence and the universe become illuminated within our consciousness. Hence, enlightenment is not a final destination, but an ongoing process of growth, learning, and the continuous expansion of our understanding. It involves lifting the veils of illusion that cloud our perception, allowing us to see with clarity and wisdom. During this stage, we begin to perceive the interconnectedness of all things and recognize the universal laws that govern our existence.

~ STAGE 4 ~
THE DARK NIGHT OF THE SOUL

During our path of spiritual awakening, we inevitably encounter a phase known as the dark night of the soul. In this stage, we courageously face our most profound fears, uncertainties, and internal conflicts. It is a challenging yet crucial part of our journey where we directly confront our shadows and the unresolved issues that impede our advancement. This process holds significant importance in the evolution of our soul, as it allows us to break free from patterns that no longer serve our growth and liberation.

By embracing our challenges as catalysts for profound transformation and personal development, we are summoned to embark on a profound exploration of our soul's intricate history. This journey compels us to confront and heal the wounds of our past, enabling us to emerge stronger and more enlightened than before.

~ STAGE 5 ~
EMBRACING THE UNCHARTED PATH
OF TRANSFORMATION

We come to a profound precipice, a pivotal point in our lives where a momentous decision awaits us. At this crossroads of our soul's journey, we confront the vast expanse of the unknown that lies ahead. We are faced with a choice: to cling to the familiar or to courageously venture into uncharted territories. By embracing the unexplored, we embark on a soulful exploration that traverses diverse dimensions and realities. Our souls possess an expansive and adventurous nature that extends far beyond what we can currently comprehend in our physical existence. The decision to leap into this uncharted territory is essential, as it enables us to discover new facets of our existence, learn profound lessons from different realms, and wholeheartedly embrace the full spectrum of experiences that our soul deeply yearns for.

~ STAGE 6 ~
SOUL'S REBIRTH: EMBRACING AUTHENTICITY AND INTEGRATING SHADOWS

As we journey further along our spiritual path, we encounter a phase characterized by rebirth and authenticity. This transformative stage involves confronting and integrating our shadow self—the hidden and often disregarded aspects of our psyche. It entails shedding old layers and emerging anew, aligning ourselves with our true nature and essence. Rebirth necessitates confronting these shadows, comprehending their origins, and embarking on a healing process. Through this process, we integrate all aspects of our being, both light and dark, leading to a more authentic and whole self.

We can bring the darkness into consciousness by illuminating the parts of ourselves that we have denied or ignored. This process of acknowledging and understanding our shadows is crucial for personal growth and spiritual enlightenment. It enables us to move beyond self-imposed illusions and limitations and embrace an existence aligned with our innermost values and truths, rather than conforming to external expectations or societal norms. This rebirth allows us to release old identities, beliefs, and patterns that no longer serve our growth.

As we embrace our authentic selves, we open ourselves up to a more genuine, fulfilling, and enlightened way of living. This transformative journey leads us towards a deeper sense of fulfillment and a more profound connection to our true essence.

~ STAGE 7 ~
ONENESS UNVEILED: EMBRACING INTERCONNECTED CONSCIOUSNESS

In the transformative journey of spiritual awakening, we eventually attain a profound realization of oneness and interconnectedness. This stage signifies a significant shift in our perception, moving beyond the notion of separate entities and recognizing our inherent connection with all that exists. The entire universe is intricately linked together. The sense of separation we often experience is an illusion, arising from our limited physical senses and societal conditioning. By transcending these illusions, we come to comprehend the fundamental interconnectedness of all beings, accessing a higher level of awareness known as the collective consciousness.

In this state, the individual self merges with the larger whole, and we begin to perceive life not only from our personal perspective but as an integral part of a vast, interconnected tapestry of existence. This realization fosters a deep sense of unity with all beings, cultivating empathy, compassion, and a profound sense of belonging. We recognize that we are all interconnected threads within the fabric of existence, and our actions ripple through the interconnected web of life. This heightened awareness encourages us to act with love, kindness, and respect towards ourselves, others, and the world around us.

~ STAGE 8 ~
THE DANCE OF SYNCHRONICITY: TRUSTING INTUITION AND EMBRACING LIFE'S FLOW

As we delve deeper into our spiritual journeys, we enter a phase characterized by heightened sensitivity to the subtle intricacies of life. This stage is marked by an awareness of synchronicities and intuitive guidance. We begin to observe meaningful coincidences and signs that appear to guide us along our path. These synchronicities are not mere chance happenings but messages from the universe, offering guidance on our soul's journey. They serve as affirmations that we are on the right track and that the universe is conspiring to assist us in fulfilling our spiritual purpose.

Central to this stage is the concept of flowing with the rhythms of life. It involves cultivating a deep trust in the wisdom and timing of the universe. Instead of resisting the natural flow of life, we learn to move with it gracefully. This entails placing our trust in our intuition, which acts as a subtle internal compass guiding our decisions and actions. Listening to our intuition involves paying attention to those inner nudges and following them, even when they may not make logical sense in the present moment. When we develop trust in the universe as a friendly and supportive force that is working in our favor this trust allows us to release the need for controlling every aspect of our lives and instead be open to the experiences and lessons that come our way. It involves embracing the unknown and recognizing that some of the most profound growth and learning arise from unexpected and unplanned circumstances. By surrendering to the flow of life and trusting in the universe's guidance, we create space for transformation and expansion.

In this stage, we learn to navigate life with a sense of curiosity, openness, and receptivity. We cultivate a mindset that welcomes the unexpected, knowing that it holds the potential for deep growth and insight. By embracing the synchronicities, trusting our intuition, and surrendering to the unfolding of life, we align ourselves with the greater wisdom and purpose of the universe.

~ STAGE 9 ~
SOUL'S UNVEILING: EMBRACING AUTHENTIC EXPRESSION AND PURPOSEFUL LIVING

In the journey of spiritual awakening, there is a pivotal phase known as authentic expression. In this phase, we wholeheartedly embrace and manifest our true selves, aligning our external lives with our innermost thoughts, feelings, and beliefs. Living authentically is a fundamental aspect of our spiritual growth and personal development.

Each soul enters life with a unique purpose and a set of lessons to learn. Authentic expression entails aligning ourselves with this inner purpose and living a life that reflects the true intentions of our soul. Before incarnating, we engage in soul contracts and pre-life planning, making agreements with other souls to meet and interact in specific ways for mutual growth and learning. Honoring these contracts involves living and relating in a manner that is authentic to our soul's purpose. It entails forming genuine relationships that resonate with our true selves and support us in fulfilling our roles in these soul agreements. Through authenticity, our connections with others deepen, and relationships become vehicles for mutual growth and spiritual evolution.

Purposeful living is another essential dimension of authentic expression. It involves making choices and taking actions that align with our highest values and aspirations. It means living deliberately and consciously, making decisions that truly reflect who we are and what we genuinely desire to experience in life. By living in alignment with our authentic selves, we create a life that is meaningful, fulfilling, and in harmony with our deepest truths.

Authentic expression allows us to embody our true nature, fully embracing our individuality while honoring the interconnectedness of all beings. It empowers us to shine our unique light, contributing to the collective tapestry of human experience. Through authentic living, we align ourselves with our soul's purpose, cultivate genuine connections, and create a life that is purposeful, meaningful, and in resonance with our deepest essence.

~ STAGE 10 ~
TRANSCENDING BOUNDARIES: THE JOURNEY OF CONSCIOUSNESS ELEVATION

As we continue on our spiritual journey, we enter a significant phase of conscious elevation. During this stage, we experience a profound shift in awareness, transcending the limitations of our physical existence and accessing higher dimensions and states of being. We expand beyond our ordinary experience, connecting with realms of existence that offer greater understanding and broader perspectives of the universe and our place within it.

The evolution of consciousness does not solely rely on accumulating more knowledge; it is about experiencing life in a deeper and more interconnected way. At the core of this phase is the concept of the higher self. The higher self is part of our soul that resides in the spirit world, consistently guiding and supporting us. It holds the wisdom and knowledge of all our past experiences and life lessons. As we elevate our consciousness, our connection with the higher self strengthens, granting us access to the vast reservoir of wisdom it holds. This connection provides us with guidance, intuition, and a profound comprehension of our life purpose.

A fundamental aspect of this elevated consciousness is understanding the interconnectedness of our thoughts, feelings, and the cosmos. We recognize that our thoughts and emotions are not isolated occurrences but energies that interact with the energy of the universe. This realization instills in us a sense of responsibility for the energy we emit into the world and a profound understanding of our deep connection to the cosmic web of life.

~ STAGE 11 ~
EMPOWERED CO-CREATION:
AWAKENING THE CREATIVE FORCE WITHIN

In the transformative journey of spiritual awakening, we reach a profound realization about our role as co-creators with the universe. This phase revolves around understanding and embracing our innate ability to manifest our reality. We are not passive bystanders in the universe; rather, we actively participate in the creation of our own experiences. This co-creation process aligns with the purpose of our souls and the lessons we are meant to learn.

Our life experiences are not random happenings but reflections of our inner state and the energies we project into the world. This perspective empowers us to take ownership of our lives, recognizing that we play a significant role in shaping our own path. The power of thoughts and beliefs holds great importance in the concept of co-creation. Our minds possess tremendous power and can influence and shape our reality. What we consistently believe and think has a significant impact on what we attract and manifest in our lives.

This concept aligns with the teachings of the law of attraction, which suggests that like attracts like. By directing our energy towards what we desire, we set the process of manifestation into motion. As Einstein famously said, "Everything is energy, and that's all there is to it. Match the frequency of the reality you want, and you cannot help but get that reality. It can be no other way. This is not philosophy; this is physics." At the core, the universe is comprised of energy and consciousness. By aligning our own energy—our thoughts, emotions, and beliefs—with the frequencies of our desired outcomes, we actively co-create our experiences and shape our reality.

~ STAGE 12 ~
RADIANCE OF THE HEART:
EMBRACING UNCONDITIONAL LOVE,
COMPASSION, AND ACCEPTANCE

As we ascend to the apex of our spiritual journey, we wholeheartedly embrace the profound virtues of unconditional love, compassion, and acceptance. These qualities embody the highest frequencies of our existence and serve as vital keys to achieving spiritual growth and enlightenment. Unconditional love and compassion, in particular, hold a foundational role in our spiritual evolution. They are the most potent vibrations in the universe, possessing the transformative power to impact not only individual lives but also the collective consciousness.

Unconditional love transcends physical boundaries and ego-driven desires, representing the purest form of energy. It is a selfless love that seeks nothing in return, reflecting the true essence of our spiritual nature. Compassion, too, plays a significant part in our spiritual journey. It involves empathetically understanding the struggles and pain of others, leading to a deep desire to alleviate suffering. This quality nurtures a sense of interconnectedness, reminding us that we are all interconnected in the fabric of the universe. By practicing compassion, we not only assist others in their healing process but also accelerate our own spiritual growth, gaining valuable lessons in empathy, kindness, and the human condition.

Acceptance is another transformative virtue. It involves embracing ourselves and others as they are, without judgment or the desire to change. Acceptance acknowledges the perfection and imperfection, as well as the uniqueness of each individual's path. It recognizes that every experience, no matter how challenging, is a valuable part of our soul's evolution.

The transformational power of unconditional love, compassion, and acceptance is profound. These qualities have the capacity to heal not only at the individual level but also collectively, dissolving barriers, healing old wounds, and fostering a sense of unity and oneness. When we embody these qualities, we contribute to the healing and evolution of the entire planet, elevating the vibration of the collective consciousness.

In conclusion, the phases of the spiritual journey offer a transformative path of self-discovery, growth, and enlightenment. As we awaken to higher consciousness and strengthen our connection with the higher self, we tap into profound wisdom and guidance. Through co-creation and manifestation, we recognize our role as active participants in shaping our reality. Embracing the virtues of unconditional love, compassion, and acceptance, we elevate our existence, fostering unity, healing, and spiritual evolution. These phases invite us to embark on a profound quest of self-realization, leading to a deeper understanding of our purpose, our interconnectedness with the universe, and our capacity to make a positive impact on the collective consciousness. As we traverse these phases, we embark on a journey of profound transformation that expands our awareness, brings us closer to our true selves, and aligns us with the boundless potential of the universe.

19

AWAKENING THE DIVINE WITHIN: EXPLORING THE SPIRITUAL BODY AND CHAKRAS

WHEN YOU CONSCIOUSLY ELEVATE THE ENERGY OF LIFE WITHIN your physical being, you unlock the potential for an elevated state of consciousness. By raising the vibrational frequency of your being, you open yourself up to expanded awareness and deeper spiritual experiences. As you cultivate and channel this heightened life force energy, you connect with the essence of your true self and tap into the vast realms of wisdom and understanding. The journey of raising the energy of Life within you is a transformative path that leads to a greater sense of purpose, clarity, and connection with the divine. Through this process, you awaken to the profound truth that the elevation of your consciousness is intricately intertwined with the elevation of the energy flowing through your physical vessel.

When we consciously and intentionally raise our energy and life force to their utmost potential, we unlock a pathway to elevation and transformation. By infusing each moment with vitality, enthusiasm, and a vibrant presence, we invite a higher level of consciousness to permeate our being. This deliberate cultivation of elevated energy empowers us to transcend limitations, expand our horizons, and connect with the vast reservoirs of wisdom and divinity within us. As we consistently nurture and raise our energy to its highest expression, we embark on a remarkable journey of self-discovery, empowerment, and spiritual evolution.

When we begin to recognize the immense creative potential inherent within us. Our thoughts serve as the architects of the inner pathway, the intricate network of energy centers known as the chakras. Through the power of focused thought and intention, we have the ability to shape and activate these energetic portals within us. By consciously aligning our thoughts and intentions with the harmonious flow of energy, we unlock the transformative potential of our chakras. With each thought, we sculpt the inner landscape, activating and harmonizing the chakras to facilitate a deeper connection with our higher selves and the realms of spiritual wisdom. Embracing this understanding empowers us to become conscious creators of our inner reality, harnessing the incredible power of our thoughts to shape our spiritual journey and unlock the boundless potential within.

Chakras are often depicted as spinning wheels or vortexes of subtle energy that are closely linked to various aspects of our physical, mental, and spiritual well-being. They are in a constant state of movement and rotation at different speeds, ensuring balance and harmony within the body. Each chakra governs distinct facets of our physical and mental health. The human energetic or subtle body comprises seven primary chakras that align along the spine, from the base to the crown of the head.

While the concept of the energetic field is not commonly discussed unless one has been exposed to practices like acupuncture or reiki through their parents or friends, it is an integral part of our bodies. Every individual, including humans, plants, and animals, possesses an energetic system. Our thoughts, emotions, and beliefs carry an energetic value that is present in our energetic field. Chakras communicate through patterns of energy within this field.

The origins of the chakras can be traced back to ancient Vedic texts, which are among the oldest Hindu writings dating from 1500 B.C. to 500 B.C. In these texts, the chakras are described as the centers of consciousness and energy that the sages and seers meditate upon, as they are considered the vehicle of the soul. The Brihadaranyaka Upanishad emphasizes this, as does the concept presented in the

Tantras that working with the chakras enables us to awaken our inner potential and realize our true nature.

It is important to note that while the origins of chakras can be traced back to Eastern spirituality, chakra healing itself is not a religion. Instead, it is regarded as a complementary therapy that can be practiced alongside various spiritual and religious approaches. Moreover, chakra healing can be pursued independently as a secular form of self-care.

The focus here principally revolves around the seven main chakras within the subtle body, although there are numerous other energy centers connected to us. These chakras are approximately the size of a golf ball, and each has its own unique spin. By simply directing our focus towards these centers, we can establish a connection with them and access valuable information from within ourselves. Spending dedicated time exploring each chakra through meditation and spiritual practice can be highly valuable. personally found that being patient and persistent in carving out this sacred time within myself was of great importance.

Growing up in the New Age movement, I had the unique upbringing of being exposed to books, lectures, and various gurus who explored the concept of the energetic body. While these ideas fascinated me during my teenage and young adult years, it wasn't until I experienced a spiritual calling in my late 30s that I truly delved into understanding chakras and other aspects of the energetic body.

It was during this time that I embarked on a journey to learn about chakras, perceive auras, and read the energy of the energetic body. I sought out resources, books, and teachings that could expand my knowledge and deepen my understanding of these concepts. This quest led me to join a transformational chakra class taught by a shaman, where I had the opportunity to immerse myself in the practical application of working with chakras.

Through this transformative experience, I not only gained a wealth of knowledge about the intricacies of the chakra system but also developed practical skills in perceiving and working with energy. It was a profound exploration that allowed me to connect more deeply with my own energy and spiritual essence.

By engaging with the teachings of the shaman and actively participating in the chakra class, I was able to integrate the theoretical knowledge with practical experiences. This integration enhanced my understanding of the energetic body and opened doors to new levels of personal growth and spiritual development.

Overall, my journey into chakras and the energetic body began in my late 30s, sparked by a spiritual calling and fueled by a deep desire to explore and understand the unseen aspects of our existence. It is a journey that continues to unfold, enriching my understanding of the interconnectedness of mind, body, and spirit.

The heart is the gateway to experiencing multidimensional realities. Living our lives with love is a universal language of the spirit within us. It is important to recognize that our true nature is made of high-frequency energy and we are always connected to spirit. We bring the light of consciousness that we are into this realm. Jesus, in his sacred photographs, exemplifies the radiant light that he calls upon us, his brothers and sisters, to also be. He encourages us to be the light of the world, to walk as children of the light, and to confront darkness without condemning it.

In meditation practices, the Kundalini energy rises through the spinal column, opening the seven chakras. These chakras have been traditionally used as focal points for meditation to invite divine energy into different areas of our subtle body. By mastering energy within this physical dimension through our body and breath, we can connect with the spirit that resides within us. We are made of the same elements found in the cosmos and have the capacity to be self-sufficient creators of our own reality because we originate from the spirit and are inherently spiritual beings.

HARMONIZING YOUR CHAKRAS: PRACTICES FOR ENERGETIC BALANCE AND CLARITY

When we cultivate awareness of our energy system, we gain the ability to harmonize and balance its energies. By attentively listening to our body's needs and embracing self-acceptance, we can enable the free flow of energy without encountering blockages. It is essential to reflect upon our experiences, emotions, and individual needs to determine the most suitable path for our energetic well-being.

There exist numerous methods to engage with and support our energetic system. Visualization, mantras, mudras, yoga, nutrition, and connecting with nature are powerful tools I explored in my journey of connecting with the spiritual body. These practices can be easily incorporated into our daily lives, allowing us to establish a profound connection with our inner energy centers.

To begin, familiarize yourself with the locations and unique properties of each chakra within your being. By consciously directing your attention to each chakra, you can work with its specific energy and immerse yourself in its distinct energetic vortex. Observe the sensations, emotions, and insights that arise from this exploration.

Deep, intentional breathing is highly effective in restoring chakras to their natural and balanced state. With each inhalation, consciously direct your energy towards the specific chakra. As you exhale, allow your awareness to relax and merge with it, facilitating a harmonious energetic alignment. Guided meditations can be a wonderful tool for interacting with our chakras.

Utilizing mantras or affirmations serves as a form of sound healing that can restore and harmonize your energetic fields. Connecting with nature is another potent method. Spend time outdoors, walk barefoot on grass, and allow yourself to be grounded as you absorb the healing energy of the natural world.

Nutrition plays a significant role as well. Each chakra corresponds to certain foods, so incorporating these foods into your daily meals can help rebalance and cleanse your energy system. Movement practices like yoga are beneficial in releasing blocked or stagnant energy, allowing the flow of revitalizing energy back into your body.

Essential oils can be used to rebalance your chakras, and tapping, also known as Emotional Freedom Techniques (EFT), combines principles from traditional Chinese medicine and psychology. By tapping on specific meridian points and repeating positive affirmations, you can facilitate the release of emotions that may be blocking your chakras.

By embracing these practices and incorporating them into your daily routine, you embark on a powerful journey of energetic self-care and balance. Harmonizing your chakras fosters a deeper connection with your spiritual essence, leading to heightened clarity, inner peace, and a greater sense of well-being.

CULTIVATING ENERGETIC WELL-BEING: NURTURING YOUR INNER BALANCE

Nurturing your energetic well-being becomes an experiential journey that not only impacts you but also those around you. You can seamlessly integrate this practice into your daily routine, much like a familiar ritual such as brewing a cup of tea or tending to a garden. Just as you lovingly tend to the soil and plants, you can devote a few moments to each spiritual center. With focused intention, gently guide your awareness towards each chakra, using a gentle circular motion or a rhythmic sway to create a harmonizing effect. This mindful engagement with your energetic centers allows you to cultivate a deeper connection with your inner self and the subtle energies that permeate your being. By embracing this practice, you embark on a transformative journey of self-care and spiritual nourishment, facilitating a radiant presence that is felt not only by yourself but also by those who interact with you.

RESTORING HARMONY: UNDERSTANDING CHAKRA IMBALANCES AND THEIR IMPACT ON HEALTH AND WELL-BEING

Experiencing chakra imbalances can profoundly impact your overall health and well-being. These imbalances occur when there is a disruption or excess in the natural flow of energy within a chakra, which in turn leads to a range of physical, emotional, and spiritual discomfort. Let's delve deeper into this concept to gain a clearer understanding.

Imagine your chakras as spinning wheels of energy, each responsible for a different aspect of your being. When these wheels spin harmoniously, you experience a sense of balance, vitality, and inner peace. However, when the energy flow becomes disrupted or excessive, imbalances occur, causing a ripple effect throughout your entire being.

For example, a blocked root chakra, located at the base of your spine, can leave you feeling insecure, disconnected, or ungrounded. It may seem as if you're constantly floating in a state of uncertainty. On the other hand, an overactive throat chakra, situated in the throat area, can lead to an incessant need to talk, difficulty in listening to others, and challenges in effective communication.

These imbalances don't just affect your energetic system; they have tangible effects on your physical, emotional, and spiritual health. You may find yourself grappling with heightened anxiety, deep-seated depression, persistent fatigue, unexplained physical pain, or troublesome digestive issues. These symptoms act as signals, urging you to pay attention and address the underlying imbalances within your chakras.

It's crucial to recognize that chakra imbalances are not isolated issues. They are interconnected and can create a domino effect, impacting various aspects of your well-being. By acknowledging and addressing these imbalances, you empower yourself to reclaim balance, vitality, and harmony in your life.

Are you ready to embark on a transformative journey of self-discovery and healing? Let's explore the ways in which you can restore harmony to your chakras and unlock your true potential for holistic well-being.

ROOT CHAKRA: 1ST CHAKRA

> **Muladhara** - The Root Chakra: Nurturing Your Foundation and Support
> **Name:** Muladhara- [moola-dah-rah] Mula means "Root" and adhere meaning "support," "base," and "foundation"
> **Mantra:** I AM

> **Inherent Empowerment:** The innate right to exist and thrive
> **Element:** Earth
> **Foundational Aspects:** Establishing roots, cultivating grounding, nurturing, fostering trust, promoting health, creating a supportive home and family, setting healthy boundaries, fostering prosperity, ensuring survival, embracing purity, seeking security and self-preservation, cultivating strength and courage.
> **Location:** base of the spine, coccygeal plexus, perineum, the base of the tailbone
> **Identity:** Physical Existence
> **Orientation:** Self-preservation
> **Challenge:** Fear (To be liberated from fear you have to choose to not be in fear, the action of fear is to create more fear).
> **Color:** Red
> **Musical Note:** C
> **Sense:** Try this: The sense organ that corresponds to the first chakra is smell. While meditating, focus on the tip of your nose to help align the root and bring forth the qualities you need to balance your root chakra.
> **Affirmations:** I am safe and secure in this moment. I am grateful for the challenges that have facilitated my growth and transformation. I am rooted deeply, and I am connected to my body. The core essence of consciousness that establishes this base is the innate drive for survival. When our survival is jeopardized, fear arises within us.
> **Petals of the lotus:** four
> **Stones that can help balance root chakra:** Garnet, Hematite, Tourmaline, and Red Jasper.

EMBRACING THE DIVINE MOTHER
AND OUR TRUE ESSENCE

Meditation serves as a firm foundation, akin to the solid ground beneath our feet, supporting and embracing us. Within this foundation, we discover the nurturing presence of the heavenly Holy Mother. Conceptually, it represents the root of creation, symbolizing our true essence, our "I Am-ness." Just as a mother nurtures and protects a baby in the womb, we are cradled in our spiritual bodies by the Divine Mother, who grounds us through our root chakra.

To connect with your root chakra, ask yourself, "Where am I in relation to my root chakra?" Direct your attention to the corresponding area in your body, such as the perineum or the tailbone at the base of your spine. You may experience sensations like tingling, resonance, or a swirling feeling. Center yourself within this energy, exploring, observing, and forging a connection.

When you feel ready, visualize merging with this energy and descending deep into the Earth, connecting with its heart. Envision roots growing from the soles of your tailbone, firmly anchoring you to the ground. Take deep breaths, allowing a sense of stability and security to flow up through your roots and permeate your entire being.

Take time to establish a connection with your ancestral roots, embracing their profound wisdom. Express gratitude, honor your true "I Am-ness," and give thanks for the essence of who you are.

Here are some questions you can ask yourself to explore and understand your Root Chakra:

1. How do you feel about your sense of safety and security in your life? What factors contribute to these feelings?
2. Reflect on your relationship with your physical body. How connected do you feel to your body? How do you care for and nourish it?
3. What is your relationship with your home and physical environment? How does it support your sense of stability and grounding?
4. How do you handle and cope with stress and challenges in your life? What strategies do you use to maintain resilience?
5. Reflect on your relationship with money and material possessions. How do you approach financial stability and abundance?
6. Consider your connection to nature. How do you engage with the natural world, and how does it impact your sense of grounding?
7. Reflect on your family and ancestral roots. How do these connections influence your sense of identity and belonging?

8. How do you establish and maintain healthy boundaries in your relationships? How do you prioritize your own needs?

9. Reflect on your sense of purpose and how it aligns with your physical existence. How do you find meaning in your daily life?

10. Consider your overall sense of self-preservation and the actions you take to ensure your well-being. How do you prioritize self-care?

These questions can help you explore various aspects of your Root Chakra, including security, stability, grounding, physicality, boundaries, and connection to the material world. Take your time with these questions, allowing yourself to reflect deeply and honestly. The insights gained can provide a greater understanding of your Root Chakra energy and areas for growth and balance.

SELECTED HOLY SCRIPTURE

Blessed is He who Finds Wisdom.

PROVERBS 3:17-19

The one who discovers wisdom is truly blessed, for her ways are delightful and her paths bring peace. She is like a tree of life, providing nourishment and vitality to those who embrace her teachings. All who hold onto wisdom firmly are filled with happiness. It is through divine wisdom that the Lord established the foundations of the earth, and with understanding, He crafted the heavens.

Wisdom has built her house; she has set
up its seven pillars.

PROVERBS 9:1

Wisdom is not merely a concept but a dwelling place, a sanctuary that has been carefully constructed. Her house stands tall, supported by seven sturdy pillars. Each pillar symbolizes a fundamental aspect of wisdom, representing its strength, stability, and completeness. Within this dwelling, wisdom invites all who seek her guidance to enter and partake in her profound wisdom.

There is no fear in love, but perfect love drives out fear, because fear involves punishment. The one who fears has not been perfected in love.

1 JOHN 4:18

Love and fear are intertwined, but perfect love transcends fear. It banishes fear's grip, for fear is rooted in the anticipation of punishment. When one remains in a state of fear, they have yet to experience the fullness of perfected love. Love, in its purest form, casts out fear, allowing one to embrace a state of harmony, trust, and deep connection.

SACRAL CHAKRA: 2ND CHAKRA

> **Core Essence:** Embracing Dynamic Movement and Deep Connection
> **Name:** Svadhisthana [Sawa-dee-stah-nah] meaning "dwelling place of self"
> **Mantra:** I Feel
> **Foundational Rights:** Embracing and Experiencing Pleasure
> **Element:** water
> **Essential Aspects:** Exploring Movement, Sensation, Emotions, Sexuality, Desire, Pleasure, Creativity, Self-Worth, Intimacy, Passion, Sensuality, Connection, and Life Force Energy
> **Location:** lower abdomen approximately three inches below the navel, at the center of your lower belly. Physical association: womb, genitals, kidney, and bladder
> **Identity:** Emotional
> **Orientation:** Self-gratification
> **Challenge:** Guilt

> **Affirmations:** I Feel
> **Petals of the lotus:** six with the crescent moon
> **Color:** Orange
> **Musical Note:** D
> **Sense:** Taste
> **Stones that can help to balance sacral chakra:** coral, carnelian, and amber.
> **Affirmations:** I embrace love and have enjoyment for my body. I am open to fully experiencing the present moment through my senses. I am a sensual and sexual being, embracing my authentic desires. I am creative and adaptable, finding inspiration in every situation. I establish and maintain healthy boundaries that honor and protect me. I deeply value and respect my body, nurturing it with care and gratitude.

The energy of this chakra enables release, movement, and the sensation of change and transformation within your physical being. It empowers you to embrace the present moment in all its richness and entirety.

Creative Visualization: Close your eyes and imagine a vibrant orange energy centered in your lower abdomen. Visualize this energy expanding and flowing freely, revitalizing your creativity and passion. Focus on sensations of joy and pleasure associated with this chakra.

Here are some questions you can ask yourself to explore and understand your Sacral Chakra:

1. What does sensuality mean to you, and how do you embrace and express it in your life?
2. How do you nurture and honor your creative energy? What activities or outlets allow you to tap into your creative flow?
3. In what ways do you connect with your emotions? How do you process and express them?
4. Reflect on your relationship with pleasure. What brings you joy and satisfaction? How do you prioritize pleasure in your life?
5. Explore your relationship with passion. What ignites your passion? How do you pursue and cultivate it in your life?

6. Consider your attitude towards intimacy and connection. How do you form and maintain healthy, fulfilling relationships with others?

7. Reflect on your self-image and body acceptance. How do you embrace and celebrate your physicality?

8. How do you balance personal boundaries with vulnerability in your interactions with others?

9. In what ways do you honor and connect with your inner child? How do you nurture your playful and spontaneous nature?

10. Reflect on your relationship with abundance and flow. How do you invite abundance into your life, and how do you share it with others?

These questions can help you explore various aspects of the Sacral Chakra, including creativity, emotions, sensuality, intimacy, passion, and self-expression. Remember to approach these questions with curiosity, openness, and honesty to gain deeper insights into your Sacral Chakra energy.

SELECTED SCRIPTURES

Understanding is a wellspring of life unto him that hath it.

PROVERBS 16:22

True understanding is a source of abundant life for those who possess it. It serves as a wellspring, nourishing and enriching the depths of one's being. Through understanding, one gains insight and clarity, leading to a more fulfilling and purposeful existence.

Who is worthy? The divine self manifests in physical form. The Creator in form. Know yourself, know your worth. We are Christed beings, spiritual beings having an experience in physicality:

The question of worthiness arises, highlighting the profound truth of our divine nature. We are not separate from the Creator, but rather an embodiment of the divine essence in physical form.

Recognizing our true selves, connected to the Christ consciousness within, allows us to understand our inherent worth. We are spiritual beings navigating a physical journey, infused with the divine spark of creation.

> *Therefore if anyone is in Christ, he is a new creation.*
> *The old has passed away. Behold, the new has come.*

2 CORINTHIANS 5:17

In the recognition of our divine essence and alignment with the Christ consciousness, a profound transformation occurs. We are reborn, shedding the limitations of the past. The old ways and patterns dissolve, making way for the emergence of a new self. This scripture encapsulates the potential for radical personal growth and spiritual evolution that comes from embracing our true nature.

These scriptures emphasize the significance of understanding, the recognition of our inherent worthiness as divine beings, and the transformative power of aligning with the Christ consciousness. They offer valuable insights that can be explored through the lens of spiritual growth and self-realization.

SOLAR PLEXUS: 3RD CHAKRA

> **Essential Objective:** Embracing Transformation as a Core Purpose
> **Name:** Manipura [Mahn-ee-pooh-rah] meaning "lustrous gem"
> **Mantra:** I act
> **Inherent Entitlements:** Empowering Individuality and the Right to Take Action
> **Element:** Fire
> **Location:** Solar Plexus, Digestive system, Liver, Gall Bladder
> **Issues:** Energy, activity, autonomy, individuation, will, self-esteem, proactivity, power, responsibility, and reliability
> **Identity:** Ego identity, power
> **Orientation:** self-definition

> **Challenge:** Shame
> **Affirmations:** I acknowledge and honor the inherent power within me. I have the ability to manifest my desires and pursue my chosen path. I embrace self-love and self-acceptance. I assertively stand up for myself and my needs. I recognize my worthiness of love, kindness, and respect. I am empowered and utilize my power with wisdom and integrity.
> **Petals of the lotus:** 10 petals
> **Color:** yellow, it's your Sun, let it shine!
> **Musical note:** E
> **Sense:** Sight
> **Stones:** Topaz, Citrine, and Tiger's Eye

Breathwork Meditation: Sit comfortably and take deep, diaphragmatic breaths. As you inhale, imagine drawing in bright yellow energy into your solar plexus area. As you exhale, release any tension or stagnant energy. Visualize the yellow energy expanding and filling your entire abdominal area, instilling confidence and personal power.

Here are some questions to ask yourself in order to explore and understand your Solar Plexus Chakra:

1. How do you feel about your personal power and confidence? Do you feel empowered to take action and make decisions in your life?
2. Reflect on your relationship with success and achievement. How do you define success, and how do you pursue it?
3. How do you handle and navigate your emotions? Are you able to express your emotions in a balanced and healthy way?
4. Consider your relationship with your self-worth. How do you value yourself, and how does this influence your interactions with others?
5. Reflect on your ability to set and maintain boundaries. How do you assert yourself and protect your personal space and energy?
6. How do you handle criticism and judgment from others? How does it affect your self-esteem and confidence?
7. Consider your relationship with personal responsibility. How do you take ownership of your actions and choices?

8. Reflect on your relationship with personal autonomy and independence. How do you assert your individuality and honor your unique identity?

9. How do you cultivate and express your creativity? In what ways do you tap into your inner creative energy?

10. Consider your relationship with personal goals and ambitions. How do you align your actions and intentions with your aspirations?

These questions can help you explore various aspects of your Solar Plexus Chakra, including personal power, self-confidence, self-worth, emotional balance, boundaries, and autonomy. Take your time to reflect on each question, allowing yourself to gain deeper insights into your Solar Plexus Chakra energy and areas that may require attention or growth.

SELECTED HOLY SCRIPTURE

But for you who revere my name, the sun of righteousness will rise with healing in its rays. And you will go out and frolic like well-fed calves.

MALACHI 4:2

For those who hold deep reverence for the divine, a powerful transformation awaits. The sun of righteousness, symbolic of divine illumination and purity, will ascend, casting its healing rays upon them. This radiant light brings forth restoration and wholeness, permeating their being with divine grace. In the presence of this healing radiance, they will experience a profound sense of joy and liberation, like contented calves frolicking freely.

This scripture conveys the promise of divine healing and rejuvenation for those who honor and revere the divine. It speaks of the transformative power of divine light, bringing forth healing and the experience of unbridled joy. Through the lens of spiritual growth, it encourages us to cultivate reverence, embrace divine illumination, and revel in the freedom and delight that come from being in harmony with the divine presence.

HEART CHAKRA: 4TH CHAKRA

- › **Core Essence:** Embracing Love and Harmony
- › **Name:** Anahata [Ahn-ah-ha-tah] "unstruck"
- › **Mantra:** I Love
- › **Inherent Entitlements:** Embracing the Right to Love and Be Loved
- › **Element:** Air
- › **Location:** Heart, chest, cardiac plexus
- › **Aspects to Explore:** Love, Equilibrium, Self-Love, Relationships, Intimacy, Inner and Outer Balance, Devotion, Reaching Out and Receiving, Openness, Connection, Trust, Emotional Stability, Compassion, Letting Go, and Surrender.
- › **Identity:** Social
- › **Orientation:** Self-acceptance, Acceptance of others
- › **Challenge:** Grief
- › **Affirmations:** I am deserving of love and embrace it fully. I express love towards myself and others with compassion. Love resides abundantly within my heart. I am open and receptive to love and kindness. I am wanted and cherished by those around me. I cultivate inner peace within myself.
- › **Petals of the lotus:** 12 petals
- › **Color:** green, pink
- › **Musical Note:** F
- › **Sense:** Touch
- › **Stones that can help balance heart chakra:** Jade, Emerald, and Rose Quartz and Malachite

Meditation for the heart: Find a quiet moment for yourself sit in peace. Ask yourself out loud, "Where am I in correlation to my heart chakra?" This question should bring you to the center of your chest, to your heart, and bring your attention to your heart center. With each inhale, imagine breathing in love and compassion. With each exhale, send that love and compassion out to yourself, loved ones, and all beings. Visualize a green or pink light radiating from your heart, expanding with each breath. Now, with your awareness on this energy center of your spiritual body, you might feel it vibrating, it might feel like it's twirling and pulsating now allow yourself to drop down into it. See what that feels like, explore, and look around. You might see a light, a flame. That is your God center. That is where God dwells in you. That is Christ in us. There is a deep love in the abode of your being, and it is a sacred place that you can go to any time you need. Observe the flame in you, nurture it and love it, be at peace and thanksgiving.

Here are some questions to ask yourself in order to explore and understand your Heart Chakra:

1. How do you express love and compassion towards yourself and others? Are there any areas where you can deepen or expand your capacity for love?
2. Reflect on your ability to forgive and let go of past hurts. Are there any unresolved emotions or grudges that are hindering the flow of love in your life?
3. How do you cultivate and nurture meaningful relationships in your life? Are there any relationships that require healing or more attention?
4. Consider your connection with empathy and understanding. How do you practice empathy towards others and seek to understand their experiences?
5. How do you show gratitude in your life? Do you cultivate a sense of appreciation for the blessings and beauty around you?
6. Reflect on your relationship with self-acceptance. Are there any aspects of yourself that you find challenging to accept and love unconditionally?
7. Consider your ability to set healthy boundaries in your relationships. Are there any areas where you can establish clearer boundaries to protect your heart's energy?

8. How do you express and communicate your emotions authentically? Are there any emotions that you find difficult to express or express in a healthy way?

9. Reflect on acts of kindness and compassion that you have extended to others. How do these acts align with your heart's values and desires?

10. Consider your connection with nature and the beauty of the world around you. How do you connect with nature to nurture your heart chakra?

These questions can help you explore various aspects of your Heart Chakra, including love, compassion, forgiveness, empathy, gratitude, self-acceptance, and healthy relationships. Take your time to reflect on each question, allowing yourself to gain deeper insights into your Heart Chakra energy and areas that may benefit from healing, growth, or further nurturing.

SELECTED HOLY SCRIPTURE

I will give you a new heart and put a new spirit in you;
I will remove from you your heart of stone and
give you a heart of flesh.

EZEKIEL 36:26

Divine transformation is promised to those who are open and receptive. A profound change awaits, as the divine bestows a new heart and spirit within. The hardened heart, rigid and unyielding, will be replaced with a heart that is tender, compassionate, and alive with divine love. This transformative process allows for a deeper connection with the divine and a renewed capacity for love and empathy.

Love the Lord your God with all your heart and with all your soul and with all your strength and with all your mind and Love your neighbor as yourself.

LUKE 10:27

The essence of true devotion is found in wholehearted love for the divine. It encompasses the fullness of one's being—heart, soul, strength, and mind. This love extends beyond oneself to encompass love for one's neighbor, treating others with the same care, respect, and compassion one holds for oneself. It is a call to embody love in all aspects of life, fostering harmonious relationships and interconnectedness.

Love Comes from God: And we have come to know and believe the love that God has for us. God is love; whoever abides in love abides in God, and God in him.

1 JOHN 4:16

Love originates from the divine source, and through the recognition and acceptance of this truth, we can experience and embrace divine love. As we deepen our understanding and trust in the love that God has for us, we come to realize that God is love itself. By abiding in love, we dwell in God's presence, and God resides within us, fostering a profound union and connection.

Behold, you delight in truth in the inward being, and you teach me wisdom in the secret heart.

PSALM 51:6

The divine essence rejoices in the truth that resides within the depths of our being. In the inward sanctuary of our hearts, divine wisdom is imparted and revealed. As we attentively listen and nurture our inner wisdom, we gain profound insights and understanding. The divine presence guides us and imparts wisdom that leads to growth, transformation, and alignment with divine truth.

These scriptures highlight the themes of divine transformation, wholehearted love, the origin of love from God, and the pursuit of wisdom within. They invite us to open ourselves to divine renewal, embody love in our relationships, recognize the divine love within us, and seek wisdom in the depths of our inner being. Through these teachings, we are encouraged to embark on a journey of spiritual growth, connection, and alignment with divine truth.

THROAT CHAKRA: 5TH CHAKRA

- > **Core Essence:** Embracing Communication and Creativity
- > **Name**: Vissudha [Vish-ooh-dah] means "purification"
- > **Mantra:** I speak
- > **Inherent Entitlements:** Embracing the Right to Express and Be Listened to
- > **Element:** Sound
- > **Location:** Throat, pharyngeal plexus
- > **Issues:** Communication, creativity, listening, resonance, finding one's own voice
- > **Identity:** creative
- > **Orientation:** Self-expression
- > **Challenge:** Lies
- > **Affirmations:** I am attuned to the truth and express it with clarity. I confidently communicate my thoughts and feelings with purpose. My voice holds significance and contributes to the world. I embody integrity in my words and actions. I have the inherent right to speak my truth and be heard.
- > **Petals of the lotus:** 16 petals
- > **Color:** Blue
- > **Musical Note:** G
- > **Sense:** Hearing
- > **Stones that can help balance throat chakra:** Soladite, Celestite, and Turquoise

The primary obstacle of the fifth chakra lies in doubt and negative thinking. By acquiring knowledge and validating it through meditation and firsthand experience, doubt and negativity dissipate.

Affirmation Meditation: Sit or stand with an upright posture. Take a few deep breaths to relax. Repeat positive affirmations related to clear communication and self-expression, such as "I speak my truth with confidence" or "My voice is authentic and powerful." Visualize a bright blue light emanating from your throat area with each affirmation.

Here are some questions to ask yourself in order to explore and understand your Throat Chakra:

1. How effectively do you express your thoughts & ideas? Are you able to communicate your needs & desires clearly and assertively?
2. Reflect on your listening skills. How well do you listen to others without judgment or interruption?
3. How do you express your authentic self through your words and communication style? Are you able to be true to yourself and speak your truth?
4. Consider your relationship with honesty and integrity. Do you speak and communicate with honesty and integrity?
5. Reflect on your ability to set healthy boundaries in your communication. Are there any areas where you need to establish clearer boundaries to protect your energy?
6. How do you use your voice to inspire and uplift others? Do you share your wisdom and knowledge to benefit those around you?
7. Consider your relationship with silence and the practice of stillness. Are you comfortable with silence and able to listen to your inner voice?
8. Reflect on your ability to express and process your emotions verbally. Are there any suppressed emotions that need to be expressed and released?
9. How do you engage in meaningful and authentic conversations with others? Are there any areas where you can deepen your connections through communication?
10. Consider your relationship with creative self-expression. How do you use your voice, whether through singing, writing, or other artistic forms, to express yourself?

These questions can help you explore various aspects of your Throat Chakra, including communication, self-expression, authenticity, listening, setting boundaries, and creative expression. Take your time to reflect on each question, allowing yourself to gain deeper insights into your Throat Chakra energy and areas that may require attention, healing, or growth.

SELECTED HOLY SCRIPTURE

In the beginning was the WORD,
and the WORD was with God,
and the WORD was GOD.

JOHN 1:1, BSB

At the very inception of creation, the divine Word existed. The Word, inseparable from God, held the essence of divinity itself. It encompassed the power of creation, the wisdom of truth, and the expression of divine love. It was through this eternal Word that all things came into being.

The Word became flesh and made His dwelling among us.
We have seen His glory, the glory of the one and only Son
from the Father, full of grace and truth.

JOHN 1:14, BSB

The divine Word took on human form, incarnating as a living embodiment of divine presence in the world. The Word became flesh and dwelled among humanity, revealing divine glory. In the person of the one and only Son, the fullness of grace and truth was manifested, offering a profound revelation of divine love and wisdom.

And you will know the truth, and the truth will set you free.

JOHN 8:32

The pursuit and embrace of truth lead to liberation. Knowing the truth, not only intellectually but also experientially, brings about a profound sense of freedom. The truth dispels illusions, falsehoods, and limiting beliefs, allowing one to live authentically and in alignment with divine wisdom.

Sanctify them by the truth; Your word is truth.

JOHN 17:17

Through the power of truth, individuals are sanctified, purified, and set apart for sacred purposes. The truth, inseparable from the divine, holds transformative power. The very Word of God is truth itself, and by aligning with this truth, one is consecrated and brought into closer union with the divine.

Since you have purified your souls by obedience to the truth, so that you have a genuine love for your brothers, love one another deeply, from a pure heart. For you have been born again, not of perishable seed, but of imperishable, through the living and enduring word of God. For, "All flesh is like grass, and all its glory like the flowers of the field; the grass withers and the flowers fall, but the word of the Lord stands forever." And this is the word that was proclaimed to you.

1 PETER 1:22-25

THE THIRD EYE: 6TH CHAKRA

> **Core Essence:** Embracing Pattern Recognition
> **Name:** Ajna [Ah-jnah] "to perceive and command"
> **Mantra:** I See, I sense
> **Basic Rights:** to see, to observe
> **Element:** Light

> **Location:** Forehead, brow, carotid plexus, the third eye also known as the pineal gland is a pea-sized gland shaped like a pine-cone, located in the middle of the brain.
> **Aspects to Explore:** Image, Intuition, Imagination, Visualization, Insight, Dreams, and Vision
> **Identity:** Archetypal (the original pattern or model from which all things of the same kind are copied or on which they are based; a model of the first form; prototype).
> **Orientation:** self-reflection
> **Challenge:** illusion
> **Affirmations:** I perceive things with crystal clarity. I am receptive to the wisdom that resides within me. I have the ability to manifest my visions into reality. I am intimately connected to the profound wisdom of the universe. I am attuned to my inner guidance, trusting its wisdom. I am the wellspring of my truth and love.
> **Petals of the lotus:** 2 petals
> **Color:** Indigo
> **Musical Note:** A
> **Sense:** 6th sense
> **Stones that can help balance third eye chakra:** Opal, Azurite, Lapis Lazuli

The "way of the third eye" is seeing everything as it is from a point of "witness" or "observer," or from simply being mindful – moment by moment. When your third eye is open, you not only see but you also understand.

Guided Visualization: Begin by gently closing your eyes and directing your attention towards the space between your eyebrows—the location of your third eye chakra. As you bring your awareness to this area, envision a radiant, vibrant indigo or violet light emanating from within.

Allow this luminous light to grow and expand, gradually opening your third eye and creating a gateway to your intuitive abilities and inner wisdom. Feel the gentle warmth and energy of the light as it fills the space, inviting you to explore the vastness of your spiritual perception.

Now, let us delve deeper into this experience by actively engaging your third eye vision. Start by giving yourself a prompt—an invitation to imagine various scenes or objects with vivid detail. For instance, picture a delicate pink rose delicately unfurling its petals, each revealing its unique beauty. Visualize a pure white snowflake gently descending from the sky, its intricate patterns mesmerizing your senses.

As you continue, envision a graceful bird or a gentle deer gracefully moving through an expansive field, harmoniously coexisting with nature. Witness the effortless elegance of a fish swimming gracefully through crystal-clear waters, its every movement reflecting a sense of tranquility.

Allow these prompts to serve as bridges, connecting your physical and spiritual realms. Embrace the power of your imagination, knowing that actively envisioning these scenes through your third eye vision enhances your connection to this sacred energy center.

As you engage in this practice, remain open to any images, insights, or sensations that arise. Trust your intuition and embrace the wisdom that flows from deep within you. Take your time to explore the depths of your inner knowing, allowing the guidance of your third eye to illuminate your path.

When you are ready, gently bring your awareness back to the present moment, carrying with you the newfound clarity and heightened intuition that comes from opening the doors of perception through your third eye chakra.

Here are some questions to ask yourself in order to explore and understand your Third Eye Chakra:

1. How in tune are you with your intuition? How do you recognize and trust your inner guidance?
2. Reflect on your ability to see beyond the physical reality. Are you open to exploring and understanding the deeper aspects of life?
3. How do you engage with your imagination and inner vision? Do you allow yourself to dream and envision possibilities?
4. Consider your relationship with knowledge and wisdom. How do you seek and learn new information? How do you integrate it into your life?
5. Reflect on your ability to perceive patterns and connections in your experiences. Are you able to see the bigger picture and make insightful connections?

6. How do you cultivate and maintain a balanced perspective? Are there any beliefs or biases that cloud your clarity of vision?

7. Consider your connection with your higher self or inner wisdom. How do you tap into this inner wisdom for guidance and understanding?

8. Reflect on your relationship with meditation or other practices that enhance your awareness and deepen your connection with your inner self.

9. How do you engage with your dreams and the messages they may hold? Are there any recurring themes or symbols that require your attention?

10. Consider your openness to spiritual experiences and the exploration of metaphysical realms. How do you connect with and explore your spiritual nature?

These questions can help you explore various aspects of your Third Eye Chakra, including intuition, insight, inner vision, wisdom, imagination, and spiritual connection. Take your time to reflect on each question, allowing yourself to gain deeper insights into your Third Eye Chakra energy and areas that may benefit from cultivation, healing, or expansion.

SELECTED HOLY SCRIPTURE

*For where your treasure is, there your heart will be also.
The eye is the lamp of the body. If your vision is clear, your
whole body will be full of light. But if your vision is poor,
your whole body will be full of darkness. If then the light
within you is darkness, how great is that darkness?*

MATTHEW 6:21-23

The scripture highlights the interconnectedness between our treasures, our hearts, and our perceptions. Our true treasures, the things we value most deeply, shape the orientation of our hearts. Just as the eye serves as a lamp, illuminating our physical body, our vision, and perception guide our spiritual being. When our vision is clear, and aligned with divine truth, our entire being is filled with light, representing clarity, understanding, and spiritual enlightenment. However, if our vision is clouded by falsehoods or distorted perspectives, our inner being is shrouded in darkness. If the light within us is actually darkness, it represents profound spiritual blindness. This passage urges us to examine our hearts, align our treasures with divine values, and ensure that our perception is rooted in truth, so that we may experience the radiance of spiritual illumination.

> *Your eye is the lamp of your body. When your vision is clear, your whole body also is full of light. But when it is poor, your body is full of darkness. Be careful, then, that the light within you is not darkness. So if your whole body is full of light, and no part of it in darkness, you will be radiant, as though a lamp were shining on you.*
>
> LUKE 11:35

Similar to the previous scripture, this passage emphasizes the significance of clear vision and its impact on our spiritual well-being. The eye is likened to a lamp, illuminating our entire being. When our vision is clear and unclouded by falsehoods or distorted perspectives, our inner being is filled with radiant light. This light symbolizes spiritual understanding, wisdom, and the presence of divine illumination. However, if our vision is poor, distorted, or lacking in truth, our inner being becomes enveloped in darkness. The passage cautions us to be vigilant and discerning, ensuring that the light within us is not darkness. When our entire being is filled with light and devoid of darkness, we radiate spiritual brilliance, akin to a shining lamp.

These scriptures remind us of the profound influence our treasures, hearts, and vision have on our spiritual state. They encourage us to align our treasures with divine values, cultivate clear and truthful perceptions, and ensure that the light within us is not obscured by darkness. By doing so, we can experience spiritual illumination, wisdom, and radiance, allowing our inner light to shine brightly in the world.

CROWN CHAKRA: 7TH CHAKRA

- **Core Essence**: Embracing Understanding
- **Name:** Sahasrara [Sah-hah-swah-rah] "thousandfold" Paradise, Heaven
- **Mantra:** I know, the mantra sound is the universal sound of OM
- **Inherent Entitlements:** Embracing the Right to Seek Knowledge and Learn
- **Element:** Thought
- **Location:** Crown of the head, Cerebral cortex
- **Aspects to Explore:** Transcendence, Immanence, Belief Systems, Higher Power, Divinity, Union, Vision, Wisdom, Understanding, Awareness, Bliss, Unity, Intelligence, Miracles
- **Identity:** universal, connected to Spirit and wisdom
- **Orientation:** self-knowledge, understanding, connecting to the divinity of God
- **Challenge:** attachment
- **Affirmations:** The essence of divinity resides within me. I am receptive to new ideas and knowledge effortlessly flows to me. The world around me serves as a profound teacher. I am guided by a higher power, supported by its wisdom. I trust and follow the guidance of my inner wisdom. I am open to releasing attachments that no longer serve me. I recognize my oneness with the Divine, embracing my sacred connection. I honor and acknowledge the Divine that dwells within me.
- **Petals of the lotus:** one thousand
- **Color:** Violet, White, Gold
- **Musical Note:** B
- **Sense:** Beyond Senses
- **Stones that can help balance crown chakra:** Diamond, Amethyst, Selenite, and Clear Quartz

The authentic self naturally attracts experiences and circumstances that align with its essence. It manifests and attracts elements that contribute to its own growth and actualization.

Mindfulness Meditation: Begin by finding a quiet and comfortable space where you can relax without any distractions. Take a moment to settle into a comfortable position, either sitting or lying down, and gently close your eyes.

Take a few deep, cleansing breaths, allowing your body to relax with each exhale. Feel the weight of your body sinking into the support beneath you, letting go of any tension or stress.

Now, bring your attention to the top of your head, the area where your crown chakra resides. Visualize a brilliant, radiant light above your head, shining down upon you like a loving and gentle beam of energy.

As this divine light touches your crown chakra, feel a subtle tingling or warmth spreading throughout the area. Sensitize yourself to this energy, allowing it to gently open and activate your crown chakra.

Imagine this luminous light expanding and enveloping your entire body, permeating every cell, every space within you. Feel its soothing and nurturing presence, connecting you to the higher realms of consciousness and divine wisdom.

As you bask in this celestial light, feel a profound sense of peace and serenity washing over you. Allow any thoughts or worries to effortlessly dissolve, as you surrender to the divine guidance and love that flows through your crown chakra.

Now, bring your awareness to the top of your head once more, and envision a gentle lotus flower blossoming at the crown of your head. Picture its petals unfolding, revealing a vibrant and radiant energy.

With each breath you take, imagine the lotus flower expanding, drawing in divine energy from the cosmos. Feel its petals reaching higher, connecting you to the infinite wisdom of the universe.

As you remain in this state of openness and receptivity, ask for any guidance, insights, or messages that your higher self, spirit guides, or the divine has for you. Trust that the answers will come in their own time and in their own way.

Take a few moments to listen, to be still, and to receive. Allow yourself to be filled with gratitude for the connection you have established with your crown chakra and the divine realms.

When you are ready, gently bring your awareness back to your physical body. Wiggle your fingers and toes, and take a few deep breaths, grounding yourself in the present moment.

Carry the sense of peace, connection, and divine wisdom with you as you go about your day. Trust that you can return to this space of inner knowing and spiritual connection whenever you need to.

Remember, you are a vessel of divine light and love. Embrace and honor the wisdom that flows through your crown chakra, allowing it to guide you on your journey of self-discovery and spiritual growth.

Take a moment to express gratitude for this meditation experience and the insights received. When you are ready, gently open your eyes, bringing the meditation to a close. May the blessings of the crown chakra continue to illuminate your path.

Here are some questions to ask yourself in order to explore and understand your Crown Chakra:

1. What is your understanding of spirituality? How do you connect with a higher power or universal consciousness?

2. Reflect on your relationship with divine guidance. How do you access and trust the wisdom and guidance that comes from beyond your individual self?

3. How do you cultivate a sense of oneness and interconnectedness with all beings? How do you experience and honor the divine in yourself and others?

4. Consider your relationship with surrender and letting go of control. Are there any areas where you can release attachment and surrender to the flow of life?

5. Reflect on your connection with higher states of consciousness, such as meditation or contemplative practices. How do you cultivate and deepen your spiritual experiences?

6. How do you find meaning and purpose in your life? What actions or practices align with your higher purpose and contribute to the greater good?

7. Consider your ability to experience and receive divine inspiration and creativity. How do you tap into this source of inspiration to express your unique gifts?

8. Reflect on your relationship with silence and stillness. How do you create space for quiet reflection and the experience of inner peace?

9. How do you integrate spiritual principles and insights into your daily life? How do you bridge the gap between spiritual knowledge and practical application?

10. Consider your connection with gratitude and appreciation for the blessings in your life. How do you cultivate a sense of gratitude for the divine presence and guidance?

These questions can help you explore various aspects of your Crown Chakra, including spirituality, divine connection, higher consciousness, surrender, meaning, and purpose. Take your time to reflect on each question, allowing yourself to gain deeper insights into your Crown Chakra energy and areas that may benefit from further exploration, alignment, or growth.

SELECTED HOLY SCRIPTURE

Draw near to God, and he will draw near to you.

JAMES 4:8

This scripture encourages us to seek a closer relationship with God. When we purposefully draw near to God, dedicating ourselves to spiritual connection and communion, God reciprocates by drawing near to us. It signifies the divine invitation for us to actively pursue a deepening of our relationship with God, knowing that God is always ready to meet us with open arms.

After all, what gives us hope and joy, and what will be our proud reward and crown as we stand before our Lord Jesus when he returns? It is you.

1 THESSALONIANS 2:19

These scriptures emphasize the importance of seeking a close connection with God, finding hope and joy in the community of believers, and embodying humility in our interactions with one another. They remind us that drawing near to God leads to a reciprocal relationship, that faithful believers are a source of encouragement and reward, and that humility is a virtue that aligns us with God's grace. By embracing these teachings, we can grow spiritually, foster meaningful relationships, and align ourselves with the values of God's kingdom.

In conclusion, working with our spiritual centers, the chakras hold great significance in our personal growth and spiritual journey. These energy centers serve as vital gateways to explore and align with the deeper aspects of our being.

By engaging with our chakras, we open ourselves to a profound understanding of our physical, emotional, and spiritual well-being. Each chakra represents unique qualities and aspects of our lives, offering us opportunities for self-awareness, healing, and transformation.

Through practices such as meditation, breathwork, energy healing, and mindful living, we can activate, balance, and harmonize our chakras. This process allows for the free flow of vital life force energy, promoting overall balance, vitality, and spiritual expansion.

Working with our chakras enables us to cultivate a deeper connection with our true selves and the divine essence within us. It empowers us to tap into our intuition, creativity, and inner wisdom. It helps us recognize and release energetic blockages, emotional patterns, and limiting beliefs that hinder our growth and well-being.

Furthermore, by nurturing our chakras, we enhance our ability to experience unity, oneness, and interconnectedness with all of creation. We recognize that we are part of a greater whole, and our actions ripple out into the world, influencing the collective consciousness.

Ultimately, working with our chakras is a transformative journey that allows us to awaken to our fullest potential, embody our authenticity, and live a life of purpose, love, and joy. It is an invitation to embrace our spiritual nature, expand our consciousness, and create a harmonious and fulfilling existence.

May we embark on this sacred path of chakra exploration and integration, honoring the divine within us and fostering our spiritual evolution for the highest good of ourselves and the world around us.

20

BEYOND THE VEIL: ILLUMINATING ESCHATOLOGY'S HIDDEN TRUTHS

ESCHATOLOGY, ([ES-KUH-TOL-UH-JEE]) FOUND WITHIN THEOLOGY and philosophy, is an area of investigation that centers on the ultimate occurrences of human history, the future of humanity, and the characteristics of the realm beyond our world. It delves into inquiries concerning the purpose of existence, the concept of life after death, divine evaluation, and the destiny of the cosmos. Within religious contexts, eschatology frequently encompasses the faith in a messianic individual or an enlightened entity who will facilitate harmony, fairness, and spiritual illumination. It also encompasses ideas such as resurrection, ultimate judgment, and the creation of a new heavenly and earthly realm.

In the realm of understanding the ultimate destiny of humanity, it is increasingly evident that we cannot overlook our inherent inclination to explore the nature of the world. Our society must reevaluate its understanding of classical physics and adopt a fresh scientific paradigm that recognizes consciousness as a fundamental element. This new perspective should be integrated into our educational systems. By failing to broaden our worldview and acknowledge our responsibility for our actions, we risk bringing about our downfall. However, by recognizing our interconnectedness with the cosmic consciousness and embracing our creative potential, we can make progress and facilitate positive transformations. The phenomenon of consciousness holds immense significance, and within each of us lies the potential for experiencing a heavenly realm. Nevertheless, we must awaken to this truth. Classical physics, in its traditional framework, fails to align with this perspective, necessitating a shift towards a more holistic understanding of reality and the role of consciousness within it.

From my perspective, it holds great significance to approach the study of eschatology with the understanding that we are co-creators, actively working towards the goals of peace and the improvement of humanity. Each individual carries the weight of responsibility for their spiritual journey, while also sharing in the collective responsibility for the state of the world. I believe God bestows upon us the power to bring about our desires, rather than solely taking charge of their fulfillment on our behalf.

The fusion of science and religion holds immense importance, as famously expressed by Einstein: "Science without religion is lame, religion without science is blind." We find ourselves presently at a critical juncture in the evolution of humanity, where the theory of knowledge (epistemology) is merging with the concept of conscious creation. We are coming to the realization that our existence is not isolated, and a collective transformation is unfolding within our cosmic consciousness. We are uncovering our place within a broader narrative and recognizing our multidimensional nature, enabling us to engage with cosmic consciousness, extraterrestrial beings, and interdimensional entities. Free will is a precious gift that propels us toward the development of an advanced civilization, teeming with infinite possibilities. The power held within our minds is of tremendous significance, as our thoughts can mold reality. Nurturing positive and empowering thoughts in the face of darkness and negativity is imperative. By comprehending and embracing our free will, we can elevate the vibrational frequency of our collective consciousness and catalyze positive transformations.

As humanity progresses, we are rediscovering our inherent bond with the vast expanse of the galactic universe and harnessing the potential of the quantum field. This connection allows us to access valuable knowledge, wisdom, technology, and information that can contribute to the creation of a revitalized and enlightened Earth.

In addition to the presence of Jesus, numerous enlightened beings exist among us and throughout the cosmos. When we unite as individuals with the freedom to make choices, embracing the radiance within us and the love that permeates our beings, we can elevate our energetic frequency. Through this elevation, we can serve as guiding lights, shining brightly amidst times of darkness.

It is of utmost significance to illuminate the darkness by allowing our inner light to shine, as this act plays a pivotal role in dispelling ignorance and facilitating profound transformation. The quote by Joseph Goldstein underscores the immense power of wisdom and knowledge in triumphing over darkness. Goldstein's words, "Just as the light of a single candle can dispel the darkness of a thousand years, the moment we light a single candle of wisdom, no matter how long or deep our confusion, ignorance is dispelled," highlight the transformative potential of even a small spark of wisdom in dispelling ignorance, regardless of the extent of our confusion or lack of understanding.

Eschatology encompasses a holistic approach that integrates science and spirituality. It recognizes the profound role of spirituality in understanding our connection to a higher power or cosmic consciousness. It acknowledges that humanity is undergoing a collective evolution, awakening to our true nature and interconnectedness. This perspective invites exploration of alternative realities, such as encounters with extraterrestrial or interdimensional beings, and accessing higher realms of knowledge. It emphasizes the power of intention and manifestation, urging individuals to cultivate positive thoughts and beliefs to shape a harmonious reality. Personal responsibility is highlighted, emphasizing the individual's role in their spiritual journey and the shared responsibility for the collective well-being. The potential for transformation and transcendence is emphasized, allowing individuals to move beyond limitations and embrace higher states of consciousness. Love and compassion are seen as vital, fostering unity and promoting the well-being of all beings.

Jesus teaches us that death does not have the final say, and He serves as a testament to this truth. Through His resurrection, He becomes the first among those who have passed away to be raised to new life.

The order of resurrection is described, with Christ being the first to rise, followed by those who belong to Him. This sequence culminates in the ultimate defeat of death as the final enemy. The belief in resurrection and the afterlife is fundamental to the Christian faith, as it affirms the assurance of eternal life beyond earthly existence.

It provides comfort, hope, and a sense of purpose, knowing that death is not the end but rather a transition into a new and everlasting existence. The resurrection of Jesus serves as foundational proof, offering comfort and certainty that the afterlife is not only a possibility but a reality to be embraced. It assures believers that death is not the end, but a door to a glorious, everlasting realm.

How can we transform the outdated belief systems surrounding the concept of the End Times? Our perspectives on the End Times have a profound impact on our present circumstances and the way we choose to live today. It is vital to dismantle old paradigms and belief structures that no longer serve our growth and well-being. Letting go of these obsolete frameworks creates room for new ideas, expanded consciousness, and positive transformation in our current reality.

The historical Jesus, the living Jesus, and the biblical Jesus each offer distinct perspectives. The historical Jesus, an apocalyptic Jew, embraced the belief in a future cataclysmic event and the triumph of God's righteousness. The biblical Jesus, as portrayed in the New Testament, includes theological interpretations and teachings from the early Christian community. Meanwhile, the living Jesus transcends historical and intellectual understanding, representing a personal encounter and ongoing influence in individuals' lives.

The living Jesus extends beyond specific religious frameworks, symbolizing love, compassion, and enlightenment. It emphasizes the idea that we're divine beings, created in the image and likeness of God. The living Jesus invites us to recognize our role as co-creators in a participatory universe, responsible for our own salvation.

In exploring these dimensions of Jesus, we are encouraged to embrace personal growth, ethical living, and a deeper connection with the transcendent. Ultimately, the living Jesus beckons us to experience a transformative relationship that transcends mere historical knowledge and engages us in an intimate journey of self-discovery and spiritual awakening.

This process of releasing outdated beliefs enables us to embrace fresh perspectives, nurture personal development, and actively participate in the collective evolution of our world.

In challenging times, as the Earth changes and a rebirth of consciousness arises within us, a path forward is determined by the choices we make. We can follow the example set by our beloved Jesus, who demonstrated the importance of creating and containing light within ourselves. By doing so, we can radiate positive energy that has the potential to inspire and uplift those around us.

This positive influence can create a ripple effect, gradually contributing to a collective shift in consciousness and elevating the overall vibrational state of the planet. It is within the power of each individual to make a meaningful difference by consciously aligning with and embodying qualities that foster beauty, harmony, and positive vibrations in their thoughts, actions, and interactions.

If we do come to understand that the universe is a conscious being it will have profound implications for the worldview of humanity. Here are some ways in which such a realization could change our perspective.

◊ **Interconnectedness:** Recognizing the universe as a conscious entity would emphasize the interconnectedness of all things. We would understand that every aspect of existence, from galaxies to individual beings, is part of a vast unified system. This awareness could foster a sense of unity and collective responsibility among humans, encouraging us to consider the consequences of our actions on a cosmic scale.

◊ **Purpose and Meaning:** Discovering the universe's consciousness might lead us to question the purpose and meaning of our existence. We might wonder if we have a function within universal consciousness. This could stimulate philosophical and spiritual inquiries, prompting us to explore deeper questions about our place in the cosmos.

◊ **Ethical Considerations:** We might also question the ethics of our actions. We would recognize that our choices and behaviors impact not only other humans but also the conscious fabric of the universe itself. This awareness could motivate us to adopt more compassionate and responsible attitudes toward the environment, other living beings, and our fellow human beings.

◊ **Expanded Awareness:** Understanding the universe as a conscious being could expand our perception of reality. This could lead to advancements in fields such as science, spirituality, and arts as we explore new dimensions of knowledge and expression.

◊ **Transcendence of Anthropocentrism:** Anthropocentrism is a philosophical perspective that places human beings at the center of significance and value in the world. It is a belief that human beings are the most important or central entities in the universe and that human interests and welfare should be the primary focus of our moral and ethical considerations. If we recognize the consciousness of the universe, it will challenge our anthropocentric worldview, which places humans at the center of importance. We would understand that human concerns are just a part of a much larger cosmic tapestry.

If the universe is indeed a conscious entity, intricately woven with the fabric of our being, then each of us carries a profound responsibility. We are not mere spectators but active participants in the ongoing evolution of consciousness. Let us awaken to this truth and strive to embody and express the highest aspects of ourselves - love, compassion, wisdom - for in doing so, we honor the sacred interplay of the universe and contribute to its ever-unfolding journey towards greater unity and harmony.

The world is transforming, leading us towards a new paradigm. The true battle we are confronted with is for our attention and awareness. As we become more conscious of our energetic nature and the frequencies we embody, it is crucial to be mindful of what influences we allow into our lives, whether it be the media we consume or the thoughts we entertain.

The collective consciousness of humanity is currently experiencing a period of profound introspection, often referred to as the Dark Night of the Soul. In this stage of our spiritual journey, it is important to remember that when individuals unite in light, their collective power surpasses that of darkness. Despite the challenging and burdensome times we face, we must hold on to hope and trust that the universe is supportive.

Taking personal responsibility and recognizing our individual capacity for change is one of the initial steps in this transformative process. It starts by examining whether we are in conflict with ourselves, our neighbors, or our communities. By cultivating love within ourselves, we gain the ability to recognize it in others since everything ultimately reflects back upon us. When we embrace inner peace and love, and actively contribute to peaceful resolutions in our lives, we engage in positive ways.

In conclusion, the exploration of eschatology and the nature of the universe's consciousness leads us to a profound understanding of our interconnectedness and the transformative power of our choices.

We can shape our reality and contribute to the evolution of consciousness by embodying qualities such as love, compassion, and wisdom. By recognizing our responsibility for personal and collective well-being, we can create a ripple effect of positive energy that uplifts not only ourselves but also those around us.

As we let go of outdated beliefs and embrace new perspectives, we open ourselves to infinite possibilities for growth and transcendence. Let us remember that we are co-creators in this cosmic journey, and by aligning with the highest aspects of ourselves, we honor the sacred interplay of the universe. May we embrace our role in the ongoing evolution of consciousness and strive to create a world filled with beauty, harmony, and positive vibrations.

FIGURES

NOTES

Introduction

1. "The New York Times Magazine" (1930, August 10). Conversation with Tagore and Einstein: On the Nature of Reality.
2. Walsch, N. D. (2018, October 12). Facebook quote. Retrieved from https://www.facebook.com/NealeDonaldWalsch/

Chapter 1

3. Latin Vulgate. (1899). Bible. Douay-Rheims 1899 American Edition (DRA). Genesis 3:15.
4. Walsch, N. D. (1998). Conversations with God: an Uncommon Dialogue: Book 3 (p. 232). Hampton Roads.

Chapter 2

5. Easwaran, E. (1985, 2007). The Bhagavad Gita. Nilgiri Press, p. 153.
6. United States Conference of Catholic Bishops. (n.d.). Daily Bible Readings, Audio, and Video Every Morning | USCCB. Retrieved from https://bible.usccb.org/
7. Singer-Towns, B., (2004). The Catholic Faith Handbook for Youth. Saint Mary's Press, p. 273 (paraphrased).

Chapter 4

8. Planck, M. (1932). Where is science going? The universe in the light of modern physics (pg. 98). New York, NY: W.W. Norton & Company.
9. Walsch, N. D. (2006). Home with God: In a Life that Never Ends. New York, NY: Atria Books, p. 87 (paraphrased).
10. The Institute of Art and Ideas. (2019, October 9). How Panpsychism Can Explain Consciousness [Video File]. https://youtu.be/2xTzwLulRAA?si=q2uOcAl-WIVQ8u9zf
11. Science and Nonduality. (2022, September 19). The Hard Problem of Matter: A Conversation with Deepak Chopra and Rupert Spira. Retrieved from https://youtu.be/iHXgRFOOEB4?si=9BWDFZ6bRIJ6yc1P
12. Walsch, N. D. (1998). Conversations With God, Book 3 (3rd ed., p. 114). Hampton Roads (paraphrased).

Chapter 5

13. Einstein, A. The quote "We cannot solve problems with the same thinking we used when we created them" is commonly attributed to Albert Einstein, though there is no verifiable source for this attribution.
14. Meyer, M. (Ed.). (2007). The Gospel of Thomas (p. 153). Harper One.

15. According to the Gospel of Thomas (saying 3), "Rather, the Kingdom is inside you and outside you at the same time. When you come to know yourself, then you will be known. You will realize then that it's you who are the sons of the living Father. But as long as you do not know yourself, you will live in poverty, and you will be that poverty".

Chapter 6

16. Levy, P. (2018). The Quantum Revelation: A Radical Synthesis of Science and Spirituality (p. 37). SelectBooks (paraphrased).

17. Wheeler, S. A. (1994). At Home in the Universe (p. 45). American Institute of Physics (paraphrased).

18. Heschel, A. J. (1962). The Prophets (pp. 26-27). New York: Harper & Row (paraphrased).

19. Spinoza, B. d. (1951). The Chief Works of Benedict De Spinoza Vol 1: a Theological-Political Treatise (TTP i.23). Place of publication not identified: New York (paraphrased).

Chapter 7

20. Meyer, M. (2009). The Nag Hammadi Scriptures: The Gospel of Philip, Truth, and Nakedness (67,9-27) (p. 173). HarperOne (paraphrased).

21. Meyer, M. (2007). The Nag Hammadi Scriptures: The Gospel of Thomas Prologue (3) (p. 139). New York, NY: Harper Collins.

22. Meyer, M. (2007). The Nag Hammadi Scriptures: The Gospel of Thomas Prologue (77) (p. 149). New York, NY: Harper Collins.

23. Catechism of the Catholic Church: Second Edition. (1994, 1997). Libreria Editrice Vaticana, p. 347 (paraphrased).

24. Chopra, D. (2008). The Third Jesus: The Christ We Cannot Ignore (p. 40). New York, NY: Harmony Books

25. Radin, D. (2017, September 9). Interview with Rick Archer. Buddha at the Gas Pump, 33:49-34:14 (paraphrased).

Chapter 8

26. Heschel, A. J. (1962). The Prophets (p. 558). New York: Harper & Row (paraphrased).

27. Heschel, A. J. (1962). The Prophets (p. 8). New York: Harper & Row (paraphrased).

28. Heschel, A. J. (1962). The Prophets (pp. 28-29). New York: Harper & Row (paraphrased).

29. Fox, M. (1985). Illuminations of Hildegard of Bingen (p. 24). Santa Fe, New Mexico: Bear and Company (paraphrased). *Illuminations of Hildegard of Bingen* Edited by Matthew Fox published by Inner Traditions International and Bear & Company, ©2002. All rights reserved. http://www.Innertraditions.com Reprinted with permission of publisher.

30. King, U. (1997). Christ In All Things: Exploring Spirituality with Pierre Teilhard de Chardin (p. 93). Maryknoll, NY: Orbis Books (paraphrased).

31. Walsch, N. D. (1998). Conversations With God: An Uncommon Dialogue, Book 3 (pp. 50-51). Hampton Roads Publishing (paraphrased).

Chapter 9

32. Weitzmann, K. (1978). The Icon. New York, NY: George Braziller, Inc. (paraphrased).

33. Walsch, N. D. (2020). The God Solution: The Power of Pure Love (p. 36). Phoenix Books, Inc. (paraphrased).

34. Walsch, N. D. (2020). The God Solution: The Power of Pure Love (p. 83). Phoenix Books, Inc. (paraphrased).

35. Walsch, N. D. (2020). The God Solution: The Power of Pure Love (p. 131). Phoenix Books, Inc. (paraphrased).

36. Walsch, N. D. (2017). Conversations With God, Book 4: Awaken The Species: A New and Unexpected Dialogue (p. 183). Watkins Media Limited (paraphrased).

37. Heschel, A. J. (1955). God in Search of Man: A Philosophy of Judaism. New York, NY: Farrar, Straus & Cudahy (paraphrased).

Chapter 10

38. Walsch, N. D. (1997). Conversations With God, Book 1 (p. 90). Hodder and Stoughton (paraphrased).

Chapter 11

39. Walsch, N. D. (2017). Conversations With God, Book 4: Awaken The Species: A New and Unexpected Dialogue (p. 84, 88). Watkins Media Limited (paraphrased).

40. Wheeler, J. (1990). Information, Physics, Quantum: The Search for Links. In Proceedings of the Third International Symposium on Foundations of Quantum Mechanics in the Light of New Technology. Tokyo: Physical Society of Japan (paraphrased).

41. Levy, P. (2018). The Quantum Revelation: A Radical Synthesis Of Science And Spirituality (p. 7). SelectBooks, Inc. (paraphrased).

42. Heitler, W. (1970). The Departure from Classical Thought in Modern Physics. In A. Einstein, Philosopher-Scientist, edited by P.A. Schlipp (pp. 196). Chicago: Open Court (paraphrased).

43. Walsch, N. D. (2014, August 6). Facebook post. https://www.facebook.com/NealeDonaldWalsch/ (paraphrased).

44. Walsch, N. D. (1998). Conversations With God, Book 3 (p. 329). Hampton Roads (paraphrased).

45. Lin-Chi, Master (n.d.). The Zen Teachings of Master Lin-Chi: A Translation of the Lin-Chi Lu. 'If you meet the Buddha on the road, kill him.'

46. Josephson, B. (1987). Physics and Spirituality: The Next Grand Unification? Physics Education, 22(1), 15-19 (paraphrased).

47. Wikipedia contributors. Four Noble Truths. In "Wikipedia". Retrieved from https://en.wikipedia.org/wiki/Four_Noble_Truths

48. Wheeler, J. A. (1994). At Home in the Universe (p. 226). American Institute of Physics (paraphrased)

49. Levy, P. (2018). The Quantum Revelation: A Radical Synthesis of Science and Spirituality (p. 283). SelectBooks (paraphrased).

50. Zajonc, A. (ed.). (2004). The New Physics and Cosmology: Dialogues with the Dalai Lama (p. 221). Oxford University Press (paraphrased).

51. Levy, P. (2018). The Quantum Revelation: A Radical Synthesis of Science and Spirituality (p. 283). SelectBooks (paraphrased).

52. Walsch, N. D. (1998). Conversations with God: an Uncommon Dialogue: Book 3 (p. 366). Hampton Roads (paraphrased).

53. Levy, P. (2018). The Quantum Revelation: A Radical Synthesis of Science and Spirituality (p. 210). SelectBooks (paraphrased).

54. Walsch, N. D. (1998). Conversations with God: an Uncommon Dialogue: Book 3, (p.366) Hampton Roads (paraphrased).

55. Walsch, N. D. (2006). Home with God In A Life That Never Ends (p. 100). New York, NY: Atria Books (paraphrased).

56. Walsch, N. D. (1997). Conversations with God: Book 1 (p. 30). Hodder and Stoughton (paraphrased).

57. Walsch, N. D. (1997). Conversations with God: Book 1 (p. 10). Hodder and Stoughton (paraphrased).

Chapter 12

58. GotQuestions.org. (2023). What is YHWH? What is the tetragrammaton? Available at: https://www.gotquestions.org/YHWH-tetragrammaton.html

59. Nassim Haramein - Tree of Life - YouTube https://youtu.be/1R8AihKoWrw?si=IfVSN6M8dqrnFaVZ

60. Image of a TETRAGRAMMATON rendered by author.

61. Image of ICOSAHEDRON rendered by author.

62. Image of DODECAHEDRON rendered by author.

Chapter 13

63. Ryan, R. E. (1999). The Strong Eye of Shamanism: A Journey Into the Caves of Consciousness. (p. 208). Rochester, Vermont: Inner Traditions International (paraphrased).

64. Einstein, A. (1929, October 26). What Life Means to Einstein [Interview by G. S. Viereck]. The Saturday Evening Post.

65. Easwaran, E. (1985, 2007). The Dhammapada (p. 206). Tomales, CA: Nilgiri Press.

66. *Ibid.*

67. Easwaran, E., & Nagler, M. N. (2019). The Upanishads (26.1, p. 140). Tomales, CA: Nilgiri Press.

68. Easwaran, E., & Nagler, M. N. (2019). The Upanishads (p. 249). Tomales, CA: Nilgiri Press.

Chapter 14

69. Moore, T. (1779–1852). The Meeting of the Waters. [1868]. New York: Published by Currier & Ives, 152 Nassau St. New York.

70. Walsch, D. (2021, February 20). Facebook post. Retrieved from https://www.facebook.com/NealeDonaldWalsch/

71. Bible Hub. (n.d.). Exodus 15:6-7,13 (Parts of Moses' Song of Deliverance) [Online]. Available at: Bible Hub website: https://biblehub.com/exodus/15-6.htm

72. Meyer, Marvin, The Nag Hammadi Scriptures, HarperCollins 2007, The Gospel of Thomas, Pg. 140

Chapter 16

73. Walsch, N. D. (2013, October 8). Facebook post. Retrieved from https://www.facebook.com/NealeDonaldWalsch/ (paraphrased).

74. Walsch, N. D. (2005). Tomorrow's God: Our Greatest Spiritual Challenge, Atria Books (paraphrased).

Chapter 17

75. A Course in Miracles (2007). Scribed by Helen Schucman, T-2. VIII.3, (p.34) Foundation for Inner Peace.

76. A Course in Miracles (2007). Scribed by Helen Schucman, T-2. VIII.4, (p.34) Foundation for Inner Peace.

ABOUT THE AUTHOR

JAMIE DUNSTON IS A CONTEMPO-
RARY MYSTIC WHOSE SPIRITUAL
journey has been shaped by a
non-religious upbringing, granting
her the freedom to explore diverse
paths of spirituality. Influenced by
the New Age movement, Jamie has
developed a unique perspective on
the nature of the divine.

In 2014, a transformative experience forever changed Jamie's life, as
she received an unexpected visita-
tion from the Blessed Holy Mother, who bestowed upon her a divine
revelation of love. This sacred encounter deepened Jamie's faith and
opened the doors to subsequent mystical experiences.

Driven by an insatiable quest to understand consciousness and
the world, Jamie engaged in soul-stirring conversations with God,
allowing her vessel to be filled with profound truths and insights.

Jamie extends profound gratitude to the Almighty Lord, known as
the great I AM THAT I AM, and acknowledges Jesus as her spiritual
teacher, dear friend, and advocate.

Residing amidst the serene landscapes of southern Colorado, Jamie
expresses deep gratitude for her readers and the unwavering support
of the universe. It is within this tranquil setting that she continues to
cultivate her spiritual path and generously shares profound insights
with others, guiding them on their own journeys of self-discovery.